Moral Argument and Social Vision in the Courts

A STUDY OF TORT ACCIDENT LAW

Moral Argument and

Social Vision

in the Courts

A STUDY OF TORT
ACCIDENT LAW

Henry J. Steiner

The University of Wisconsin Press

Published 1987

The University of Wisconsin Press
114 North Murray Street
Madison, Wisconsin 53715

The University of Wisconsin Press, Ltd.
1 Gower Street
London WC1E 6HA, England

First printing

Printed in the United States of America

For LC CIP information see the colophon

ISBN 0-299-11010-9

To Pam

Contents

Preface

This essay has been long in the making. It grew out of a project begun during a free semester made possible by a faculty Program for Basic Research in Law, funded by the Ford Foundation. My first draft of September 1981 had the basic structure of this completed work. It "went public" that autumn as the subject of a faculty seminar at the University of Wisconsin Law School. Under the pressure of other obligations, I left for my summers the several revisions and expansions of this essay. Its publication now by the University of Wisconsin Press brings to a happy conclusion what has become the essay's five-year association with that university.

The book explores the elements of legal argument through a study of the evolution of tort accident law. In so doing, it concentrates on what courts have said in appellate opinions, rather than on scholarly writing. But in the background lie some established schools of legal thought that have influenced courts' reasoning, observations, and decisions. Those schools, as well as scholarly movements now growing within law faculties, have also influenced the structure and concepts of my essay. Although notes refer to the relevant writings, brief explanatory remarks seem in order here.

In the more distant background lie the messages of legal realism. What particularly informs my work is that movement's stress upon law as regulation, upon the degree of indeterminacy and hence of choice in judicial decision-making, and upon the diverse sources influencing how courts exercise that choice. Such related strands all bear upon another theme, the realists' denial of a coherent public-private distinction in legal ordering. Moreover, my emphasis upon social vision, upon ways in which courts express their understanding of social actors and social structures, derives partly from the attention of the realists and their successors in legal scholarship to economic and political contexts and to social facts relevant to litigation.

The resurgence in recent decades of writing about moral theory in law has influenced my perception of courts' arguments, and thus the essay's framework. I refer less to abstract work in moral theory than to writing which has portrayed the process of reaching judicial decision or portrayed a given field of law as exemplifying and working out the implications of one or another moral ideal—an ideal of fairness or of right or of welfare. Some of this scholarship has in fact addressed tort accident law, from perspectives as distinct as distributive justice and the premises of an economic analysis of law. It will be evident that my essay contradicts some central tenets of this scholarship. Nonetheless, such writing has heightened my awareness of the ideal element in legal argument and of the significance of courts' moral justifications.

Most recent is the developing movement of critical legal studies. Given the variety of insights and methods of scholars identified with that movement, I must speak of a few prominent themes within it rather than of the influence on my essay of critical legal studies as a whole. For example, I have not employed concepts figuring in some critical scholarship such as legitimation or alienation, nor have I followed such new directions in legal analysis as the deconstruction of doctrine. Rather, the themes influencing my essay consist principally of ways in which critical scholars have gone beyond the insights of the realists by rendering the description and understanding of law more systematic and structured, and by drawing on other traditions of thought exploring the significance of concepts like ideology. Their writings have portrayed law's inner structure in ways similar to my own portrait of courts' justifications and social vision—for example, a stress on the competing moral and political premises to and ideals in legal argument, on the structured choices and the contradictions before courts. Surely my essay shares the conviction of realists and critical scholars of legal doctrine's historically contingent rather than necessary character.

The powerful scholarship within these three movements in legal thought helped me to shape my project. But in the end, the method and structure of this essay are of course my own, developed out of these diverse bodies of thought and out of my understanding of the judicial opinions in tort accident law which my concepts are meant to illuminate.

Over the course of the essay's revisions, I benefited greatly from the reactions of friends and colleagues. At the start were the probing remarks of Robert Gordon and David Trubek at the Wisconsin seminar. Thereafter a number of colleagues at Harvard Law School read one or another draft. I appreciate all their suggestions. Duncan Kennedy's comments about an early version were particularly challenging. But I should single out Lewis Sargentich for my special thanks, and not simply for his astute criticism. Years of our conversations about torts and legal theory pushed my own thinking in a more conceptual direction and thereby contributed greatly to this project. I also benefited from reading some unpublished manuscripts of colleagues, particularly one by Richard Parker that is cited in my essay.

Two students, Peter Lake '84 and Marc Granetz '86, gave valued assistance in helping me to prepare the manuscript for publication. Norma Wasser provided able secretarial help. I appreciate all their aid.

Moral Argument and
Social Vision in the Courts

A STUDY OF TORT
ACCIDENT LAW

1   Purposes

Theme and Illustration

My theme in the large treats characteristics of common law change. The essay sketches a framework for understanding relations among vital elements of such change, and thus for understanding the nature of legal argument in adjudication. It does so through an examination of recent and arresting developments in the tort standards governing compensation for accidentally caused harm to persons or property. But analysis of this modern tort law of accidents is not the point of the essay. Rather, through a study of the evolution of that body of law I mean to develop a conceptual framework for understanding the dynamics of change that informs other bodies of law as well.

To elaborate this framework, I probe the trend in the common law of tort that dates generally from the 1950s but that has intensified during the last fifteen years. Although the doctrinal trend has stopped well short of the "strict liability" by which it is sometimes characterized, it has unmistakably heightened liability relative to the version of the fault system that took form by the late nineteenth century and slowly developed into the mid-twentieth century.

In examining this trend, I look closely at the work of courts rather than of scholars. The scholarly contributions have not been insignificant or without consequence. To the contrary, academic writing on tort theory relevant to the trend has influenced a growing number of appellate opinions and to that extent it figures in this essay.

But the opinions of judges are my focus—and for their rhetoric and mode of argument rather than for their holdings or doctrinal ambiguities or instrumental effects. My project is to explore judges' assumptions, perceptions of society, and reasoning, and thereby to reveal the patterns of rhetoric and argument that emerge from this movement toward heightened liability. Critical evaluation of the developing tort law, typically undertaken by scholars through some ideal norm against which doctrinal change could be assessed as healthy or pathological, is not my purpose. At this essay's conclusion, I do reflect on the character and prospects of this trend toward heightened liability. Those views are in the nature of a postscript, comments on rather than integrally a part of the preceding analysis. My essay would have much the same character and thrust, merely a reversed chronology in its description of the evolution of tort rules, had doctrine moved in recent decades to restrict rather than expand liability.

The essay looks not at what courts "do" in any instrumental sense but at what they "say." It is concerned not with examining the effects of the developing tort doctrine on corporate or individual behavior or on the toll of accidents, but rather with exploring courts' beliefs about what those effects might be. It takes what courts say seriously, by asking how courts resolving accident cases grasp the situation or problem before them, how they perceive the world of accidents, how they argue toward a better or juster world. It suggests the ways in which courts' perceptions and arguments help to construct the social reality that their rulings are meant to address.

A range of questions becomes relevant to such an enterprise. For example, do judges view accidents as tragic but isolated events, or as a systemic social problem? How do they describe the behavioral characteristics of typical injurers and victims? What understanding do their opinions suggest of the changing contexts, socioeconomic or political or ideological, in which accidents occur and arguments for liability are assessed?

The answers to such queries all bear upon a related set of questions treating the ways in which courts explicitly justify their decisions. What are the characteristic justifications for this liability-expanding trend? Generally, what relationships exist among courts' perceptions of society, their justifications, and the rules of tort law?

I respond to these questions by systematizing what, at first encounter with the opinions, hardly appears systematic. Consider the typically varied, loosely related features of opinions: logical or analogical reasoning linking rules or precedents to the stated facts, barely expressed intuitions of justice, formal argument pointing toward and justifying the decision from the perspective of one or another moral ideal, characterizations of social actors, understandings of social goals or ideologies. Such typical features form the three principal categories of my description and analysis: doctrine, moral justification, and social vision. My aim is to develop the roles of those categories within the structure of legal argument as a whole, and thus to elucidate relationships among them as adjudication forms and transforms doctrine.

How are these three elements of legal argument to be understood? Imagine a characteristic modern appellate decision awarding damages to an accident victim, and consider the diverse strands of the court's argument. Suppose that defendant corporation is held strictly liable because plaintiff's injury stemmed from its "abnormally dangerous activity"—perhaps blasting during building construction that injures a pedestrian. A typical appellate opinion might invoke prior decisions imposing strict liability for such abnormally dangerous activities. It would seek support in opinions that characterized analogous activities, or perhaps characterized blasting itself, as abnormally dangerous.

The court may recite reasons for imposing strict liability in these circumstances and employ those reasons to help resolve any ambiguities in characterization of the relevant activity. (Blasting, for example, would find specific historical precedent, but other activities such as crop dusting or the transportation of inflammable fuel would be more problematic.) Such reasons may include a "policy" such as the attribution of accident costs to the business that "caused" the harm or to the party that can best control such costs. They may involve a "principle" of fairness, such as one requiring those who benefit from the activity—the defendant and third-party consumers of the defendant's services—to share the victim's loss. In the course of developing reasons that justify its decision, the court may observe that the accident victim was helpless to protect himself against this risk of injury, that the defendant corporation is better situated than the victim to reduce that risk, and that business will not be unduly burdened because it can spread the losses assigned to it.

That each of these arguments or observations could be countered by other arguments or observations antagonistic to strict liability, is here beside the point. They illustrate the three interrelated strands of common law adjudication and change— doctrine, moral argument or justification, and social vision— that form this essay's framework.

Doctrine refers to the formal, conventional expression of law through rules and standards. It is captured in the Restatements' black letter. In the imagined opinion, doctrine enjoys a typically prominent role as the court draws on precedents characterizing the defendant's or analogous activity as abnormally dangerous, as well as on the strict-liability rules that those precedents have developed to resolve claims growing out of such activities. Argument based primarily on doctrine may proceed in a formal and even mechanical way, perhaps by the extrapolation of rules from precedents and the application of those rules to the present case through deductive logic. Doctrinal argument may proceed more complexly, as courts support their conclusions by drawing analogies to prior decisions.

However absorbed into courts' argument and decision making, doctrine constitutes the core of most lawyers' and teachers' discourse. It is also our clearest indicator of changes or trends in the law. Given such characteristics, my analysis of tort accident law and the judicial argument informing the doctrinal trend begins with a description in chapter 2 of ways of understanding the standards of that body of law, and with a summary of the liability-expanding changes in doctrine. By justification I mean the moral argument supporting a decision. Justificatory argument seeks to demonstrate why one rule or standard is to be preferred to another, why doctrine is what it ought to be or why it ought to be changed. It means to ground an opinion in reason, to put a rational face on it. The reasons in the imagined opinion for imposing strict liability, the policies or principles invoked, come within the category of justification.

Chapter 3 inquires into the types of moral argument that have yielded the "oughts" or "ought nots" of tort accident law. It portrays the variety of ideals that have influenced the judicial development of tort law. Its purpose in so doing is both to make clear the historical choices and contradictions among justifications, and to systematize the leading judicial justifications supporting the older negligence system as well as modern heightened liability.

This essay employs two general and traditional modes of moral justification within the Western liberal tradition, utilitarian theory and theories of right or fairness, to organize the many judicial justifications that have figured in the evolution of accident law. Chapter 3 traces ways in which courts once advanced justifications growing out of utilitarian and right-fairness theories to build and maintain what will be referred to as the classical fault system, covering roughly the period from the late nineteenth century to the mid-twentieth century. It also traces ways in which contemporary courts draw upon such traditional frameworks for moral thought to build distinct justifications supporting modern heightened liability.

Social vision, a more amorphous category described in chapter 4, constitutes the pivotal and unifying concept within this portrait of common-law adjudication and change.[1] It refers broadly to perceptions of courts about accidents, about the socioeconomic context for the resolution of accident claims, and about the character and capacities of the victims and defendants before them. It embraces empirical statements, observations about social actors, evaluative characterizations of social life, and understandings of older and prevailing ideologies. Relative to justification, it has a less abstract and more contextual and graphic character. It enters opinions less as reasoned argument than as fragments of description, evaluation, or insight. The observations in the imagined appellate opinion about victims, business defendants, and corporations' capacity for loss spreading illustrate this notion.

This essay portrays a shift in courts' social vision which accompanies and informs the changes in doctrine and justificatory argument. The description emphasizes three interrelated trends in ways that courts see accidents, the parties to them, and the sociopolitical or ideological context in which they occur. Courts perceive accidents less as random encounters between two parties (dyadically) and more as incidents of systemic social interaction. They visualize the parties before them less as individual persons or discrete organizations and more as representatives of groups with identifiable common characteristics. They understand accidents and the social losses that accidents entail less as unique events and more as statistically predictable events. Modern social vision tends then toward the systemic-group-statistical in contrast with the vision more characteristic of the fault system, the dyadic-individual-unique.

Were it possible to grasp these phenomena—doctrine, justification, social vision—independently, each would lead to only a partial understanding of this recent transformation of tort accident law and of the legal argument that brought it about. It is not sufficient to consider separately the ambiguities

in or alternative paths of doctrine, the choices among competing justifications, the polar social visions. Rather these phenomena must be understood in their complementary
relationships within adjudication, in their interdependence
and totality. The task of the essay is to trace relationships
among these elements of change, to explain why each implies
and requires the others, and thereby to illuminate the nature of
legal argument.

More than merely ornamenting or influencing doctrine,
justification and social vision form and inform it. They give it
life and meaning. These two elements of argument are as
much a part of doctrine as distinct from it. They are themselves
mutually dependent, reciprocally influential categories of
thought and imagination, complementing and indeed shaping
each other even as both shape doctrine. A systemic, group-
oriented, and statistical social vision, for example, has come to
inform vital elements of both the utilitarian and fairness justifications for heightened liability. Such vision and justifications
are at the core of and inhere in modern tort doctrine. It is this
distinctive configuration of doctrine, justification, and social
vision that best illuminates the evolution, character, and dilemmas of modern accident law.

However dramatic their doctrinal expression may seem,
these interrelated changes do not bring about radical change
within tort law. The new doctrine imposing heightened liability resembles the prior law of the classical negligence system
in ways as significant as those in which the new and old di-
verge. What this common law change does express is not then
a radical shift in political or legal premises, but rather a trend in
liberal thought from the vision and ideology of a more individualistic society stressing a facilitative state framework for private activity to the vision and ideology of a more managerial,
redistributive, and welfare state.

If not fundamental, these doctrinal changes are nonetheless important. Of course, they underscore the degree to
which our legal arrangements, common law as well as legis-

lative, are open to reconceptualization and change. They signal both the significance of the choices open to courts, and the significance of the traditional constraints within which those choices are made.

Moreover, the study of this evolution of tort accident law illuminates relationships between changes in legal ordering within the common law and changing premises of the larger political system. More radical and structural innovation in accident law has occurred, and is likely to occur, through legislation implemented by administrative schemes providing compensation to victims and generating safety regulations. The common-law evolution, influenced by and viewed together with the novel directions being explored by these schemes, suggests the degree to which accident law in its totality is being transformed. In parts of this essay and particularly in its concluding section, I comment about the nature and significance of this transformation.

My plan in executing this study is to keep the text systematic and self-contained, at a level of general description and analysis that remains free of observations about or quotations from particular cases. Nonetheless, support for much of what I say lies in the argument and rhetoric of judges. For that reason many notes to the chapters treating justification and social vision consist of extended excerpts from opinions that are meant to provide the broad foundation for my description, concepts, and analysis. At a few points—particularly note 7 to chapter 3 and note 2 to chapter 4—I make my method clearer by indicating the degree to which the quoted opinions are intended to provide a basis for general inference and extrapolation throughout the essay as well as to support in detail the immediate text.

The Scope of Accident Law

Accident law serves then as a convenient vehicle for developing my themes. But some clarification of the ways in which I use the term is necessary. In different contexts it will signify different phenomena. "Accident law" refers primarily to the common law of tort's central concern: working out the consequences of unintended physical injury to people or property. It thereby embraces harms stemming from phenomena as diverse as auto accidents, medical malpractice, workplace mishaps, blasting, pollution, and product defects.[2]

Tort law bears upon accidental injuries in two principal ways: regulation of defendants' behavior (and thus of the generation of risk) through the award of money judgments or (rarely) the issuing of injunctions, and help for the accident victim by providing financial compensation.[3] Since the turn of the century, accident law has expanded beyond the work of courts to embrace legislative and administrative schemes. The accident schemes have similar functions to tort law in that they both regulate and compensate. To some extent, they seek to reduce the number and severity of accidents by regulating behavior through a variety of techniques and sanctions. To some extent, they also relieve accident victims of distress, either through cash payments or the direct provision of medical or other services.

Three types of legislation form part of this enlarged field of accident law. I here differentiate those types—as the essay later does in its concluding section—in terms of their varying emphasis on regulation of defendants' behavior or on relief of victims, and of their relation to tort law. The first type includes legislative-administrative schemes, ranging from the long-established workers' compensation plans to the contemporary no-fault auto plans. Such schemes regulate behavior only *indirectly*. That is, they do not mandate change in employers' or drivers' behavior through such forms of *direct* regulation as safety standards or driving restrictions. Rather, they may stimulate changes in the behavior of such actors indirectly by imposing insurance and accident costs upon them. For example, workers' compensation plans may use variable insurance ratings to create financial incentives for employers to design safer workplaces. These schemes also provide compensation for victims. Similar to the common law of tort in their blend of indirect regulation and compensation, they may displace tort law in whole or part.[4]

The second type of legislation consists of safety regulations—workplace safety, environmental protection—that are enforced by orders or criminal sanctions.[5] It aims primarily at the regulation of behavior. It may regulate directly (prohibitions or requirements of precisely defined conduct) or indirectly (imposing a tax on rather than prohibiting the emission of pollutants). Of course, safety schemes may also open avenues to compensation for accident victims by creating statutory actions for them against a violator.[6] Moreover, proof of violations of safety requirements can facilitate tort recovery by victims through doctrines such as negligence per se (showing that the defendant was negligent because of its unexcused violation of a statute).[7]

Third, I occasionally employ the term "accident law" more broadly, to include compensation schemes like social insurance and welfare programs that support categories of the population such as the needy or aged.[8] Programs like Medicare or Medicaid cover medical needs whatever their cause. Hence, they incidentally provide relief for accident victims. Such programs, funded partly or wholly from general tax revenues, do not attempt to regulate behavior, directly or indirectly. They are exclusively compensation systems. But they could affect a tort action brought by an accident victim through doctrines such as the collateral source rule, which determines whether payments to an accident victim from such "collateral sources" as health insurance are to be deducted from any tort recovery.[9]

Generally I use the term "public law" simply to refer to statutory and administrative law as opposed to common law. I suggest relationships between this category of public law bearing on accidents—the plans and schemes referred to—and the common law of accidents.[10] But my focus is on the common law. Despite its contemporary ascendance and bolder invention in developing accident law, public law here remains a subsidiary theme. Its importance to this essay lies in its powerful influence on the moral argument and social vision of the courts transforming tort accident law.

Public law and tort law do not comprise the only important institutions relevant to the accident problem. Another figuring importantly in this essay is the private insurance industry. As with respect to public law, my interest herein does not lie in the institution of private insurance as such. That is, I do not treat matters like the total relief that it affords accident victims, its expenses and who bears them, the types of legal regulation to which it is subjected, or the causes and consequences of the current crises in the rates and even availability of insurance in several fields of accidents. Rather, I examine the influence of private liability and loss insurance on the justifications and visions of the courts.

CHAPTER

2   Doctrine

Within the triad completed by justification and social vision, doctrine expresses most clearly the trend toward heightened liability. The familiar and compact expression of law, the typical "law talk" among professionals, doctrine first summons lawyers' or the public's attention to a judicial decision. It is doctrinal change that best defines the trend here described.

In the complex orchestration of common-law adjudication and change, doctrine carries the melodic line through this essay. Doctrine renders my thesis concrete. It provides an immediately recognizable framework for and anchors the related discussions of justification and social vision. It embodies these other elements of legal argument, gives them a practical significance, and carries them forward through time.

Until given doctrinal expression, justification and social vision remain abstract and indeterminate, susceptible to different and inconsistent doctrinal realizations. Their concrete historical character, the meaning and significance attributed by courts to a moral ideal or a social perception, become known through the doctrine to which they lead and within which they are captured. To anticipate what will follow, the image is one of a complex interweaving of these three elements of legal argument, rather than of hegemonic determination of doctrine by the other two. It is the distinctive configuration of the three elements that characterizes and best describes the modern tort law of accidents.

14

Much of the doctrine here relevant fits within the typical setting of tort accident law—namely, accidents involving previously unrelated parties, strangers. A car strikes a pedestrian; hazardous wastes contaminate a farm; an explosion injures a bystander. The victim, aware of the risk of injury in only the most general and abstract sense, neither adverted particularly to it nor agreed to assume it. Realistically, the victim and injurer could not have worked out in advance a mutually acceptable level of risk or the legal consequences of an accident involving them. They meet, as it were, through the accident.

In other cases relevant to my discussion, the victim and defendant were not strangers but related parties. They were linked directly or indirectly before the accident, as by status or through contract. Such links may, for example, make relevant the doctrine of implied assumption of risk: the victim (an auto passenger) recognized and chose to incure the risk of injury generated by the defendant (an obviously drunken driver). The links may be formal and explicit, such as pre-accident agreements between the (later) victim and a defendant doctor or lessor or vendor that insulate the defendant from liability to a patient or lessee or vendee under negligence or implied-warranty principles. In such circumstances, animating principles or precise rules of contract law may affect the resolution of claims for accidentally caused harm.

In some important ways, the courts have distinguished between the context of strangers and that of related parties. As later chapters show, they have developed justifications and expressed aspects of social vision that are distinctive to one or the other. But the recent course of decisions has led to heightened liability for similar reasons in both contexts. For the most part, my discussion does not distinguish between them.

The trend here described is often characterized as the continuing ascendance of strict, relative to negligence (fault), liability.[1] Surely tort doctrine has changed in ways that justify that characterization. Consider some examples. A sequence of appellate decisions from 1856 to 1965 involving water mains, escaping water, and property damage traces the shift from application of a negligence standard to the defendant, to retention of that standard accompanied by a jury charge on *res ipsa loquitur,* to imposition of strict liability.[2] Or, within a shorter time frame, we observe the shift from rules imposing liability for injury resulting from a flawed product (the car with defective steering) only when the flaw is traceable to negligent manufacture, to the current imposition of liability even when that product was carefully manufactured.[3]

But this chapter offers many more examples of tort doctrine expressing less decisive and more ambiguous movement toward heightened liability.[4] Those examples reveal the doctrinal categories of fault and strict liability to be inherently vague in scope, and thus resistant to separation by a clear dividing line. Although negligence law has defining characteristics that enable us to refer to it as such, it is not rigorously a "system" that can be understood to be internally coherent and self-contained. Much liability under negligence law fits one or another characteristic of what is often called "strict" liability. Similarly, concepts that were developed within, and were basic to, the negligence system are now applied to limit liability rules that are commonly described as beyond-fault or strict. Beyond-fault liability therefore includes both instances of a genuinely strict liability—a concept defined below—and instances of a liability somewhere between the classical negligence system and genuine strictness. Both forms of liability are referred to in this essay as heightened liability.

One should understand the recent trend toward heightened liability against the background of the fault system as it had developed to the mid-twentieth century.[5] Even as that system took form and became dominant during the nineteenth century, some changes within it expanded liability.[6] No illustration is more pungent than the erosion of some defenses to suits by employees against their negligent employers, particularly the fellow-servant rule, which, together with contributory fault and assumption of risk, composed a related and powerful trinity of defenses.[7] Further and more general expansion of liability within the fault system occurred during the period up to the 1950s—for example, through the collapse of contract-privity notions and the related growth of liability for injury to users or bystanders from negligently manufactured products.[8]

Of course, the fundamentally restrictive character of liability under the fault system, the requirement that the defendant be found to have acted unreasonably, remained implanted throughout this period. There were numerous additional bars to recovery. Even in the mid-twentieth century, the end of the period referred to herein as classical negligence law, constituent rules of the fault system like contributory fault, and such important protections for defendants as immunities or enclaves of limited duty or no duty, meant that the faulty actor often escaped liability.

The heightened liability of recent decades stems both from liability-expanding changes within negligence law, and from a trend toward the distinct conceptual and doctrinal structure of strict liability. The section on negligence illustrates modern accident law's expansion of liability within the formal framework of the negligence system. That expansion highlights the degree to which the negligence system is permeated with principles and methods for their application that border on strict liability. The second section treats judicial approaches toward strict liability.

Opinions involving both types of heightened liability figure in my later discussions of modern justifications and social vision. Similar phenomena were vital to the development of both types. For example, the institution of insurance transformed the older negligence system into something very different, a negligence-with-liability-insurance system, and then spurred modern strict-liability theory. It is not, then, a simple contrast between negligence and strict liability that provides a doctrinal counterpart to the later discussions distinguishing between older and contemporary justifications and social vi-

sions. Rather, the contrast providing that counterpart is between the classical negligence system and modern heightened
liability, whatever its doctrinal formulation.

Negligence: The Trend Toward Heightened Liability

"Negligence" means the conduct of a party that fails to satisfy a
socially required minimum of care, one generally expressed to
juries as the care to be expected of a reasonable person in the
circumstances. The negligent defendant imposes an undue or
unreasonable risk of harm on the accident victim. The defendant is therefore judged to have been at fault. Negligence's
formal distinction from strict liability lies in the necessity of a
conclusion that the defendant failed to act as one ought to have
acted in the circumstances. Thus liability for damages rests on
a criticism of the defendant's conduct. The defendant must
compensate the victim precisely because the conduct was
wrongful.

But what constitutes wrongful conduct? It is one matter to
articulate a reasonable-person standard, and quite another to
apply it. Courts have developed three broad tests for determining whether a defendant ought to have acted differently.
Rarely explicit ingredients of a reasonable-person jury charge,
these tests emerge principally through appellate opinions that
have sought to clarify the meaning of an external standard of
reasonableness. Of course, they bear both on a defendant's
negligence and a victim's contributory negligence.

First, what most social actors do may acquire a normative
character and stand as an indication of what the defendant
ought to have done. Social or professional practice or general
custom within a given activity thereby constitutes a test of
reasonableness, though not necessarily a decisive one. Compliance with general practice (such as a medical practice) at

least bears on the ultimate issue and may insulate the defendant from liability, whereas deviation from such practice that generates a higher risk of injury will likely lead to liability.[9]

Second, courts employ a cost-benefit methodology that is now typically understood in terms of the Hand Formula.[10] That formula determines what is reasonable conduct by weighing the burden of the defendant's precaution or care (B) against the accident loss (L) to be foreseen as a consequence of the defendant's conduct discounted by its probability (P). If the care (B) amounts to a defendant's surrendered opportunity (lower driving speed and later arrival, or foregoing an activity such as selling a dangerous product to minors) rather than an out-of-pocket cost (the expense of repairing brakes), its valuation (the cost of the surrendered opportunity) depends on courts' assessment of that opportunity's social utility.[11] When B (the cost of repairing brakes or the opportunity cost of curtailing the activity of driving by reducing speed) is evaluated as less than the reduction in $P \times L$ (the loss anticipated through collisions discounted by its probability) to be achieved through incurring that B, a defendant is judged negligent for having failed to take the proper care. Defendant ought to have incurred the marginal safety costs since they were less than the marginal savings to be expected in accident costs. In cost-benefit terms, the benefits of safety measures in reducing accident costs exceeded those measures' own out-of-pocket or opportunity costs.

Third, courts invoke safety requirements in statutes and administrative regulations that are backed by criminal sanctions in order to set a standard of reasonable care in tort.[12] Thus violation of a statutory requirement of periodic car inspection may constitute negligence if the accident would have been avoided through detection and repair of a defect. (Additional tests of due or reasonable care appear in some opinions, particularly in contexts where prior contractual links exist between the victim and defendant—for example, care consistent with expectations about a product's safety that were induced by the defendant manufacturer,[13] or the care stipulated by a contract between the parties.[14])

These three principal tests for negligence offer a good starting point for considering the covert changes within negligence law that have contributed to heightened liability. Since the content of each test is indeterminate and manipulable, it is possible to imagine that each could generate different liability trends, either liability-expanding or liability-contracting.

Custom and practice, for example, leave ample room for debate.[15] Practice will often be diverse and disputed. The defendant may be held to the more rigorous standard of care within an industry characterized by divergent practice. An ascendant but minority practice may set the standard. Indeed, a general practice within an activity may be rejected in favor of more demanding requirements stemming from some other test of negligence.[16] That is, custom may be treated as a floor of what is legally required rather than as a ceiling.

The Hand Formula poses the same dilemmas that are associated with the use of a cost-benefit methodology in other institutional settings.[17] There are, of course, many instances where its application seems unproblematic, such as a drunken and speeding driver who strikes a child in a school zone. The burden of precaution, socially valued, is trivial compared with the related reduction in $P \times L$. But in all cases, the court examining a defendant's conduct within this framework must explicitly or implicitly resolve a complex range of issues.

It must, for example, decide what counts as the private or social costs (the losses within the Hand Formula) of the way that the defendant conducts its activity. In so doing, it must be aware of the gap between the legal measure of such losses— say, the damages awarded for bodily injury—and the larger measure of social losses that are not accounted for in a judgment of liability. For example, through notions such as unprotected interests or proximate causation, tort law excludes from damages many losses stemming from the victim's injury and suffered by persons or enterprises related to the victim—

the pain of family members or friends, economic losses in the victim's workplace, and so on. Often, application of the formula requires the court to evaluate an act's or activity's social utility, an evaluation necessary to a conclusion that defendant ought (or ought not) to have foregone an activity because the expected reduction in accident costs would (or would not) exceed the relevant opportunity costs.[18]

Rarely do courts explicitly consider and evaluate these factors, nor do evaluations take precise numerical form. Rather, the appellate opinions suggest that the process of decision remains impressionistic, often as much an exercise of ordinary common sense as the application of a complex methodology. Obviously, such a flexible test for negligence and framework for decision leave ample room for choice. A more exacting notion of foreseeability imposed on a defendant (P, within the Hand Formula), or a more expansive conception of loss (L) stemming from the defendant's activity, or a lower valuation of the burden of precaution (B) that the defendant is to be charged with, may change the calculations sufficiently to turn the balance against the defendant.

Consider, for example, the inescapably retrospective judgment in the adjudication of negligence about the risk of accident stemming from the defendant's conduct. That judgment may heighten liability by finding the probability of a harm that the defendant in fact foresaw (the risk that the victim would become addicted to a prescribed drug) to have been higher. That is, the defendant as a reasonable person ought to have assessed the risk correctly and acted responsively to it. Or that judgment may charge the defendant with knowledge of an unperceived risk (the defendant as a reasonable person ought to have foreseen that its product might be misused by the victim in a dangerous way and thus ought to have taken precautions against such a misuse). What determines decision lies in the "ought," in the rigor of the standard of reasonable care with which we compare the defendant.

That "ought" speaks the language of negligence. But the more exacting the "ought," the more the judgment goes beyond requiring a common understanding of reasonable foresight and risk assessment to require foresight that is close to perfect. The "ought" may ambiguously straddle the worlds of fault and beyond-fault liability. Nonetheless, the rhetoric of reasonableness and fault formally governs the case. The defendant is liable because of wrongful conduct. Despite that rhetoric, despite the explicit criticism of the defendant's conduct, we are within a continuum from lesser to greater liability rather than on the near side of a well-marked boundary between legal regimes of negligence and strict liability. Setting a high requirement of what is reasonable conduct marks a well-travelled route toward heightened liability.

As for the third test of negligence, the criteria to determine the relevance of criminal regulations for civil liability are in flux. If the violation of a safety standard constitutes negligence despite a defendant's reasonable effort to comply with it, liability again approaches the strict. It may be impossible to conclude that defendant ought to have acted differently, that the violation "ought" to have been avoided. Here, too, fault may almost imperceptibly approach beyond-fault liability, without judicial resort to the rhetoric, doctrinal structure, or justifications of strict liability.[19]

In making the familiar observation that fault and beyond-fault liability systems may blend, much depends on how one identifies the determining characteristics of one or the other system. Scholars have pointed out, for example, that application of the external standard of care to defendants of low cognition and intelligence amounts in one sense to a strict liability.[20] From the perspective of personal morals, one could not meaningfully say that people lacking the capacity to do better (to comply with a socially necessary standard of care) nonetheless ought to have done better.

In such circumstances, fault could be better understood as a characterization of defendant's conduct that was attached to a judgment of liability rather than invoked as a moral and legal premise of that judgment. That is, defendant was faulty because liable, rather than vice versa. Nonetheless, in such cases as well as in fields of modern heightened liability, employing the rhetoric of fault may serve important underlying needs. It appears to ground recovery in tort in stable, uncontroversial notions about the relationship between liability and individual moral responsibility. It thereby satisfies certain ideological conceptions of the nature and social function of tort law.

Such are the ambiguities within the so-called negligence system. They illustrate how tendencies to expand or contract liability have long been accommodated, indeed secreted, within that system's highly general and indeterminate concepts and hence flexible structure. Given that indeterminacy, it is not surprising that the judicial reforms in recent decades of numerous rules and standards bearing on negligence liability illustrate more graphically than my preceding examples the trend toward heightened liability.[21] Those changes, explicit rather than covert, do not involve liability-prone applications of the flexible traditional tests but involve new rules affecting diverse aspects of negligence law. They illustrate how tort liability expands not simply through the subjection of defendants to a more demanding test of reasonableness, but also through the abolition of doctrines which shielded negligent defendants from liability.

To some extent the new rules—terminating charitable and sovereign immunities, displacing contributory with comparative fault—abolish anomalies.[22] They render the negligence system more coherent by eliminating doctrines shielding a defendant from liability despite acknowledged fault.[23] Other changes in rules, such as the decline of assumption of risk,[24] eliminate pockets of "no duty."

At least by comparison with the classical negligence system, some of the recently revised rules as well as some changes in the application of older standards suggest that so-called negligence liability is moving beyond the fault system. As a

formal matter, it remains true, however, that the courts so reforming tort law continue to require sufficient evidence for the
conclusion that defendant acted unreasonably. Whether then
to characterize some of these changes as imposing negligence
liability or beyond-fault liability is not always obvious. Consider a few common illustrations.

1. A more expansive use of evidentiary rules such as *res
ipsa loquitur* renders proof of fault less burdensome and carries
more cases from the judge to the jury, with a predictable effect
on outcomes. Some judges have understood a generous resort
to *res ipsa loquitur,* standing midway between a more liberal
application of the traditional criteria and reformulation of
those criteria, as tantamount to dispensing with proof of fault
and therefore imposing a strict liability.[25]

2. Standards for joint and several liability change to embrace defendants in a broader range of accidents, a change of
considerable importance for plaintiffs suing multiple defendants in fields such as nuisance.[26]

3. Traditional requirements of but-for causation face challenge and invite relaxation, both in cases of multiple (perhaps
synergistic) causation when the defendant represents only one
such cause, and in cases where an accident's circumstances
permit identification of a given cause but prevent victims from
showing a more-likely-than-not link between that cause and
any one defendant.[27]

4. Special categories of defendants confront more hostile
doctrine. Changes in the "locality rule" or the doctrine of "informed consent" heighten liability in medical malpractice
cases.[28] Numbers of status and special relationships—auto
hosts and guests, landowners and those on their land—have
undergone dramatic changes by which traditional pockets of
limited duty or no duty have been abolished.[29] Together with
the trends toward abolishing the defense of contributory fault
as well as some assumption-of-risk doctrine, these changes in
effect round out the fault system by making it more likely that
faulty actors will be liable to their accident victims. Perhaps the

most vivid contemporary illustration is the reformulation of the tort rules affecting landowners. New rules either redefine older categories of plaintiffs (trespasser, licensee, invitee) in a way that generally expands liability, or directly abolish some "limited duty" doctrine in favor of a general negligence standard.[30]

Modern Strict Liability as Heightened Liability

Strict liability applies independently of defendant's fault. It is not a condition to liability that a court or jury criticize a defendant's conduct. However questionable may be a judgment within the framework of the negligence system that the defendant ought to have acted differently, no such judgment is now required.

In its pure or ideal type, strict liability follows basically from proof of a cause-in-fact relationship between a given activity or given conduct (say, blasting) and the victim's harm (injury from the explosion). Compared with such indeterminate tests of negligence as the Hand Formula, it would appear that the rule in a strict-liability regime defining what accident costs are to be attributed to defendants could be relatively simple and straightforward. Companies engaged in blasting bear costs of victims of the blasting, and so on.

Of course modern strict liability in tort, the second prong of this trend of several decades toward heightened liability, lacks the rigor of this ideal type. Even the blasting cases are not simple. It is rather some statutory schemes displacing tort law that approach the ideal type of strict liability and thus can be accurately characterized as close to an absolute or insurer's liability. For example, under workers' compensation plans an employee can generally recover limited statutory damages by proving that the accident arose out of the course of employment. A simple causal nexus between the injury and the employment suffices. Even though questions will arise about the scope of an employment or the causal relationship, even though in extreme circumstances defenses such as the employee's fault may prevail, the rule attributing costs to the business activity is relatively straightforward and simple.[31]

In one or another way, the common law has necessarily qualified the concept of strictness. Victims must prove more than a causal nexus between a defendant's general activity or specific conduct and their injury. The very tests for determining if "strict" tort liability applies—whether there was a product "defect" or whether an activity is "abnormally dangerous"—retain some characteristics of fault liability. Moreover, notions of legal or proximate cause, or of boundaries to legally recognized interests of victims, continue to limit liability (the blaster may not be liable for the loss of companionship experienced by the victim's children). Defenses related to a victim's conduct (ignoring a warning to avoid the blasting site), or defenses based on a pre-accident contractual relationship between the defendant and victim (a disclaimer of legal responsibility), may reduce or avoid liability.

For such reasons, I employ the concept of "heightened" liability to embrace so-called strict tort liability (product defects) as well as expanded liability for negligence (abolish assumption of risk). I earlier noted that the relevant contrast for my discussion is not between these two related doctrinal movements. Rather, I stress the differences between heightened liability and, on the one hand, the classical fault system or, on the other, the stronger, nearly absolute liability of accident schemes such as workers' compensation. In comparing these systems, I shall continue to use the rubric "strict liability" much as the courts do, to cover tort doctrine that departs in some way from the requirement of proving defendant's fault as that requirement was understood within classical negligence law.

Modern strict liability governs tort accident law less inclusively than did the classical negligence system. Of course, the negligence system never occupied the entire field of accidents. On one side, there were the pockets of "no duty" or "limited duty" and, on the other, pockets of an explicit strict liability.[32] Nonetheless, despite these gaps in liability, variations among accident fields, and the indeterminacy of the negligence system's rules, that system constituted in a formal sense a relatively comprehensive doctrinal framework for deciding when compensation was to be paid to an accident victim.[33] The car driver, the railroad, the doctor, and the product manufacturer (at least after the fall of privity-contract doctrine) were equally subject to the reasonable-person standard in suits brought by most of their victims. Absent special contractual arrangements or other pre-accident links, fault was a condition to the liability of all such actors.

Despite its recent expansion, modern strict liability has yet to achieve a similar comprehensiveness within tort accident law. Rather, we tend to think of it within discrete doctrinal categories, within enclaves marked out from the underlying body of negligence law. The chief categories are vicarious liability, liability for harm from abnormally dangerous activities, liability in damages for trespass to land or for nuisance, and product liability. Today, to be sure, these are spacious and significant categories through which much of tort law's recent dynamism has been expressed. Together with the no-fault statutory schemes covering workplace and automobile accidents, they suggest how substantial a percentage of contemporary accident claims are resolved within one or another beyond-fault liability regime.

Several of these fields of modern strict liability have roots deep in the common law. They precede the development of negligence law and figure in the battles since roughly 1850 between negligence and strict principles—battles originating in divergent understandings of the liability principles secreted within the old forms of action.[34] Contradictory justifications supported contradictory lines of doctrine. Maxims pointing toward strict liability such as *sic utere tuo ut alienum non laedas* (use your own property in such a manner as not to injure that of another), or "between two innocents, he who caused the harm should pay," coexisted with other maxims ("no liability without moral fault") that were invoked by courts to build the framework of negligence law.[35]

The field of vicarious liability—a hybrid of negligence and strict-liability principles because the servant's fault, though not the master's, is a condition to that liability—represents the most entrenched example of a modern strict liability in tort. It long ago imposed liability on a faultless master for injuries stemming from the negligent conduct of a servant acting within the scope of employment. Even there, liability has increased—for example, through expansion of the category of servant by relaxing notions of a master's necessary "control," through a more expansive view of the "scope of employment," and through an erosion of the exception for independent contractors.[36]

The ambiguous principles of *Rylands* v. *Fletcher*[37] have influenced several fields of strict liability, particularly "abnormally dangerous activities." The liabilities from such activities have gradually expanded. Now they cover harm to a victim's land stemming from a broader range of uses of defendant's land (the historically dominant instances, but going beyond the traditional blasting cases to activities like crop dusting), as well as harm to a victim (such as injury from fire following a collision with a defendant's truck transporting inflammable fuel) unrelated to either the use of or injury to land.[38]

Nuisance law, a complex blend of principles of fault and strict liability in its cyclical movements and interaction with trespass law, tends in its contemporary form toward strictness, at least with respect to liability for damages.[39] To these three traditional fields with elements of strict liability, modern accident law has added an important fourth—liability for harm traceable to product defects.[40]

Apart from the central role of the servant's negligence, the vicarious liability of a master most closely approaches a genuine strict liability. If the negligent tortfeasor is characterized as a servant acting within the scope of employment, and if no defenses based on the victim's conduct are available, the master's liability is literally strict.

Each of the other important fields of modern strict liability employs threshold tests for the liability of a nonnegligent defendant that bear some affinity to the tests for negligence. Although not requiring criticism of defendant's conduct as wrongful, the tests include considerations that are at least potentially relevant to such a criticism. For example, courts deciding cases involving abnormally dangerous activities or nuisances and characterizing their decisions as going beyond the classical negligence system nonetheless consider relevant to liability such considerations as the utility of a defendant's activity, or the degree of risk and gravity of harm stemming from the defendant's activity.[41] The weighing of risk of harm from the defendant's product against the defendant's burden of precaution figures in the field of product liability treating design defects.[42] Such considerations are of course closely related to the cost-benefit reasoning required to perform the Hand Formula's calculation of negligence. Moreover, apart from the ambiguity in these threshold tests, questions continue to arise as to whether defenses endemic to negligence law such as a victim's advertent negligence will benefit the defendant in a strict-liability action.[43]

In such fields we are then far from the simple attribution rule—the rule indicating which accident costs are to be attributed to and thus covered by the defendant—of a workers' compensation plan. Nonetheless, the judicial habit is to characterize many of these liabilities as strict. Such terminological and conceptual confusion stems partly from the long-shared occupation of accident law by mixed regimes of negligence and strict liability, and their resulting interpenetration. Much of modern beyond-fault liability finds its nineteenth-century predecessors in vicarious liability, in strands of nuisance or land trespass, and in a *Rylands*-style liability.

It is not then surprising that each of the main contemporary fields of strict liability retains its specific character and tests, the mark of its peculiar history. This occurs despite the inevitable cross-fertilization among these fields through the common justifications that courts direct to them.[44] Nor is it surprising that such fields today experience gradual expansions or contractions in coverage, as courts feel the pull of the older negligence law and wrestle with the practical and conceptual dilemmas that a stronger version of strict liability would pose.

Consider the degree to which the provisions of the Second Restatements of Agency and of Torts[45] which treat the four identified fields bear out the preceding remarks. Each field has its distinctive doctrinal structure, unlike the Torts Restatement's effort to elaborate general principles of negligence liability embracing diverse actors and activities. We look in vain within the Restatements' discrete rules for each field for some overarching directive principles that would bind the doctrine among these fields within a general formulation and explanation of strict liability, or that would adequately distinguish the fields from other activities or conduct where one or another version of the negligence standard continues to govern.

The comments to the black-letter statements of the varied rules for strict liability merely summarize common explanations of courts for the evolving doctrines or stress one among them, without elaboration or critical appraisal. Sometimes the explanations have a tautological character; doctrine appears to justify itself. Liability for harm from abnormally dangerous activities is said to rest on a "policy of the law" imposing on one who creates an abnormal risk of harm a responsibility to compensate for it. The enterprise "is required to pay its way . . . because of its special, abnormal and dangerous character."[46]

In several instances, we are left with black letter law lacking even the character of a rule or standard. Consider the attempt of the Restatement of Torts to define an abnormally dangerous activity. It notes six relevant considerations and warns that they resist precise weighing. The presence or absence of any one factor is not decisive.[47] No one rationalizing principle guides us in making the vital preliminary characterization that generates a strict liability. We are left with a catalog uninformed by a methodology, a phenomenon all too apparent in opinions seeking to characterize an activity as unusual or atypical or highly dangerous.[48]

The sections dealing with monetary damages for nuisance blend concepts of intent, negligence, and strictness.[49] Relative to the First Restatement the upshot is heightened liability. These provisions retain criteria for liability that are compatible with a negligence regime: consideration of the utility of a defendant's enterprise, the reasonableness of the interference, or the gravity of the victim's harm. At the same time, they include distinctive criteria for liability that could, as applied, lead to beyond-fault liability. For example, the Restatement deems it relevant whether compensation by a defendant will affect its ability to continue in business—an ingredient of one version of so-called feasibility analysis in contemporary safety regulation.[50] And it inquires whether the victim's harm "is greater than he ought to be required to bear under the circumstances, at least without compensation."[51] We are now explicitly beyond negligence (because liability may exist without criticism of the defendant's conduct), but shy of the genuinely strict liability attaching, say, to a master after the preliminary characterizations for vicarious liability have been made (because defendant's ability to absorb the loss as well as the seriousness of the nuisance for the victim bear on liability).

Consider finally Section 402A of the Second Restatement of Torts treating liability for harm from defective products. It provides that one in the business of selling a product is liable for injury to the product's user or consumer if the product is sold "in a defective condition unreasonably dangerous to the user or consumer." It tells us that liability obtains although the manufacturer or seller "has exercised all possible care" in preparing or selling the product. In some contexts this section's departure from the classical negligence system is clear—for example, when the injury stems from an atypical flaw in a nonnegligently manufactured product.

Nonetheless, extensive judicial interpretation has given varied meanings to these provisions: different versions of the notion of a "defect," when a product's condition is "unreasonably dangerous," the relevance of a defendant's compliance with industry custom or a "state-of-the-art" standard, the distinction between flaws and design defects.[52] Despite its rulelike formulation of the basis for liability, Section 402A is now better viewed as a standard, as imprecise and manipulable as was the negligence standard for product liability that it formally displaced, subject to a variety of defenses, and less distanced from negligence law than was initially thought.

Given the Restatement's dominant aspiration to be photographer of a moment in the evolution of the common law, one would not have expected it to impose order on the unruly trend toward heightened liability. My point is simply that the fuzziness of contemporary black letter law and of any conception of strictness accurately reflects the confusion of opinions from which the restaters have drawn. In turn, the frequent invocation by the courts of the Second Restatement, as a peg and justification for expanding liability, can give no more coherent direction to doctrine than the Restatement itself possesses. Courts at once cite and interpret. They rely on the Restatement even as they qualify or creatively develop its rules and comments. Throughout they wrestle with the Restatement's ambiguous implications for doctrine and justification.

A phenomenon vital to my later discussion emerges from a review of these principal fields of modern strict liability. In each field, the defendant subject to such liability constitutes a business activity. In two fields, the doctrinal formulation signals this fact: harm from abnormally dangerous activities (such as blasting or crop dusting), and from product defects stemming from the activities of manufacturers and sellers.

Nuisance, on the other hand, is generally understood as a type of interference with the use and enjoyment of the victim's land, rather than as harm traceable to a particular kind of business activity. Nonetheless, liability for nuisance grows principally out of the pollutants that business activities generate. Even vicarious liability has become ever more linked to the forms of modern business organization. Indeed, decisions may either hold a corporation vicariously liable for an employee's fault, or simply treat the corporation and its employee as one business unit that is directly liable for negligence.[53]

The corporation as the characteristic instrument for substantial business activities becomes the characteristic defendant. A similar phenomenon can be observed as liability has expanded within the negligence system, either covertly or through explicit doctrinal change. In modern life, apart from auto accidents and self-inflicted harms, accidental injuries to persons or property are typically related to business activities or defective industrial products.

We shall see that the justifications for expanding liability within or outside the framework of negligence law underscore the business character and activity of the defendant. Moreover, the social vision expressed within modern accident law emphasizes the market context, corporate organization, and related capacities of the characteristic modern tortfeasor.

3   Justification

Outlines of doctrine, the Restatement's black-letter formulation of tort rules, give us sparse information about the
character and direction of accident law. Rules' indeterminacy,
their susceptibility to one or another interpretation or application, provide part of the explanation. In the hands and imagination of different judges, the same rule or standard can
express different perceptions of social life and advance different goals.

But the problem is deeper. One can be aware of the divergent meanings attributed to the "same" rule and yet fail to
perceive their origins in social life or moral thought. A doctrinal summary may inform us both of rules and counterrules,
or advise us of the range of judicial interpretation of a given
standard. But it will generally confine itself to that task, and tell
us little of the roots of or reasons for such diversity and contradiction. The recognition of indeterminacy and contradiction in
doctrine, vital as it is to an understanding of law and the work
of courts, carries us only to the threshold of more significant
questions and insights. How can we explain contradictions?
Given the extensive freedom of choice of courts in making and
remaking law, how has that choice been exercised and justified?

To explore such questions, we cannot view rules in isolation
from their animating goals or principles, or from the social
vision informing them. Chapter 3 examines the moral arguments that courts have used to justify their decisions, and the

justifications for tort accident law. Chapter 4 describes the social visions of courts and their complex relationship to justifications. The two together enable us to perceive tort rules both in
their historical realization and in their potential form, to understand them as dynamic rather than static in meaning, as contingent rather than necessary.

Moral justifications give meaning to the structure or competing structures of doctrine. They permit us to organize our
understanding of law at a level different from the formal rule.
Moral argument in opinions—its premises, assumptions, and
structure—lifts our comprehension of law from a mass of mi-
nutiae to their animating ideals. Rule and justification are
joined within a larger understanding. Given that relation, we
can imagine that a Restatement of Justifications would better
illuminate the law's significance and movement than one on
doctrine. Clarification of the ambiguities and contradictions
among justifications would form part of that illumination.

What relation then does moral justification bear to doctrine? In one sense, justifications are distinct from legal norms.
They confirm or criticize or develop such norms from moral
vantage points extrinsic to law. We can develop many policies
or principles of moral thought independently of the formal
structure of a legal system and the opinions of courts. The
ideals in judicial justifications—an ideal of mutual respect or
distributive justice or material growth—can then be said to
originate "outside" law, in social existence and the broad do-
main of moral and political thought.

But can we grasp the nature of the tort rules described in
this essay independently of moral ideals? The very phrasing of
this question suggests that the justifications described herein
are located not outside but within law. They figure centrally in
the argument of appellate courts about doctrine, and in this
sense are as much part of as distinct from rules. Indeed, judges
often refer to justifications as policies or principles "of the law,"
as instituted in some manner within the law, as deeply implicated in the whole structure of tort accident rules.

Much of the influential contemporary scholarship in tort law develops one or another moral argument to guide the assignment of accident costs. Its dominant strand involves the economic analysis of accident law, whether within formal models of allocational efficiency or within broader and more flexible frameworks of cost-benefit analysis.[1] In both cases such scholarship evaluates tort law against the goal of optimization of accident and safety costs within the assumptions and boundaries of the posited analytic framework.

Another influential strand of contemporary scholarship has stressed conceptions of fairness that should shape liability rules. Critics arguing that liability rules should achieve fairness have emphasized diverse conceptions of that ideal—for example, that liability should follow from the imposition of a nonreciprocal risk,[2] or that liability rules should aim at the fair distribution of an activity's benefits and burdens,[3] or should express intuitions of justice that underlie commonly held notions of causation.[4]

This literature has both a descriptive and prescriptive character. The descriptive undertaking seeks to identify a theory that is said to underlie courts' discussions of both doctrine and justifications, discussions that on their surface may fail to reveal that theory as such. The justificatory theory advanced by an author, such as allocational efficiency or an ideal of fairness related to reciprocity of risk imposition, may then be presented as one that is latent rather than manifest in the work of courts, as a deeper explanation for or rationalization of doctrine.[5] The scholar-advocate invokes such judicial rhetoric as supports that latent theory and often tends to blink the rest.

The prescriptive undertaking develops a theory of justification that lawmakers—sometimes only courts, sometimes legislatures as well—ought to follow in defining liability rules. The prescription may amount to the systematization of one or another of the strands of justification within the common law. Sometimes the descriptive and prescriptive undertakings seem indistinguishable.[6] The reader is left here, as elsewhere, with the recurrent question whether history yields theory or theory yields history.

My purpose is to explore how and what courts have thought about these matters rather than to chart a preferred course. I describe not one necessary structure of justification for tort law but competing structures among the fields of accident law, or structures that change over time within a given field. Hence the essay portrays not one ideal but a variety of ideals expressed through accident law. Its analysis of justifications grows out of and generalizes from opinions in diverse fields of accident law, expanding on and rendering more systematic the terse explanations of courts.[7] But the essay holds to the major themes in the opinions, avoiding the many refinements that scholars have brought to the elaboration and criticism of moral theory.

What I describe is a trend, not an abrupt dichotomy between older and modern justifications. The older and modern periods each contain their contradictions among fields or within a field. Important elements of contemporary justification figured in some earlier opinions, which in turn expressed attitudes basic to the developing negligence system that survive in many contemporary opinions. But a trend there has been.

The Style and Role of Judicial Justifications

As varied as they may appear, judicial justifications for fault and beyond-fault liability fall within a few broad patterns. An observer may believe one or another pattern to be dominant or preferable, but no single pattern emerges. It would indeed be remarkable if the common law did not offer us a feast of justifications, and as remarkable if they were not barely sketched fragments of moral theories rather than systematically elaborated.

Judges have never been rigorous moral philosophers, political theorists, economists, or expounders of some historical teleology—although elements of each such perspective on law as well as sheer prophecy inform their work. We understand judging in the large not as an occasion for the intense and reasoned pursuit of one or another ideal of justice or conception of welfare or vision of social transformation, but as an imprecise, even impressionistic, art, as a vexing and awful undertaking. An ideal competes with other ideals. Conceptions once probed may appear incoherent. Visions may be blurred. Principled decisions may veil simple compassion or inarticulate intuition.

Various phenomena, ranging from judges' differing notions of their institutional role to their different intellectual capacity and moral insight, further suggest that a search in opinions for coherent and complete argument about justifications is doomed to frustration. The force of inherited doctrine and precedents; different senses of what types of moral or political argument are appropriate to judicial opinions; related conceptions of courts of their institutional legitimacy and of the constraints on their freedom of invention relative to legislatures'; the diversity of social experience and political commitments brought by judges to the bench; the socioeconomic structures and dominant ideologies within which judges decide—such phenomena, all changing over time, make unlikely the continued supremacy of any single moral frame for decision.

Surely the surface structure of most opinions belies such a conception of the work of courts. Often discussion has an exclusively doctrinal character. The conventional, unproblematic style of an opinion holds closely to prior cases. We characteristically encounter formalist or analogical reasoning based on such cases, often without clarification as to why distinctions from or analogies to them are appropriate.

Or courts may draw justifications from prior opinions, such that the discussion of justifications and precedents becomes intertwined, part of a single argument. In such circumstances, moral justification appears on the surface of things to be as rooted in law as the narrowest holdings of the precedents. It may appear as precedent-bound, as judges repeatedly make the common modern arguments for strict liability. Or courts may draw on a broader framework of moral and social thought bearing on the doctrinal decision—public purposes, intuitions or theories of fairness, moral postulates about rights.

Justifications characteristically figure briefly in an opinion, often in the guise of a quickly sketched policy or principle. Their invocation may become as incantatory as church ritual, indeed quite predictable as a familiar justification is wedded to a given rule. Moral justification may consist of a sentence or two, perhaps no more than the bare statement of a conventional maxim, unreasoned and but another way of stating the doctrinal result. Rare are the opinions, and therefore much cited by courts and gathered by scholars, which attempt a systematic statement of the moral good or right to explain the decision.

As sparse as justificatory argument typically is, the important fact is that it constitutes an explicit and recurrent feature of judicial opinions. Why should courts seek to justify their decisions by moral argument rather than, for example, purport to rely exclusively on the shaping of doctrinal argument by a professional "legal technique" divorced from moral or political values?

First and fundamentally, there may be no escape. The need for an appellate opinion arises only because a losing party below thought a legal issue sufficiently debatable to merit an appeal. In such circumstances, courts will generally confront an important degree of doctrinal choice. A plausible opinion could decide for either party. The court struggles over different ways of characterizing the facts, conceptualizing the issues, or interpreting a rule. It may debate which of competing rules to follow. The mere reporting by a court of each party's argument, and surely a dissenting opinion, make the necessity of choice apparent on the face of things.

Resolution of these characteristic choices of appellate courts will not be achieved through a formal logic of decision making, through a refined legal technique. Of course, as Holmes observed, "You can give any conclusion a logical form."[8] But dressing a decision as routine deductive logic within a model of rule or concept formalism, or applying some "neutral" rule of interpretation to resolve ambiguity, or using unexplained doctrinal analogies, simply may not suffice. It may be impossible to conceal the choice made through such strictly "legal" argument. The opinion may appear too transparent or evasive. Or apart from such appearance, it may violate a judge's sense of obligation to explain why the particular decision was made.

Justificatory argument thus makes explicit, however tersely and incompletely, what must be present in many appellate cases—the beliefs underlying judges' choices whether one or another rule or decision is right or wrong or good or bad, according to some goals or principles or purposes or postulates. Justifications, often competing ones, may probe and clarify the implications of the choices that must be made. They may thereby influence the decision, no matter whether the court's justificatory argument confirms an extant rule or through its critical thrust promotes doctrinal change.

A second and related explanation of courts' explicit resort to justification would stress their perception of their institutional role and responsibility. Given that appellate cases generally involve some serious doctrinal choice, the problem arises of how a court will explain its choice in a way that convinces others. An important goal and function of that explanation will be to make the opinion appear legitimate. That is, the decision should appear to rest on broadly accepted norms and reasoned argument. It should not appear as an unconstrained exercise of power, as arbitrary preference.

Justificatory argument seeks to demonstrate that the decision was correct. It will be obvious on the face of things that the case could not be decided within the law's "autonomous" materials of rules and standards, pursuant to an "internal" or "legal" technique for reasoning about their application. Those materials and that technique were exhausted. Nonetheless, the opinion announces, as it were, that the court was not without moorings, was not left to whim or to inarticulate and unexplainable moral intuition.

Justification puts this rational face on the opinion, on the lawmaking work of courts, on the law. The moral ideals invoked by the judge, one or another conception of welfare or of right or fairness, serve the political and ideological function of presenting normative order as indeed ordered, as rational and just. Justification will tend to clothe an opinion with a form of legitimacy. It does so despite our awareness that a plausible competing justification could often generate a different decision, that choice has not been bypassed but simply raised to a level of insight and reflection above the formal rule.

Perhaps this purpose of legitimating individual decisions as well as the general lawmaking work of courts helps to explain why justification occupies a more prominent place in legal argument during periods of doctrinal turbulence (such as the recent decades of tort accident law). When courts adhere to a substantial body of inherited doctrine, when counterrules or competing justifications are less prominent in doctrine, judges may resort less to explicit justification. Adherence to the dominant, broadly accepted rules provides, as it were, sufficient legitimation for the opinion—perhaps because that adherence rests on a broadly shared conception of the proper institutional role of courts, or on the root ideal that like cases be decided alike.

In contrast, doctrinal innovation, or an inescapable choice between contradictory lines of doctrine, appears to arouse the sense of a judicial obligation to justify decisions. There can be no pretense that precedents resolve the matter, that decision did not require a lawmaking choice. Resort to justification may indeed underscore how deeply rooted are the conflicts within the doctrinal tradition, how significant are the choices to be made. Nonetheless, if not made to appear inevitable within some carefully bounded concept of the judicial role, the decision can at a minimum be made to appear reasoned and reflective, a considered exercise of a court's established authority rather than a random or mindless act of power.

Even in such circumstances, justifications often have a groping character. Essential for decision and vital to legitimation they may be. Nonetheless, justifications resemble less a comprehensive framework for the development of accident law than bits and pieces of a changing moral and political outlook.

Utilitarian and Right-Fairness Theories

This essay organizes the justifications for contemporary accident law within the two familiar modes of moral justification of conduct or rules within the Western liberal tradition: utilitarian theory and theories of right or fairness. These traditions of moral thought recurrently inform courts' debates about tort liability rules.[9] Hence, I begin with a statement of contemporary understandings of them, one that stops shy of exploring their shadings, deeper premises or historically varying forms.[10]

The strand of utilitarianism here relevant treats collective rather than personal morals—that is, the moral framework for a collective decision maker such as a judge rather than for individual decisions about personal conduct. The relevant decisions here amount to definitions of the rules or standards for tort liability. The question posed is how the judge making a utilitarian argument reaches and justifies these decisions.

Utilitarianism, a teleological structure of moral thought, posits one moral "ought." In contemporary terms, that "ought" can be described as the maximization of welfare or the satisfaction of wants. Utilitarian argument must then identify both a welfare goal and a means of realizing it. Analysis and prescription rest on the relation between ends (the goal) and means, hence, on means-to-end or instrumental rationality. Rules (means) are justified by virtue of their tendency to achieve the desired goal, ultimately by their consequences.

When described so abstractly in its barest structure of argument, utilitarianism is necessarily indeterminate about prescription. Consider the problem of defining the relevant end. Courts (or legislatures) rarely if ever imagine the *concept* of welfare and its maximization in the abstract, as a vast and comprehensive goal to which every rule of every character should be immediately and demonstrably responsive. At so general a level the concept can hardly be grasped or made to function as a guide to decision. Rather, courts invoke in different contexts more precise and limited *conceptions* of welfare—for example, a conception appropriate to accident law (whatever its breadth and complexity) such as the optimization of accident costs.[11] Such conceptions are tacitly understood to be a part or an intermediate realization of the ultimate goal of maximizing welfare. They may, of course, have considerable breadth and complexity, such as the welfare-related conception of optimization of accident costs. They may be disputed and contradict each other. Surely they have changed over time. In courts' decisions, one or another conception is simply posited.

Once the end is defined, the judge is left with the problem of means to realize it. The court must form a view or resolve competing views of what rule would best achieve a given conception of welfare. Such views rest on gross predictions about the consequences of a rule. Probabilities about outcomes under different rules (say, the different effects of negligence or strict-liability rules on the control of accident costs) depend on assumptions about cause-and-effect relationships in social life (say, the effect of higher product prices on consumer demand), particularly about the reactions of individuals and institutions to liability rules (say, whether companies will increase safety-related research as liability heightens). After all, the welfare goals stressed by the courts developing accident law must be realized through extant social institutions and patterns of social interaction.

The consideration of what rule is appropriate will generally involve cost-benefit calculations. Indeed, those calculations inhere in the test for liability for negligence that was earlier described, a test that explicitly absorbs justification—the Hand Formula's conceptualization of reasonable behavior. But such cost-benefit calculations within a utilitarian framework are more impressionistic than precise. They conceal as much as they reveal.

The problem reaches beyond the difficulty of quantification, hence of assessing whether or not benefits exceed costs.[12] A tacit but vital process of selection determines the kinds of costs and benefits that are to figure in the decision of courts or juries. Consider the Hand Formula. What types of harm (physical, mental, or economic; immediate or distant) are to be included within a prediction of the probable losses related to an activity? How will the court assess the social utility of the activity creating the risk of those harms? Which and whose benefits will be accounted for when courts consider the advantages of a liability rule?

Characteristically, the rule chosen in preference to another will be to the advantage of some but disadvantage of others. That is, it will have systemic distributional consequences. Victims, for example, generally benefit as liability grows stricter (although potential victims, when contractually related to the defendant through perhaps product purchases, may as a group bear a significant part of the heightened liability costs). Such trade-offs are inevitable within a utilitarian framework for decision making that posits the single moral imperative of maximization, an aggregative rather than distributive concept.[13] From the court's perspective, loss to some (diminished personal welfare, frustration of wants) will be justified by the larger gains and satisfaction of wants of others, and thus by the gain for society as a whole. Utilitarian calculations of judges cannot avoid such interpersonal comparisons of welfare.[14]

On the whole, courts are straightforward and unsophisticated in their utilitarian justification. They do not wrestle as do scholars with its problematic assumptions or argument. For example, the academic literature vigorously debates classical utilitarianism, the contemporary analysis of accident law within the framework of welfare economics, and relationships between the two. But rare is the opinion that suggests an awareness of the difficult methodological problems in deriving liability rules from utilitarian premises.

The current academic debate over the economic analysis of liability rules[15] remains alien in many respects to the judicial debate over, say, negligence and strict liability. Courts, for example, do not parrot some of the academic literature by self-consciously seeking to identify that liability rule which the concerned parties, in the absence of transaction costs, would have realized through bargain. Nor do they probe accident law's relation to such welfare-economics conceptions of efficiency as Pareto or Hicks-Kaldor criteria.

What courts do employ is a broad and unexamined welfare-oriented methodology. They engage in rough consequentialist reasoning.[16] Frequently, they simply allude to a rule's assumed or likely support of one or another policy, such as the effect of *res ipsa loquitur* doctrine on ferreting out information from defendants in negligence cases. (The term "policy" is frequently associated in opinions with utilitarian argument, whereas the term "principle" frequently suggests right-fairness argument.[17])

The same lack of methodological rigor or philosophical sophistication characterizes judicial justifications expressing the moralities of right or fairness. In their historical versions, such moralities have rested on different methods and derivations: ethical intuition, theological premises, a concept of natural law, abstract reason, contractarian images within the notion of a state of nature or of another form of original position.[18]

Right-fairness theory posits duties and correlative rights that are superior to the "good" (of, for example, welfare maximization): the duty to respect the human personality of others, the right to a fair distributive share of the benefits of social life. The rhetoric of right-fairness thought communicates a sense of unchanging principles of moral and legal conduct, of rights and duties that have an absolute character, and thus are not subject to erosion and trade-offs to realize one or another goal. Such rhetoric is distant from the assumption of utilitarian argument that legal rights are contingent on time and circumstances, subject to changing conceptions of welfare goals and changing beliefs about the proper instruments (rules) to reach them.

Nonetheless, different starting points within the right-fairness tradition—as well as different intuitions of justice, unadorned and direct—have led courts working within that tradition to different conclusions about what rules are justified. Despite its implicit claim to universality and timelessness, right-fairness theory has proven to be no more determinate or stable than utilitarian argument with respect to legal prescription.

Such theory rests not on maximizing or aggregative notions of welfare but on basic distributive criteria, whether the entitlements that it posits are defined in terms of equal rights against stated interferences by others, or in terms of rights to redistribution within a theory of fair shares. Relative to utilitarian calculations, which tend to stress material phenomena (such as optimization of accident costs or adequate legal encouragement for entrepreneurial activity), right-fairness thought emphasizes nonmaterial and intangible values such as those inhering in human personality or in a theory of distributive justice.

My analysis of the justifications inhabiting tort accident law draws on these distinctions between the utilitarian and right-fairness traditions. It does so in order to underscore the differences among such justifications' premises and structures of argument. Despite their conventional character and utility, these distinctions can however be readily overstated. Each tradition can be seen as containing important elements or responding to important concerns of the other. For example, courts justifying their decisions by a theory of fair distribution are not blind to the implications of their rulings for social life. Implicitly or explicitly, their arguments based on right-fairness theories take account of the consequences of court-made rules for social actors and interaction. By the same token, some of the welfare-oriented arguments considered below can also be understood as expressing conceptions of right.

Other considerations further qualify the significance of these distinctions. Because of the terseness and ambiguity of their arguments, or because of their blend of concepts identified in the present discussion with one or the other tradition of moral thought, numerous opinions are open to alternative classifications. Moreover, it will become clear that whether a court justifies a decision within one or the other tradition of moral thought has little independent significance for the content of legal norms. There is no reason to believe, *a priori*, that argument within either utilitarianism or right-fairness theory will point toward a fault rather than a strict system of liability. Abstractly, the logic or assumptions of utilitarianism or fairness theory have no such inherent bias. Within the classical negligence system as it developed to the mid-twentieth century, judicial justifications within each of the two traditions sometimes supported the same structure of rules. On the other hand, at times one or the other mode of justification was employed to challenge negligence principles and support strict liability. Utilitarian and fairness justifications have been employed both to support and criticize the trend toward heightened liability.[19]

Such indeterminacy with respect to legal prescription stems principally from the abstract character of these structures of moral thought. Each can embrace diverse aspirations for and beliefs and information about the world. Only when fleshed out with facts or assumptions about and understandings of social life will they yield a reasonably concrete theory of justification and hence reasonably concrete prescription. Rather than probe the abstract logic of justificatory arguments, much of chapter 3 and the discussion of social vision in chapter 4 emphasize just those elements in judicial opinions that flesh out justifications.

The Content of Justifications

My discussion treats separately the justifications for what I have termed the classical negligence system and for modern heightened liability. The first section therefore includes a variety of justifications, changing over time, as negligence law developed from its nineteenth-century formulation to the mid-twentieth century. For example, the form of utilitarian justification now captured in the Hand Formula became prominent only toward the end of this period.[20] Although concentrating on the four major fields of contemporary tort law with doctrinal aspects of strictness, the second section on heightened liability also draws on decisions expanding negligence liability (abolishing immunities, eliminating pockets of limited duty).

THE CLASSICAL NEGLIGENCE SYSTEM

I shall characterize as either affirmative or negative the recurrent justifications for negligence liability. Imagine a chart meant to describe the fault system (intentional tort and negligence). It is divided into three vertical columns: (1) a characterization of defendants' conduct as reasonable or as unreasonable, (2) the related doctrinal conclusion about liability, and (3) the related justification for that conclusion.

The chart is also divided midway up by a horizontal "fault line." Below that line, defendants' conduct (the first column) is characterized as unreasonable within one or another of the described tests for negligence. Therefore tort doctrine (the second column) indicates that they are liable. Above the line, defendants' conduct (first column) is characterized as reasonable within these same tests. Hence, tort doctrine (second column) indicates no liability. The victims bear the loss even though they are as "innocent" as the defendants.

The *affirmative justifications* supporting the tort doctrine of liability for fault appear (in the third column) below the fault line and argue *for liability* up to that line. They explain why the intentional or negligent tortfeasor ought to compensate the victim. The *negative justifications* supporting the negligence system appear (in the third column) above the fault line and argue *against liability* for conduct above that line.[21] They explain why the defendant characterized as behaving reasonably ought not to be required to compensate the victim.

It is difficult to imagine a system of tort liability after the development of industrial society that did not reach at least to the fault line on the chart—for example, to imagine a tort system confining liability to the traditional intentional torts such as battery. During the growth of negligence law in the nineteenth century, when the forms of action bowed to modern substantive conceptions of the bases for tort liability, courts rarely took pains to justify why there should be liability when the defendant acted negligently. That did not seem to require justification.

Of course, there were pockets of "limited duty" or "no duty": landowners' limited duties of care to others on their land, aspects of assumption-of-risk doctrine that effectively insulated negligent defendants from liability, contract-limited duties in product liability that shielded a negligent manufacturer against liability to remote users of its product, or the limited duty to aid persons in physical danger.[22] Apart from such increasingly anomalous fields of tort law, and apart from defenses and immunities and doctrines like proximate cause, courts simply took for granted the liability for physical harm of a negligent as well as an intentional tortfeasor. That liability was not problematic.

When outside the areas of limited-duty or no-duty, what courts were more apt to wrestle with was the choice between liability only for fault and strict liability. There lay a battle. In waging that battle, the nineteenth-century courts developed negative justifications for the fault system. Those justifications served primarily to ward off liability above the fault line, where defendants were "innocent."

We start with the affirmative justifications. Although such justifications for fault liability figured more significantly in the work of scholars than of courts, let us begin with their judicial exposition. Within the tradition of right-fairness thought they were more implicit than explicit in opinions. They appeared to rest on familiar moral principles within the Western liberal tradition of individual rights and autonomy (with correlative duties of others to honor those rights and respect autonomy): the right to be accorded equal respect, to be viewed as an end rather than as a means to another's purposes, to be treated by others as they would be treated. Tort doctrine on the strong intentional torts most vividly illustrates the force for the fault system of these postulates about human personality and dignity—for example, the right not to be intentionally interfered with by a blow (and the correlative duty not to strike).[23] These indeed are the classic libertarian rights to be left alone. Violation of a duty not to interfere, it was assumed, led quite naturally to a further duty to make reparation for the resulting harm, to rectify a wrong or moral imbalance and set the world straight.[24]

Apart from intentional torts like battery, it is advertent negligence—the conscious imposition on the victim of an unreasonable risk to serve the imposer's purposes—that most readily falls within such principles of moral rights and duties. Again there is a failure (the driver speeding through the school zone) in the duty to show equal respect (to those within it). However, when negligence consists of the inadvertent failure to meet an external standard of care (defendant failed to notice and thus to advise others of the defective stairs to his house), those principles have a more doubtful application. If defendants are capable of greater care, the justification may assume that liability will educate them to a higher degree of attention to and respect for others. But at a certain stage that assumption becomes untenable. When, for example, mental incompetents are held liable, the rigor of the external standard of care may render impossible the equation of fault liability with personal moral fault.[25]

Affirmative justifications within the utilitarian framework figured prominently in the negligence system, particularly by the early twentieth century. Indeed one of the principal tests for ascertaining negligence, the Hand Formula, drew upon that framework.[26] Marginal safety costs (B) were compared with the marginal reduction in accident costs (PL). Where B was greater than the reduction in PL, the risk-generating conduct of a defendant was justified, for more precaution would have diminished social welfare. The imposed risk was therefore reasonable. But where reduction in PL would have exceeded B, defendant was judged negligent. By failing to take greater precaution, defendant diminished welfare.

It is possible to view the Hand Formula not only within the framework of welfare-maximization, but also as expressing a duty of care resting on conceptions of right and respect. Social actors should not impose serious risks and costs on others to achieve less significant goals of their own. To do so disrespects and uses others. Rather, they should act as prudently as they would if they were to experience the risks and costs of their conduct as well as realize its benefits—if, that is, they were to internalize the costs as well as benefits of their conduct. Under that hypothesis, actors would so conduct themselves as to assume a burden only for a greater benefit. And they would treat others with equal respect.[27]

But the Hand Formula and the judicial rhetoric accompanying it in many opinions speak more vividly to notions of utility. The general belief, implicit in judicial opinions, was that the attribution of accident costs to a defendant through such cost-benefit calculations would encourage cost-rational social actors to modify their behavior by taking cost-justified precautions that would avoid tort liability. Requiring compensation served less as a way of rectifying an injustice or alleviating the victim's suffering than as a means of persuading potential defendants to modify behavior.[28] Businesses, the typical defendants, would spend ninety-nine cents more in safety costs to spare themselves the one dollar in projected liability costs that courts would impose in tort actions. The affirmative justification for liability appeared to rest dominantly on this purpose—one that would be described in contemporary terms as resource-allocational, encouraging the movement of resources to their highest valued use and thereby achieving a socially optimum investment in safety. Waste would be curbed and the conditions for social life improved.[29]

Opinions generally gave scant attention to the conceptual and practical difficulties in this test *cum* justification. It amounted to a conception of tort liability as a form of regulation—not, to be sure, direct regulation involving statutory safety standards mandating changes in behavior, but rather indirect regulation encouraging changes in the behavior of enterprises by requiring them to bear certain accident costs related to their activities. It thus depended, as do utilitarian justifications in general, on instrumentalist premises, on causal relations in the world (the relation between rule and behavior) rooted in intention: the intention of the court to induce behavior modification through incentives or disincentives, and deliberative conduct of cost-rational social actors responding as self-interest suggested. This mode of justification then assumes a certain type of behavioral rationality of institutional defendants and, particularly with respect to its application to defenses such as contributory or comparative fault, of individuals as well.

Courts ignored the general barriers to realizing such indirect regulation, such as the serious transaction and information costs that reduced the likelihood of victims suing. They also blinked barriers impeding the access of particular types of plaintiffs to the legal system, barriers related to poverty and race. By making litigation or settlements less likely, such phenomena led to less internalization of accident costs to negligent actors than the justification theoretically required. Moreover, courts generally ignored the possible influence of the expanding system of liability insurance on the cost-benefit analyses and behavior of defendants.[30]

Of course, realization of the justification's goal was further threatened by the sheer complexity and uncertainties in applying the Hand Formula. The ingredients of analysis, such as the social utility of a defendant's activity or the nature and probability and quantification of loss, were indeterminate.[31] Opinions treating administrative safety standards under programs of direct regulation have made explicit, in ways that the tort opinions have not, such dilemmas in the assumptions and methods inhering in cost-benefit approaches to decision making.[32]

The negative justifications employed by courts reinforced the fault system by rejecting liability above the fault line. They were in part mirror images of the affirmative ones. For example, principles of right suggested that a defendant who had failed to give equal respect to a victim should be liable in damages, an affirmative justification. Within the negative justifications, those same principles were drawn upon to deny liability without fault. Strict liability was viewed as lacking a moral foundation for holding defendants responsible.[33] Fault was at once the occasion for and limit to liability.

Similarly, ideas within the welfare-maximizing justifications for negligence liability figured in negative justifications arguing that fault should constitute a ceiling for liability. It was apparently assumed that reaching above the fault line to assess damages against defendants who acted reasonably would not improve on the fault system's incentives to those defendants to make cost-justified investment in safety. On the other hand, a strict liability could discourage socially useful activity by requiring productive actors to bear unavoidable accident costs.[34] Entrepreneurs would hesitate to invest and innovate in a legal setting requiring compensation for harms traceable to reasonable as well as unreasonable risks. Beyond-fault liability could thereby generate costs (including surrendered opportunities) exceeding benefits.[35] It would reduce social welfare, explicitly identified with production and material progress.[36] Negligence liability functionally accommodated the goals of reducing accident costs and achieving some level of security in social life with the goal of encouraging (or at least not discouraging) entrepreneurial activity.[37]

Other negative justifications figuring in the opinions were fragmentary versions of theories of distributive fairness. Courts argued that all members of society benefited from industrial activity with its inevitable risks, and that within a long-run framework of reciprocities of risk imposition, all members more or less equally burdened and benefited from others. Hence, when an actor had not imposed an unreasonable atypical risk through negligence, there was no reason to redistribute loss.[38] Or courts noted that business could not capture many of the external benefits that it conferred on strangers, such as the heightened value of farmers' land after the railroad came through. Hence, in fairness business should not be charged with its external costs other than those traceable to fault.[39]

Two issues arise in the following comparison between these affirmative and negative justifications for the fault system and the judicial justifications for heightened liability. First, why do the negative justifications for the fault system no longer convince courts that liability should be arrested at the fault line? Second, what different affirmative justifications support heightened liability?

MODERN HEIGHTENED LIABILITY

Each of the four major fields with explicit elements of strict liability poses its distinctive problems affecting the character of justifications. Nuisance law, for example, must wrestle with the choice between negligence and strict liability in the different contexts of actions seeking damages or injunctive relief. Liability rules for product defects confront special issues that grow out of their contractual nexus—for example, the related problems of manufacturers' warnings or disclaimers and of consumers' assumption of risk. Hence, my description of the major, recurrent justifications for strict liability will not perfectly fit the peculiar character of any one field.

Nonetheless, these fields have not evolved in isolation from each other. The same judges developed them, and quite naturally employed similar justifications for heightened liability among them. Justifications initially prominent in one field have come to inform others. Vicarious liability cases, for example, invoke justifications for strict liability that were used earlier for strict product liability.[40]

Numerous opinions of recent decades expand liability within the framework of negligence law by abolishing immunities or such defenses as assumption of risk, and by eroding older fields of no duty. They employ justifications similar to those in the four "strict liability" fields. It is both from opinions with elements of strict liability and from those expanding negligence liability that we can draw and classify the major strands of contemporary justification.

The Task of Strict-Liability Justification

Justifications for strict liability must respond to difficult threshold problems. If fault is no longer to serve as the reason for attributing accident costs to a defendant, what test or principle is to succeed it? The loose notions grouped under the rubric of legal or proximate causation will not alone suffice to define the boundaries to liability. Some additional limit must be established if courts are to avoid attributing to a defendant all accident costs to which it is causally related.

Within the opinions advancing arguments for strict liability, one encounters such rhetoric as "business ought to bear all its costs," or ought to "internalize" its external costs—a version of so-called enterprise liability. Implicitly, such rhetoric assumes that a business activity alone "causes" accidents and should therefore assume their costs. But the multiple and reciprocal character of causation—both the defendant's and the victim's activities were necessary causal antecedents to the accident—suggests that such a notion, standing alone, often cannot yield a satisfactory answer. Causal assumptions or rhetoric of this character often veil the theories of fairness or utility that support charging the defendant with "its" costs and that may help to define just how courts should decide which costs are "its."[41]

The inadequacy of a simple causal rhetoric made necessary other judicial approaches toward marking and justifying the boundaries to cost internalization. But the doctrinally ambivalent character of strict liability complicates the task of marking those boundaries. As was earlier noted, "strictness" as applied to most common-law liabilities falls shy of a so-called absolute or insurer's liability, or of the rigorous beyond-fault liability of statutory schemes like workers' compensation. First, the threshold tests for liability in fields such as product defects and nuisance sometimes incorporate criteria linked to the fault system and thereby limit the accident costs attributed to a defendant. Second, defenses based on the victim's fault or assumption of risk survive.

Given the complexity of "strict liability" doctrine, including its links to negligence law, it is not surprising to find a similar complexity among the modern justifications for tort liability. For example, the negative justifications for the fault system retain force as courts confront the implications of a genuine strict liability and worry that too severe a burden on business will impair productivity.

Recurrent Themes

Modern opinions offer many explanations for strict liability. Some are rare; some predictably recur. Courts, for example, have argued that strict liability bypasses the difficulties confronted by victims in proving negligence. By imposing more costs on defendants' activities, it corrects this reason for the historical underinternalization of accident costs within the fault system.[42] But certain themes and arguments stand out. Rather than presenting an exhaustive catalog, my description here treats these major themes.

We first consider the recurrent argument that strict liability will induce defendants to modify their behavior in order to contain accident costs, a welfare-oriented argument resting on a regulatory vision of tort law. A second major category of moral argument treats justifications for compensation of the victim and the related spreading of accident costs. It stresses the situation of victims and the distribution of loss rather than the regulation of the typical defendants, namely, businesses. The final theme here considered isolates a body of cases involving prior contractual arrangements between defendants and victims that bear on liability standards, and examines justifications for honoring or invalidating such arrangements.

Behavior Modification to Reduce the Number of Accidents

Within the fault system, defendants bore accident costs up to the fault line. Modern justification urges cost internalization above that line as well. In doing so, it achieves indirect regulation by seeking to influence the resource-allocational decisions of both producers and consumers of goods and services. The modern justifications deny what appeared to be an implicit assumption in the negative justifications for the fault system, that strict liability would not provide additional incentives for safety. Rather, they argue that under a regime of strict liability, producers will allocate resources differently within their activities, whereas consumers will allocate their resources differently among the products or services offered them. The effect of these decisions will be to achieve a preferable level of safety.

Producers' Resource Allocation   Like the Hand Formula, this prominent strand of utilitarian justification aims through liability rules at modification of the behavior of potential defendants. The desired behavior, it is assumed, will lead to more cost-justified investment in safety, and hence to reduction of the total costs of safety and accidents.[43]

Perhaps by hypothesis, the goals of these two versions of utilitarian justification—the Hand Formula's understanding of negligence and strict-liability justifications—are identical. Both seek the optimization of accident costs through indirect regulation. But the means toward achieving that goal, the type of liability rules, change. That change stems from the assumptions and empirical understandings about social and institutional life that inform and render concrete any utilitarian-based prescription. Different assumptions and understandings here generate different liability systems.[44]

So we start by comparing the broad assumptions in the justifications for fault and strict-liability systems. The comparisons underscore the dynamic character of the incentives to improve safety under strict liability. The fault system works within a static rather than dynamic time frame. It contemplates life retrospectively, comparing what in fact occurred with a conception of what ought to have occurred if the defendant had acted reasonably. The court and jury engage in a historical, contextual inquiry into the risk generated by the defendant and the related accident. In deciding whether the risk was unreasonable, whether the defendant ought to have acted differently, they generally accept the technology extant at the time of the conduct as the relevant framework for a defendant's decisions—although the boundary may be hazy between the known technology at a given time and what with due diligence and research manufacturers ought to or could have known.[45] Despite its implications for behavior modification and thus for future conduct, fault liability flows only from the past mismanagement of risk.

Justifications for strict liability imagine a dynamic time frame and the further possibilities of business life. Courts speculate prospectively rather than analyze retrospectively. Their inquiry into safety is more abstract than contextual. That is, they stress not how safety ought to have been improved but rather how it might be improved through changes in defendant's ongoing management of the risk that its activity generates. They emphasize that broader *activity,* the larger technological and organizational framework for the activity, rather than defendant's particular accident-related *conduct* that dominated inquiry into fault. The defendant is before the court in the large, as a systematic business enterprise, rather than merely through a slice of its past operations.[46]

Within a future-oriented rather than historical vision, the notion of foreseeability of risk changes from the fault system's. It is not just undue risk that ought to have been avoided for which the defendant is charged. Rather, defendant is also responsible for harm traceable to unavoidable risk in an activity, a risk subject to actuarial calculation on the basis of a defendant's or an industry's experience, and foreseeable only in this abstract statistical sense.[47] There will be accidents from blasting or from auto defects no matter what care defendant takes in its activity. That the risk may have been cost-justified within the Hand Formula becomes irrelevant.

But if reasonable risk no longer establishes the boundary to liability, what does? Since all risk is in theory foreseeable, the notion of foreseeability cannot itself limit liability for causally related harm. Moreover, victims such as pedestrians or product users can also be made aware of and thus foresee bare actuarial risk, even if that awareness could not reasonably be expected to induce any modification of their behavior. So fore-sight of risk alone cannot stand as a sufficient criterion for assigning liability. Nor, as earlier noted, can a simple and workable concept of causation that treats the business defendant as "the" cause.

For many courts, the relevant question has become whether the defendant or the victim will better respond to a liability rule by seeking to reduce presently cost-justified risk. Strict liability justifications conclude that business defendants are the more likely to act under tort law's incentives to avoid liability costs.[48] Rare is the opinion that argues in any detail toward this conclusion. Characteristically, the courts simply note a business's superior knowledge and organizational capacity for ascertaining and controlling risk, particularly within the typical activities giving rise to accidents—technologically complex means of production, services, and products. They observe that the typical victim tends to be uninformed about such matters, and thus unable to guard against the many systematic accident risks in modern society.[49]

Unlike the fault system, strict-liability justifications then stress not what the defendant ought to have done within then-existing (or perhaps attainable) knowledge and technology, but what it perhaps ought to do, or at least ought to think about doing.[50] To the extent indicated by marginal cost-benefit analysis, firms will engage in research and development to gain the knowledge necessary to control accident costs economically. They will act to devise safety measures less costly than the predicted accident costs that the firms must now bear.

Courts simply guess that strict liability will thereby yield improved resource allocation.[51] That improvement may stem not only from technological advances but also from changes in the organization or structure of a defendant's activity. Perhaps routes or time schedules should be adjusted by a trucking company to reduce the predictable vicarious-liability costs from their servants' negligent driving. If an activity generates disproportionate accident costs at a high volume, perhaps its level of activity should be marginally reduced.[52] Such administrative rationalization of an enterprise, in theory within the calculations suggested by the Hand Formula, effectively escaped legal scrutiny within the fault system because of the range and complexity of the issues it poses. But the new liability rules could spur all such complex, decentralized choices by enterprises about resource allocation.

To the extent that the victim's fault reduces or eliminates the defendant's strict liability, the court's or jury's reasoning returns to negligence analysis. With respect to the victim, it becomes less abstract and future-oriented, more contextual and historically oriented.[53] The allowance of such a defense emphasizes the tension between such themes in strict-liability justification as a rigorous enterprise liability (business should bear all its costs) and allocational goals (attribution of accident costs should aim at superior resource allocation). Under the reigning behavioral assumptions, allowing the defense of a victim's fault is consistent with placing the accident loss on the party better able to have avoided the accident. The elimination or reduction of recovery because of contributory or comparative fault would encourage the victim to modify behavior.[54] Doctrine here is particularly unstable. Courts, for example, waver with respect to the effect on liability of even a victim's advertent negligence.[55]

Judicial ambivalence about allowing a fault-based defense in a strict-liability case appears to stem from several considerations. Contributory or comparative fault is a defense typically asserted by business defendants against individual (rather than institutional) victims. But there is doubt that tort rules significantly influence the safety-oriented behavior of individuals. Fear of personal injury seems more likely to affect potential victims' level of safety than fear of diminished recovery after injury. Moreover, the force of justifications stressing loss distribution rather than behavior modification has further weakened fault-based defenses.

Consumers' Resource Allocation   A related strand of utilitarian justification stresses modification of the behavior not of producers but consumers. Opinions note that strict liability makes an activity or product "bear its costs."[56] Accidents together with other costs will be expressed through the pricing of products and services. Markets will then indicate more accurately the social costs of products and services sold within them.[57]

Just as strict liability influences producers' resource allocation within an activity, the inclusion of more accident costs in the price of a service or product will influence consumers' choice about how much to buy and whether to seek a substitute.[58] Such allocational choices by consumers will be more "rational" than when fewer accident costs were captured in prices of products or services through the fault system. The negligence system "underinternalized." Consumers will now take account through the price system of reasonable as well as unreasonable risks, of inevitable as well as avoidable accidents. Price-induced changes in consumer demand—assuming, as courts appear to, sufficient elasticity of demand—will in turn affect producers' resource allocation among types of products and activities.

Compensation and Loss Spreading

This second strand of justification for strict or heightened liability shifts attention from modifying defendants' behavior to compensating accident victims. It looks initially to a victim's plight rather than to a defendant's past or future conduct. It addresses primarily the victim's postaccident costs. Even if strict liability had no influence on resource allocation different from, say, the Hand Formula's, the larger compensation of victims that it entails would still bring about this radically different outcome from the fault system. Absent fault, loss does not lie but is transferred to the defendant. The difference from the fault system is at least distributional. Victims come out ahead.

Of course, compensation may amount literally and exclusively to *shifting* from a victim to a defendant those elements of loss that the law takes into account through tort damages. Such, for example, would be the effect of an individual defendant's liability for battery. After payment of compensation, and assuming no protection through liability insurance, the legal measurement of the plaintiff's loss is concentrated on the defendant. Modern justification for heightened liability, however, typically links compensation of the victim not simply to the *shifting* of loss to a defendant, but to the related *spreading* of loss by the defendant to a broader community.[59]

The distinction is vital. Judicial opinions within the select fields of strict liability in the nineteenth century asserted a moral duty to compensate a victim. They expressed that duty partly through maxims suggesting an unproblematic notion of causation, such as "between two innocents, who caused the harm should pay."[60] But the image within that maxim is one of shifting loss from one innocent to another. The implicit premise was that loss would now "lie" with the "cause" (defendant) rather than with the victim.[61] Such earlier judicial justifications rarely linked compensation to loss spreading. Even within the long historical tradition of strict liability, the prominence of justificatory argument based on loss spreading appears to constitute a distinctive recent phenomenon.[62]

It is true that the rhetoric of loss spreading has also grown within the negligence system in recent decades. As one reason for abolishing immunities or defenses such as assumption of risk, courts have noted the availability of liability insurance and underscored its effect of broadly distributing loss. Liability could therefore avoid concentration of loss on either the victim or the defendant.[63] In this manner, insurance and loss spreading contributed to heightened liability within the negligence system. Nonetheless, in such contexts the defendant's fault remains a condition to liability. But as developed by courts to support fields of modern strict liability, justifications based on loss spreading dispense with the requirement of fault. Thus, the theme of loss spreading should be understood both as allied with judicial justifications for heightened liability within the negligence system and as underlying powerful modern arguments for going beyond that system.

It is clear that utilitarian argument underlies the development of strict-liability rules intended to lower accident costs. Loss spreading as a justification for heightened liability is, however, ambiguous. It may involve welfare-oriented argument in that courts may believe that accident costs will be lowered if they are spread rather than concentrated on the victim. And it may draw on right-fairness thought. In fact, few opinions elaborate either a utilitarian or right-fairness justification for loss spreading. But those that go beyond mere references to the goal of spreading to some explicit argument appear to be dominantly within the spirit of an ideal of fairness.

Frequently, the justificatory rhetoric of courts that argues for loss spreading is so summary and general that it is amenable to being classified within either moral framework. Statements, for example, that a defendant should bear liability because it is better situated than the victim to spread loss, which is itself a "policy" of the law, can be as readily classified within one as the other.

Utilitarian Justifications   We start with the utilitarian argument for loss spreading.[64] A few basic ideas recur. Allowing accident costs to lie with the victim entails serious social loss that reaches well beyond the victim. But this postimpact loss is not fixed or inevitable. Liability rules can reduce it by spreading the loss among others through the intermediary of the tort defendant.[65]

The frequently mentioned mechanisms for spreading include the defendant's liability insurance or self-insurance, and market mechanisms for spreading these costs of insurance.[66] Within market constraints and in indeterminate percentages, insurance costs will ultimately be borne by the consumers of the defendant's production or by other groups related to the defendant, such as shareholders or employees. Like behavior modification within fault and strict-liability justifications, loss spreading also then relies on conventional market mechanisms to achieve its goals.

In making the argument for loss spreading, courts draw on the understanding of the accident problem that informs legislative schemes of the regulatory-welfare state, such as workers' compensation or auto plans. Should medical care be unaffordable and otherwise unavailable, concentration of loss on the victim will block recovery and the victim's potential for productive activity. Whether the victim remains physically handicapped or simply economically deprived because of the accident, there will likely be adverse financial and psychological effects on those supported by the victim, as well as welfare losses for the business or activity in which the victim had been productive. Waste results for the individual and society.

Even when loss remains with the defendant to whom it is shifted, compensation still alleviates these problems of the victim. However inadequate a reparation for the injury, it will facilitate the victim's return to preaccident life—to be sure, at best a partial return in cases of serious injury. But spreading the loss beyond the defendant avoids its concentration on any single actor. Social life is thereby restored, more or less, to where it was. It will never be the same, for an accident did occur. But that welfare loss for the victim and others will be lessened through spreading.

Courts whose language suggests a utilitarian foundation for spreading accident losses do not even sketch the possible theoretical support for the view that the welfare loss from an accident can thereby be reduced. One could argue, for example, that the concept of diminishing marginal utility, when coupled with interpersonal comparisons of utility and an assumption of similar utility functions, supports loss spreading. Small burdens on many, when aggregated, will weigh less than a loss that is concentrated on the victim.[67]

Of course, potential victims could themselves arrange for spreading an important part of the loss by acquiring first-party (loss) insurance, either individually or through workplace-related insurance plans that benefit employees and grow out of collective bargaining. Opinions barely touch on the reasons for preferring strict liability to reliance by potential victims on loss insurance.[68] Courts do suggest that the business defendant is better situated than the victim to insure and plan for accident losses.[69] Businesses can better make actuarial predictions of losses and can more economically take advance precautions through liability or self-insurance and product pricing. In this sense, loss-spreading justifications, like those aiming at behavior modification, have a prospective and not simply retrospective orientation. They, too, seek to change the behavior of potential defendants, and assume that businesses will respond to the strict-liability rule by prudently managing inevitable liability costs.

Through loss-spreading arguments, courts attempt to overcome a negative justification for the fault system—the concern that heightened liability will repress production or innovation and thus burden national growth. They perceive the corporate defendant as an intermediary rather than a terminal point in the transfer of accident costs. Therefore, liabilities can be spread rather than remain with and ruin the defendant. Moreover, some decisions suggest that the older negative justifications no longer fit current circumstances. They explain liability-restrictive doctrines that have been revised or abolished—such as contributory fault or assumption of risk— as efforts to protect nascent industry. Such protection, they seem to suggest, is no longer necessary, since the country and its business enterprises are now rich enough to aid accident victims.[70] Nonetheless, the negative justifications retain their force in fields such as medical drugs or malpractice, as courts worry about the effect of heightened liability on insurance rates and on prices of products or services, or on the willingness of entrepreneurs to invest and experiment.[71]

Right-Fairness Justifications   Within this category, I treat justifications both for *compensation* (assuming no more than that a defendant covers and remains to that extent with the victim's loss) and for *loss spreading* (further assuming that defendant's compensatory payment will be spread to and borne by large communities). Some of these justifications amount to widely shared but barely expressed intuitions, though not less powerful for their brevity. Others develop bare outlines of what can be termed theories of distributive justice.

These arguments lack the instrumentalism of utilitarian justification. Courts perceive compensation as a requirement of justice rather than as a path toward the welfare goal of reducing individual and social costs of accidents.[72] The older common law and the opinions of recent decades offer three principal types of such arguments for heightened liability. The first two types of right-fairness justifications stress compensation as such; the third points to loss spreading.

1. Several justifications proceed from the unexplored premise of a near absolute right or entitlement to be free of harmful interferences—a right, it is interesting if not historically surprising to note, attaching primarily to property rather than the person. Any substantial interference with that property right constitutes a wrong, independent of fault, which entails the duty to compensate. Traditional maxims supporting strict liability such as *sic utere* capture this conception.[73] In their strong form—and *sic utere* has been rendered by courts in many versions—such maxims appear to support injunctive relief against continuing interferences such as nuisances, as well as compensatory damages. The faultless defendant, after all, acted as the maxim forbad by using its property so as to interfere substantially with another's.

2. A second strand of right-fairness justification rests on a comparison of moral positions of the defendant and the victim. The comparison stresses the nature of their activities and interaction, the way in which the accident occurred. Although the defendant's activities relevant to these cases are generally recurrent and systematic, related to an ongoing enterprise, courts tend to focus on the particular interaction producing the accident and to compare the particular position or conduct of the plaintiff and defendant. That is, their analysis and observations focus on the precise relevant events, whereas the justifications built on loss spreading tend to view the immediately relevant interaction as but one instance among many, as part of the systemic accident-producing interactions of modern life.

Opinions provide varied examples of such comparisons of moral positions, in each of which the court concludes that violation of the plaintiff's "right," or an ideal of fairness, requires compensation. In these situations, the "wrong" does not lie in the defendant's conduct, which is not criticized. Rather, it consists in the defendant's failure to compensate for the harm resulting from its activity. In this important sense, such justifications differ from a strong version of maxims such as *sic utere*.

A. The maxim, "between two innocents, he who caused the harm should pay," falls within this strand of justification. It generally enters opinions as an unargued but deep intuition of fairness.[74] Though silent itself about the complexities in the notion of causation—multiple causation, reciprocal causation between defendant and victim—the maxim appears to assume that the defendant has been an "active" party and the victim a "passive" one, and to assume a moral difference between such parties that justifies viewing the active one as the cause. Indeed, most of its applications involve contexts where it is easy to imagine one party as active and the other as passive—an industrial firm polluting a farmer's stream, for example, as opposed to the two innocent parties to a collision. In this sense, the maxim expresses the notion of an imposition that is undue because it is unilateral, and whose consequences therefore require rectification. It thus bears some relationship to our next example of judicial justifications emphasizing the nonreciprocal character of risk impositions.

B. In fields of strict liability, such as abnormally dangerous activities, courts often express a principle, fairness as reciprocity, that attaches liability to defendants imposing nonreciprocal risks on victims. This justification for a strict liability to compensate then stresses the atypical character of a defendant's risk-generating activity. Such a defendant imposing an atypical and serious risk should in fairness compensate the risk's victim.[75] The principle is applied by courts in a concrete manner and context. That is, the atypical character of defendant's activity, its nonreciprocal character with respect to the victim's conduct, and thus the unilateral character of the imposition, are apparent on the face of the court's description of the accident. The concept of nonreciprocity is here focused upon the precise, immediate situation and activities of the parties. The principle, for example, clearly covers injury to a pedestrian from blasting even when the blasting is carefully performed. It might also serve more broadly and systematically to justify the negligence system, where defendants are liable for their faulty performance of typical activities (the defendant's carelessly driven car creating an atypical and unreasonable risk collides with one carefully driven).

C. In nuisance cases involving continuing interaction between the defendant and a known victim (e.g., pollution from defendant's factory affecting victim's contiguous farmland), some opinions characterize a defendant as intentionally wresting welfare from a determinate victim for its own benefit. Therefore, defendant is strictly liable in damages even though its socially useful and cost-justified conduct imposed a reasonable risk. The rhetoric justifying such strict liability is that of fairness. Notions of unjust enrichment because of defendant's "taking" of part of the value of plaintiff's property, notions bordering on intentional tort, inform such justifications.[76] Given defendant's continuing imposition of risk and harm on a known victim, they have force. But they have less relevance to the more typical one-shot (car, blasting) accidents. Two differences appear. In one-shot accidents, we deal only with probabilities of harm and not with the certainty of a continuing nuisance that the defendant's conduct will cause harm. Moreover, the statistically predictable victims are indeterminate (the car or blasting injures a pedestrian) rather than identified at the time that the defendant acts (the factory knowingly continues to pollute farmland).

3. The most distinctive of the contemporary justifications for strict liability elaborates the moral claim for compensation in a broader social frame, so as to link it to loss spreading rather than merely compensation. It argues that the burdens of an activity, its accident costs, should be borne broadly by the activity's beneficiaries rather than concentrated on the victims. The justification posits as a requirement of fairness the spreading of loss to those beneficiaries rather than merely shifting it to a (any) defendant. In contrast, the two preceding categories of justification within right-fairness thought are satisfied even if the legal measure of a victim's loss remains concentrated on an individual defendant.

The justification rests on a comparison between those who benefit from and those who are burdened by the business activity that is causally related to the accident. It stresses the disproportionate burden that an activity places on a victim who is unrelieved of loss. It expresses sympathy with the victim. This sympathy indeed animates the justification.

The courts link the victim to broad social groups that are implicated with the activity. Thus, they emphasize the injustice of letting loss lie with an unfortunate innocent, when a profit-making enterprise and a larger community of consumers, shareholders, and others benefited from the defendant.[77] Those benefiting, those behind the enterprise and profiting through its activities, ought as a matter of fairness to assume such external accident costs. They ought to bear a share of the activity's burdens proportionate to their benefits, rather than merely profit from the enterprise's continuing imposition of risk on individually random but collectively predictable victims of the activity.[78] This predictability, this statistical certainty that over time there will be victims of the ongoing generation of risk, and the related suggestion that the enterprise causes harm intentionally because it is aware of this certainty, strengthen the courts' argument that fairness requires compensation. Of course, the victim may also have benefited from the activity (a consumer of electricity whose farm suffers pollution from a generating plant), but only as one among many.[79]

The ideal of proportionate sharing will never be fully achieved. Even if a theory of distributive justice were developed in sufficient detail to suggest the appropriate burden of accident costs to be borne by each segment of the related community, courts could hardly predict whether the imposition of liability in a given case, or over many cases, would satisfy the theory's criteria. How a defendant absorbs and spreads its liability costs depends on business strategies as well as market forces. Moreover, the costs will be spread over time. Dramatic and atypical losses for which advance arrangements could not realistically have been made may ultimately be borne by groups of consumers, shareholders, and employees in later periods. Nonetheless, the ideal is at least approached through the defendant's beyond-fault liability.

This justification for strict liability, although a distinctively modern phenomenon in its influence on a large number of tort decisions, is nonetheless consistent with much old strict-liability doctrine resting on different justifications, such as "between two innocents," or postulates of right. It can adequately rationalize and justify such old doctrine. For example, earlier nuisance or trespass cases imposing liability without fault on the basis of maxims such as *sic utere* or "between two innocents" could today be explained in terms of the moral argument for sharing the burdens as well as enjoying the benefits of business activity.

This last observation is not distinctive to contemporary right-fairness justifications. The same point could be made with respect to recent utilitarian justifications, such as the behavior-modification argument for strict liability. In the circumstances of many older cases, it was likely that the defendant was in a better position than the victim to control accident costs. Here, too, modern justifications both expand and re-explain older strict-liability doctrine. In this sense, they "fit" much of tradition even as they make new law.

Loss Spreading and Redistribution: Individualistic and Collective Images of Tort Law   In both its common law and statutory expressions, beyond-fault liability has provoked strong attacks. Some view it as amoral precisely because it imposes liability on a faultless defendant. Fault is at once the moral occasion for and the limit to liability.[80] Other critics have concentrated on the degree to which strict liability grows out of judicial sympathy toward victims and the related attention to loss spreading, phenomena which the critics associate with a redistributive, collectivist program.[81] The attack bears some examination before we turn to the question of redistribution.

Given the radically different premises of its several justifications, the fault system surely did not represent a triumph of the individualistic spirit, a pure bastion against collective thought. The Hand Formula, for example, explicitly invoked social utility or welfare as a criterion for individual responsibility. Individual action was good or bad insofar as it realized or frustrated systemic social goals. Nonetheless, negligence law's characteristics, and principally its rights-oriented justifications, were at least consistent with the ideology of liberal individualism.

One was liable only for overstepping a boundary of due care. Since in theory attention to that boundary could avoid liability, actors could control their social responsibilities through discipline and will. In this sense, tort liability resembled and indeed reinforced that understanding of contractual obligation which viewed duties as flowing only from the free exercises of will by the contracting parties. But under strict liability, the actor loses much of its apparent earlier control over tort liability. In many instances, business can avoid liability only by refraining from business activity. Of course, decentralized, cost-rational decisions may serve to reduce liability, but they cannot eliminate it. In the justifications for strict liability, good conscience and care may be assumed, but they are simply irrelevant.

Moreover, the rhetoric of the fault system stressed individual freedom over restraint or social responsibility. Principles of both right and utility required no more than reasonable, generally customary consideration of the interests of others. When meeting that requirement, social actors could advance their interests without concern for harm thereby caused others. Negative justifications indeed stressed the danger of excessive constraint on individual initiative. Business's exposure to damages was limited to what was an inevitable floor to liability in any imaginable legal system of the period, one or another version of fault liability.

The point can be illustrated through a version of the negligence standard appearing in a famous century-old opinion, the *Nitro-Glycerine* case decided by the United States Supreme Court. The Court, rejecting strict liability for trespass to real property, summarized various precedents developing the negligence standard. It then defined the measure of care that must be taken to avoid liability for negligence as "that which a person of ordinary prudence and caution would use if his own interests were to be affected, and the whole risk were his own."[82]

We can explore the moral implications of this standard by imagining contiguous parcels of land, X and Y. Assume that both parcels are owned by the same person, who makes a cost-justified decision to act on parcel X (as by spraying crops) in such a way as to injure parcel Y. The owner suffers the loss to Y in the process of securing a larger gain for X, and thus comes out with a net advantage.

Assume now that Y is owned by another (plaintiff), and that the owner of X (defendant) is confronted with the same decision under the same assumptions of costs and benefits. Under the *Nitro-Glycerine* opinion's standard, or under notions of reasonableness within a standard such as the Hand Formula,[83] defendant is not liable for the harm suffered by Y. Defendant will now gain the full advantage of the action while plaintiff suffers the loss. Defendant would indeed have followed the moral principle of treating others as he would treat himself, a principle implying some minimum of respect for others. But that principle here expresses a limited sense of obligation toward the community. Defendant reaps the benefits but no longer bears the costs of his conduct.

The rhetoric and doctrine of the fault system were innocent of notions like the just distribution of losses within a broad community including persons and firms additional to the parties to the litigation. That system's distributional principle was operative within a more limited context—that is, between the (characteristically) two parties to a dispute. If the defendant was faulty, it was just to "redistribute" plaintiff's loss, in the narrow sense of "shifting" it to the innocent defendant. But absent fault, between two innocents it was just to let loss lie.

Some notion of the fair sharing of accident losses within a broader social context could be said to have been debated in the context of the negative justifications for the fault system. To the extent that impositions could be understood as reciprocal, so that today's nonnegligent imposer on some victim became tomorrow's victim of some other nonnegligent imposer, some courts employed a diffuse notion of reciprocity to justify the limited liability of the fault system.[84] That is, larger and more systemic distributional considerations figured within the negative justifications for negligence law. The courts looked beyond the concrete or focused instance of reciprocity (the factory activity and the injured nearby landowner) to a broader context of social interaction. Such a notion of reciprocity of risk imposition and loss, a notion operating over time and many parties, did not address the individual victim's plight or the argument for distributing that victim's loss to a broader community.

Strict liability changes the situation by requiring the non-negligent defendant to bear the costs causally related to his conduct—somewhat as if, to adapt the *Nitro-Glycerine* opinion's illustration of the negligence standard, "the whole risk were his own." Indeed, in this sense strict liability better realizes the moral justification underlying the test in *Nitro-Glycerine* of the negligence standard.

But even in such circumstances of strict liability, the whole risk is not the actor's. It is the victim and not the defendant who experiences injury to health, prospects, property, and so on. No legal act—an injunction, a statutory provision or administrative regulation—forbids the taking of the victim's welfare. Tort law, within the scope of strict-liability doctrine, simply requires that if the defendant takes welfare from the victim, then he must pay. Only to that extent does it require social actors to take potential victims' interests into account. Indeed, the payment provides only the legal measure of the victim's loss, often a far cry from a more complete social measurement of the loss or even from the victim's subjective sense of loss.

Nonetheless, relative to fault liability, social actors must expect to absorb more losses that are causally related to their activities. As we have seen, the justifications for that larger responsibility express not only notions of controlling accident costs, but also ideas about the fair assumption of burdens, of sharing and spreading. Thus, elements of strict liability evoke, perhaps more generally and impressionistically than concretely, collective images of social interaction and the accident toll, images of the sharing of losses within a large social context binding all together. The theme of loss spreading—indeed, also the theme of systematic planning by business firms to reduce accident costs—link strict-liability justifications not to the ideology of individualistic capitalism but to that of the regulatory and welfare state.[85]

Safety regulation and loss spreading are now part of mainstream political discourse. They form the core of contemporary accident legislation. Once such policies and rhetoric were introduced into the mainstream of common-law discourse, earlier critics might have asked, to what will they lead? Would not ideas like liability despite customary care, or like loss distribution, come to appear neutral and conventional in their doctrinal formulation, more legal than political, more stable and imbedded in the culture, and therefore more legitimate and dangerous? From the perspective of rhetoric ("spreading," "deep pockets," "heightened liability independent of care") and ideology, the concern of political conservatives about the growth of strict liability was not without foundation.

It should, however, be clear that, despite such concern, important principles of traditional liberal political ordering continue to govern a tort regime of strict liability. Several points are here relevant. First, no more than the negligence system does strict liability require enterprises to act in specified ways. Decisions about safety remain decentralized, although made within a different structure of norms from the negligence system that is intended to spur different decisions about safety. The transition from one common-law liability regime to another is well within the mainstream liberal tradition.

Second, the concern that strict tort liability expresses a broad social principle of wealth redistribution blinks a telling distinction. Redistributive principles may look to a reform of the distribution of wealth and power in society pursuant to one or another ideal of distributive justice. Such principles are distinct from those underlying strict liability—namely, the redistribution of accident losses through tort law to approach the goal of reestablishing the distributional *status quo ante*.[86] Both types of redistributive programs—I shall call them *wealth* distribution and *loss* distribution—affect large groups and have a systemic character. Both figure in the modern liberal state. Nonetheless, their differences are as significant as their shared characteristics.

Loss distribution through accident law lacks the breadth of vision and the transformative aspirations that may animate schemes of wealth redistribution in American life, such as some welfare programs or progressive taxation. It does not aim at "deep pockets" as such, at drawing from the wealthy to raise the poor. It lacks the ideal of achieving a new pattern of wealth or power.[87] Such an ideal, with its greater potential for reconstructing aspects of society, may draw on principles as diverse as egalitarianism, or the satisfaction of minimum needs, or the maximin solution.[88] Varied principles may generate radical or ameliorative programs. But even ameliorative programs, like welfare schemes meeting minimum needs for the poor, have systemic redistributive implications, in the sense that their advocates intend some reshaping of extant patterns of wealth distribution.

Even a rigorous version of strict liability with a strong attribution rule lacks such implications or intention. Surely this is so when loss distribution rests on the utilitarian argument that total accident costs are lowered by their dispersal rather than concentration. But the point holds also with respect to the justification for loss spreading emphasizing the fairness of sharing benefits and burdens. That justification expresses an ideal of distributive justice. But the ideal is realized within the community defined by and closely related to the defendant's activity, rather than in the society at large. It treats only that community of consumers, shareholders, and employees. It treats within it only the burdens and benefits that grow out of defendant's activity. Such an ideal of fairness thus differs from ideals of greater scope and reach about a just society or fair distributive shares.

Strict liability touches, then, only the accident-related activity and its broad-ranging communities of participants, not the basic socioeconomic structure.[89] Its justifications for loss spreading as well as the measure of damages assume, build on, and maintain rather than criticize and reform the ex ante (pre-accident) distribution of wealth in society. Quite unlike schemes of wealth redistribution, its goal is to move society closer to its pre-accident situation by assuring that the accident loss is nowhere concentrated. By this token alone it should be understood as politically more conservative than programmatic wealth redistribution. Indeed, the costs that are spread express and confirm existing social stratification, for lost earnings and often medical bills will vary directly with the victim's socioeconomic status.[90]

When contractual relationships link the victim to the defendant, the rhetoric of wealth redistribution becomes the more inappropriate. Strict liability for product defects might (in theory) lead to price increases covering *all* the incremental liability costs that it imposes on the manufacturer. Within such an (unlikely) assumption, one can imagine strict liability as operating within a closed system of producers and victims, at least if we further assume that all victims are purchasers rather than strangers to the contract relationship. The feedback of liability costs through product pricing can then be understood as the judicially coerced acquisition of first-party insurance by the product purchasers (potential victims). When we realistically relax some of these assumptions, it remains true that part of the liability costs will be picked up by purchasers. As to them and those amounts, strict liability hardly amounts to redistribution of wealth, except in the limited sense of bringing about redistribution among consumers when risk among them varies but all pay the same "insurance premium" through the product price.

Limits and Alternative Paths to Loss Spreading   Loss spreading as a justification for strict liability poses some obvious dilemmas. At least where a business is the defendant and the causally related victim is an individual, the justification suggests no evident stopping point for liability. The argument that a busi-

ness defendant could spread accident losses better than probable victims would always entail liability, independently of
justifications treating behavior modification.[91]

But scholars have questioned whether businesses are invariably the better loss spreaders. They suggest that spreading
through tort law has less justification in the contemporary
welfare state with its many institutionalized facilities for
spreading. Potential victims can now protect themselves
through rapidly expanding programs of first-party (loss) insurance. Moreover, many among them benefit from social insurance or other welfare programs that cover some accident
costs.[92]

Despite such criticism and its message that the common
law ought not to be as concerned with loss spreading, courts
might expand that justification. Any defendant managing an
ongoing, risk-generating activity and able to spread liability
costs might be subjected to strict liability—vehicular transportation of business goods, for example. Doctors, lessors, and
repair services would join blasters and producers of machines
within a regime of strict liability.

So dramatic an expansion seems unlikely. Courts must first
resolve practical and conceptual problems bearing on strict
liability—for example, assigning liability in graphic instances
of reciprocal causation like car collisions, tracing but-for causation when harm allegedly stems from nonnegligent medical
treatment, determining the legal effect of a victim's earlier contractual consent or express assumption of risk, taking into account an abrupt escalation of damages and insurance rates in
fields like auto accidents or escalation of consumer prices in
specific industries.[93]

Moreover, loss spreading has yet to achieve that supremacy
among strict-liability justifications that would open large areas
of the surviving negligence law to its embrace. Despite its
significance, it constitutes but one of an interrelated group of
justifications rather than a paramount or exclusive ideal pointing toward strict liability. Perhaps, then, courts understand the

different justifications—say, behavior modification and loss spreading within a utilitarian framework—as parts of a coherent and interrelated system of goals. Perhaps they perceive trade-offs among justifications, one goal being furthered while another is thwarted. That perception might act as a check on giving free reign to the goal of loss spreading.[94]

The scholarly literature has developed such a systemic vision of interrelated goals.[95] But no such broad understanding emerges from the judicial opinions. Courts do frequently invoke the goal of behavior modification together with that of loss spreading. Indeed, they may simultaneously invoke other justifications for strict liability as well, such as *sic utere*. But the several justifications are not seen as systematically related. Rather, courts generally view them as independent and complementary, as mutually supportive of the strict-liability rule.[96]

In the context of tort law, they generally are. Advancing one goal will rarely prejudice another. For example, strict liability internalizes more accident costs to the defendant's activity than the fault system. Even if justified primarily by virtue of its loss spreading, strict liability may also lead to defendant's behavior modification. Surely the incentives given defendant for improved resource allocation—that is, the potential tort damages to be avoided—are at least as great as those within the fault system. Except where there may be reason to seek modification of potential victims' behavior rather than the business defendant's, strict liability does not thwart the goal of improved resource allocation, whatever justification it rests upon.

On the other hand, welfare schemes for compensating accident victims and spreading losses may prejudice that goal. To the extent that victims' costs are covered out of general tax revenues or special funds collected from persons other than the business causally related to the accident, cost internalization to the relevant activity is reduced. Depending on the status of the collateral source rule, incentives for behavior modification may thereby be lowered. Of course, legislative schemes may combine goals of behavior modification (through cost internalization to the activity causally related to the accidents) and compensation, as do workers' compensation plans or no-fault auto plans. Or they may independently aim only at accident reduction by imposing safety regulations on an activity.

Justifications Used to Override Contractual Liability Standards

We here view justifications for tort liability in the special setting of prior contractual understandings between the parties to an accident about what the liability standard should be. What is distinctive is precisely this contractual element. Courts shift their attention from justifying tort liability as such to justifying the invalidation of contractual derogations from established tort doctrine. Courts must overcome the traditional justifications for enforcing provisions to which contracting parties have apparently agreed.

These opinions treat contractual elimination by the defendant of either negligence liability (exculpatory clauses) or strict liability (disclaimers of implied warranties). Some of the cases involve tort claims that are based only on negligence law rather than strict liability, such as a lessee's claim for damages for an injury stemming from the lessor's negligent maintenance of the leased premises.

Nonetheless, all such cases involving contractual liability provisions appropriately figure in my description of the trend toward heightened liability. It matters not for my argument whether the tort element of the case rests on the allegation of negligence. Overcoming an exculpatory clause so as to permit a claim in negligence still heightens liability. Moreover, courts employ the same justifications to invalidate exculpatory clauses and disclaimers of implied warranties. Finally, whether treating negligence or strict-liability claims that are said to be contractually barred, all such opinions express aspects of the social vision characteristic of modern heightened liability.

In these cases, it is fair to assume that absent the contractual bar, the victim would have a substantial claim in negligence or strict liability. If the contract is judicially honored, that claim will be denied. Hence, courts must resolve a tension between contract freedom (party autonomy in the allocation of risk) and tort law as a body of mandatory norms.

The tort element in these cases stems from the accidental physical harm suffered by the victim. The situation thus differs from typical contract cases in which plaintiff alleges a breach causing economic loss and generating a claim based on reliance or expectancy damages. All the cases here drawn upon in fact involved injury to the victim's person rather than property, a distinction rarely noted but undoubtedly significant for the courts' reasoning.

The contractual relationship in these cases may be direct (contract between the victim and defendant for a lease or for medical services). It may be indirect and, since created through a third person, lack privity of contract (a retailer's sale of the defendant's product to the victim). Of course, even when the chain of events leading from the defendant's activity to the victim's harm includes contractual relationships, the victim may be external to them (a bystander injured by a defective car, a lessee's guest injured by using a defective staircase). In such cases the argument strengthens that the victim should be free to invoke tort liability standards, without regard to any contractual bar. In this discussion, I assume the stronger case for the defendant—namely, that the victim is no stranger but rather contractually related.

The last few decades of decision have moved toward the triumph of the tort norm over these contractual derogations from it. In arguing for the supremacy or compulsory character of the tort standard, courts may invoke such familiar justifications for heightened liability as behavior modification and loss spreading. But they devote less energy to building an affirmative case for tort liability than to overcoming the traditional justifications for enforcing consensual understandings. Courts seek to explain why the contract provision, viewed almost as presumptively valid, should be held void. Hence, I stress the distinctive issue of contract freedom in these cases, and refer to the familiar tort justifications for heightened liability only insofar as they become problematic because of the agreement between the parties.

The Ideology of Contract Freedom   The dilemma confronted by courts implicates the familiar liberal ideology of freedom of contract.[97] That ideology has the following structure. As much as possible, social life should be ordered through voluntary choices by social actors expressing their views of how to advance their welfare. Those choices are made through exercises of will and expressed in bargained agreements that courts enforce within the stable framework of contract law. In this sense, contract is quintessentially "private" law informed by liberal and individualist premises, a neutral framework for facilitating private interaction.[98]

Of course, tort and criminal law serve a complementary function. Through their protection against defined interferences by others, they give integrity not only to the basic entitlements to one's person or property, but also to the contractual system for their exchange. But relative to contract, tort and criminal law have an inescapably collective and public-law character.[99] Given the inability of many potential victims and defendants to stipulate in advance through contracts the required levels of care and how losses from harmful interactions are to be allocated between them, courts and legislatures must resolve the liability issue. High transaction costs impede private ordering. Most accidents link pre-accident strangers for the first time.[100] When parties can overcome transaction costs by bargaining to a contract, private decisions about required standards of behavior and risk allocation should prevail—subject to such background assumptions as the legal capacity of the parties or the voluntary and nonfraudulent character of the bargaining and agreement,[101] and subject to the rare common-law constraints of "public policy" forbidding enforcement of agreements such as those for prostitution or gambling.

Some modern justifications for this libertarian conception of freedom of contract stress its favorable consequences for welfare.[102] Contract ordering honors the individual's subjective determinations about welfare and its maximization. Social welfare undeniably increases through contract arrangements and their enforcement, for each party has chosen to contract on the terms finally stated (rather than not to) and hence has improved its welfare position.

But the paradigm of contract freedom also rests on ethical postulates of a different character that stress values of liberal individualism, free will, and autonomy of choice. Decentralized choice represents an ideal of personal freedom. Promises expressing those choices are a mode of realizing that freedom and carry a moral obligation to act consistently with them.[103] Collective decisions of courts or legislatures nullifying private choices by imposing compulsory norms that the parties eliminated thus curtail personal as well as contractual freedom.

Contract freedom thus stands as an antipaternalist and anticollectivist ideology. Courts invalidating contract terms disparage what the parties thought to be in their best interest. The consequence is striking in cases involving tort claims that are barred by contract clauses. The allocation of risks of injury from products or services will likely affect pricing. Judicial reallocation of risks to the business defendant may lead to price increases equal to part or all of the cost of bearing the relevant risk. The courts may effectively require the consumer to pay a higher price for more (insurance) protection, even though— the argument for contract freedom continues—the consumer preferred to bear the risk of accidental injury and thereby benefit from a lower price. Assuming that the contracts were voluntarily entered into through transactions not tainted by fraud, courts ought to recognize that consumers know best.

Such arguments for contract enforcement raise peculiarly sensitive issues for courts reviewing exculpatory clauses or

disclaimers. The sensitivity stems from the political importance of and the contradictions inhering in the concept of freedom of contract. Such freedom is realized through legal norms
that simultaneously recognize and limit it by setting conditions
to the exercise of the lawmaking power delegated to private
parties. The choices for courts in ruling on disclaimers are not
therefore the grand and dichotomous ones between freedom
in the abstract and collective coercion, between totally decentralized and totally centralized decision making, or between noble individualism and insulting paternalism. Rather,
the question is how to define in this special context the
character and content of the contract norms which at once
empower and constrain.

To be sure, the judicial response to that question will implicate and perhaps make explicit such larger themes. Courts are
therefore aware of the potential reach of opinions that invalidate contract clauses. Their opinions must explore the ideology
of contract freedom and the "antinomies" of contract law,
which, as a scholar has noted, are "too painful" to be brought
to the level of consciousness.[104] The courts' observations described below about the challenged contract relationships—
about such phenomena as coercion, unequal bargaining
power, lack of choice, or imperfect market structures—inevitably raise issues that reach beyond the particular context of the
case to the concept of freedom of contract in the large. After all,
contracts are often made in circumstances with coercive elements, between parties of unequal power, within imperfect
markets. How should the phenomena that the court relies on
to override contractual disclaimers affect many other contracting situations in which they are also present?

For such reasons, opinions invalidating contract clauses
touch moral and political postulates more sensitively and
deeply than does modern criticism of, say, the negligence system. The issues in tort, at least in the typical cases involving
strangers, are less threatening to any given legal or political
ideology. Both fault and strict liability systems coexist comfort-

ably with either a welfare state or with premises of individualism and party autonomy, indeed even with an extreme libertarian image of society. Unlike safety legislation, both fault liability and strict liability rely on decentralized decision making by private actors influenced by collectively established rules.

Of course, the regulatory effects on market allocation and distribution differ significantly between the two tort liability systems. One or the other may be viewed as fairer or more efficient. The social vision informing modern strict liability may be, as chapter 4 suggests, more collective and even altruistic in spirit. Nonetheless, neither liability system can be seen as potentially threatening to prevailing ideological bases within the liberal tradition for economic organization or social interaction.

The Tension and Its Attempted Resolution   Decisions invalidating contract-based defenses are short on justification and long on what chapter 4 describes as social vision. The opinions, for example, note numerous aspects of the contractual context that in different ways contribute to the decision to invalidate—for example, a defendant's use of form contracts with standard clauses, or the socially "necessary" character of the service (medical care) or product (car) provided by the defendant. They may describe consumers as unable to understand complexly phrased clauses such as disclaimers, or as lacking effective choice about contract terms because of market conditions such as short supply or oligopoly in which sellers offer identical terms. The victim's contractual assumption of risk may be characterized as compelled rather than voluntary. These types of observations then generate conclusions such as undue coercion, or subjection of the victim to unequal bargaining power with respect to matters informed by a "public interest." Such conclusions are meant to justify the invalidation of the disputed contract clause.[105]

Possibly for the reason earlier suggested, these opinions do not explore the "normal" circumstances in which courts honor contract freedom. Such circumstances might be understood to include a generally obtaining "equality of bargaining power," or a lesser degree or different character of "coercion" in contract bargains, or sufficient "consumer choice," or "competitive market conditions." But rather than attempt to elucidate some ideal type of the context in which contract freedom flourishes, courts are content to assert that the circumstances before them depart from an unspecified paradigm of contract freedom.[106] Discussion holds to the immediate circumstances. No serviceable theory of contract freedom emerges against which courts determine the legality of exculpatory clauses or disclaimers.

Justification for invalidation is then generally implicit in the courts' empirical observations and evaluative characterizations of a transaction. The consequence for contract doctrine, perhaps an intended one, is a sense of general judicial adherence to freedom of contract and enforcement of the disputed clauses, qualified by selective refusals to enforce them for one or another of a catalog of circumstances. Those circumstances are both indeterminate—a service informed by a "public interest," a "necessary" service, market conditions impairing "free choice"—and in some sense special, so that the catalog does not appear to threaten the traditional contract principle.

Moreover, the grounds for invalidation are not made sufficiently clear to indicate whether the court imagines itself to be realizing the "true" interest of the party benefited by the invalidation, or to be imposing a contract term justified on some other basis. It is difficult to draw from the reasoning and rhetoric of the opinions any pattern of motivation, such as paternalism toward the party waiving tort protection, or perhaps redistribution of wealth or power to groups seen as powerless and systematically victimized by such clauses.[107]

At best, the opinions reveal openings toward more explicit justifications. The recurrent and powerful rhetoric is that of (un)fairness—bare references to rather than elaborated notions of unfair dealing, amounting to comments about coercion, deception, or maltreatment by the defendant using the standard clause.[108]

Such justifications bear some relationship to the principles of unconscionability within contract law, typically applied to situations of economic harm without physical injury. Those principles stress elements of so-called procedural unconscionability, matters such as fraud or duress that are viewed as corrupting the process of contract formation and therefore violating the premise of free and informed choice. But the decisions that we here consider do not rest on the narrow and traditional formulations of procedural unconscionability: small print or obscure language blocking cognition or understanding, physical threats distinct from the threat inherent in all bargain of refusing to consummate it unless certain provisions are accepted. Rather, the courts justify their decisions by reference to the broader socioeconomic contexts or structures in which contracts like those before them are formed. It is those broader contexts or structures that represent the "special" circumstances justifying invalidation.

The duress or coercion found sufficient to invalidate an exculpatory clause affects many others in the victim's position: persons seeking an apartment during a housing shortage or seeking admission to a hospital, consumers purchasing a "necessary" product offered on identical terms by a small group of producers.[109] Coercion becomes less an *ad hoc* finding linked to a unique transaction than a characteristic of mass transactions bearing structural relationships to the victim's transaction.

Many of these cases, for example, grow out of clauses in standard form contracts.[110] In such circumstances, courts have been ready to characterize the contract less as the outcome of bargain and individual choice than as imposed law. But if law is to be imposed, the courts appear to say, it should be formulated and applied by the judiciary or legislature rather than by the powerful corporate drafters of contracts of adhesion. Such contracts therefore become to some degree socialized, no longer a private affair of private parties exercising party autonomy.

Other elements in these justifications resemble so-called substantive unconscionability, such as contracts for gambling or prostitution that are condemned within a broad cultural consensus as violating "public policy." The "policy" objections to liability-avoiding contract provisions are not difficult to identify. An exculpatory clause seeks to avoid a liability for negligence that rests on strong considerations of utility and fairness; the disclaimer of an implied warranty would negate a protection that is equally a creation "of the law." In the contexts of the decided cases, the victim was in no position to substitute for the defendant in taking appropriate safety measures. The patient in the negligently managed hospital, the driver of a car with a dangerous flaw are powerless to guard against the relevant risks—risks in these contexts of serious physical injury. Moreover, the loss-spreading justifications for assigning liability to, say, the car manufacturer would be frustrated by judicial enforcement of a disclaimer. From all such perspectives, the contractual restructuring of liability rules undercuts vital goals of collective justification.[111]

Within these opinions one encounters the familiar, ruthlessly perceptive insights of the legal realists: contract as a collectively determined body of public law stating the conditions for enforcement of private bargains; party autonomy and decentralized choice as relative concepts, their scope determined through collective justifications that express ideas of fairness or welfare; coercion as inhering in all bargains through the play of market forces of supply and demand, its permissible degree to be similarly determined; the market not as a natural phenomenon serviced by legal ordering but as a social artifact structured by common and statutory law to serve collective goals; all law as regulation, the relevant issue being one of its kind and degree.[112] Contract freedom becomes as flexible a concept as, for example, the protection of property rights or the conception of fault. There are no sacred givens in working out the meaning or force of contract principles in these accident cases. There is indeed no sharp boundary between contract and tort.

SIGNIFICANCE AND SOURCES OF THE TREND IN JUDICIAL JUSTIFICATIONS

Surely the content of judicial justifications has greatly changed. Today's opinions imposing one or another version of strict liability or expanding liability within the fault system employ justifications alien to typical opinions of, say, the 1930s. Nonetheless, the justifications for heightened liability should not be understood as novel contributions to accident law in the large, including its legislative expressions, let alone as radical in their technique or effects.

Consider, for example, the foundations for heightened liability. Since the collapse of the forms of action in the mid-nineteenth century, the contradictions in justification have been as notorious ingredients of the common law as were those in doctrine. Courts have long had choice. Contemporary courts give a fresh prominence to some older or deviant strands of justification, albeit within the distinctive circumstances of modern social vision.

Some of the continuing contradictions in justification pointing toward strict or fault liability could be expressed in the following pairs, the first of each pair arguing for heightened liability: *sic utere,* as opposed to the argument that all benefit from productive activity and hence must put up with inevitable nonnegligent interferences; between two innocents, who caused the harm ought to pay, as opposed to the asserted immorality of imposing liability on one innocent of fault; industry ought to internalize and spread its accident costs, as opposed to the argument that accident costs should be selectively assigned to satisfy a welfare goal such as optimization of accident costs or facilitation of industrial growth; liability disclaimers unfairly deprive the consumer of tort law's protection, as opposed to the view that no principle is more sacred than freedom of contract.[113]

Although the relative weight within each pair has shifted over time, never has one set of these paired maxims or justifications occupied the entire field. The contemporary trend toward heightened liability rests partly on the first justification in each of these pairs, but the second of the paired justifications retains vitality and moderates the trend.

To an important extent, modern justifications reach beyond common-law antecedents that were developed within earlier versions of strict tort liability. They draw on distinct but complementary sources of inspiration, including the pioneering scholarly literature whose influence is made explicit through citations in a growing number of opinions.[114] More significant are features of the political and ideological context in which modern heightened liability has developed. Surely this is true of the judicial rhetoric of loss spreading which also inhabits many schemes of the regulatory and welfare state. Vastly expanded liability insurance and loss insurance respond to similar goals of loss spreading. This growth of the insurance industry surely has deeply influenced judicial views of the accident problem.

But it was decades ago that regulatory schemes for accidents such as workers' compensation as well as private and social insurance became common features of American life. The phenomenon and rhetoric of loss spreading are not new. Despite the ring of novelty of recent tort doctrine, many underlying ideas of the courts developing it are familiar to American political culture. The utilitarian and fairness justifications in the decisional law, as well as the social vision informing such justifications, resemble those invoked in much legislation of the regulatory and welfare state.[115] Judicial and legislative justifications have tended to coalesce.

4 Social Vision

The Nature of the Concept

By social vision within accident law I mean perceptions of courts about society (its socioeconomic structure, patterns of social interaction, moral goals, and political ideologies), about social actors (their character, behavior, and capacities), and about accidents (their causes, volume, and toll).[1] The concept then includes courts' understandings about matters as varied as the incidence and social costs of accidents, the operation of market pricing mechanisms, the capacity of individuals for prudent behavior, the bureaucratic rationality of business firms, the effects of standard clauses in contracts, and ideologies of growth or distribution in the nineteenth century or today. Social vision embraces not only empirical observations (the number of auto accidents), but also evaluative characterizations of events (the absence of free choice in a given context) and feelings of disapproval or empathy toward what is described (a "sharp" bargain, or a "tragic" loss).

The breadth of my definition and of these few illustrations suggests a more amorphous descriptive category than the two preceding ones. Moreover, there is less in the way of immediately apt judicial comment for discussion to build upon.[2] But my argument is that social vision is vital to an understanding of accident law, for it permeates the preceding description of justification and thus of doctrine.

Justification and social vision are reciprocally linked, each requiring and even implying the other. A moral argument for a liability rule is necessarily informed by a social vision that gives it texture. Courts can hardly work toward a decision about legal norms through concepts or ideals that remain as abstract and disembodied as, say, welfare or distributive justice or libertarian rights. At that level, they are hollow, empty of the mediating conceptions and understandings that give them content and render them more concrete.

When considered in terms of their abstract structure of argument—say, means-to-end rationality in pursuing a welfare goal within the logic of utilitarianism—justifications are necessarily indeterminate with respect to the content of legal norms. What conception of welfare is relevant, what assumptions about social life underlie that conception, what mechanisms of social life or what tendencies in human behavior will promote the particular conception? Through the infusion of elements of social vision, concepts like welfare or fairness take on more specific content. Even though they will often remain debatable in their implications, choice may be narrowed and argument may better be joined. Ideals of, say, distributive justice become sufficiently specific to serve as a guide to decision.

Similarly, if uninformed by moral postulates or goals, social vision would amount to random, unconnected observations or insights about the social world. The observations would lack any coherence, express no identifiable point of view, and offer no direction to thought.

The substantive content of the elements of social vision, the particular perceptions about society or social actors or accidents, vary among courts and over time. So, then, inevitably the moral ideals expressed through justifications also vary. Moreover, like different justifications, social visions of radically different character may coexist in competition with each other. But it is the fusion of some vision of society with some ideal of right or fairness or welfare that enables us to describe in any detail any one justificatory theory.

By way of illustration, consider the current justifications for heightened liability. Within utilitarian justification, courts equate welfare with a more concrete conception, such as optimal reduction of accident costs. Within right-fairness thought, the ideal of justice is given a more concrete expression by some courts through a theory such as proportionality in the sharing of the benefits and accident costs of an activity. Still, without more texture and detail, each of these familiar justifications remains vague as to its prescription for tort doctrine.

But each in fact is informed by vital understandings about how the society and the parties function, about social mechanisms and causal relationships in social life, about social aspirations and ideologies. By embodying such elements of social vision as the role of insurance or market pricing, justifications aiming at behavior modification or developing benefit-burden theory reveal their historical context and relationship to culture. The moral ideals informing accident law appear to be rooted in the courts' understandings and evaluations of social life, to be integrally related to that life rather than to exist within a stable, autonomous, and isolated realm of thought.

The transformation in social vision during the period here examined has influenced the trends in justificatory theories and doctrine. But this does not suggest a one-directional causal flow from social vision to justification, the first in general determining the second, and a specific social vision determining a specific justification. Moral ideals and postulates about individuals and society themselves affect social vision. What the court "sees" and how it evaluates the social phenomena that selectively enter opinions are not divorced from moral thought.

To the contrary, moral thought may structure perception. Beliefs that tort doctrine should enable society to achieve greater efficiency or the fair distribution of losses will lead observers to see, or at least will draw their attention to, different social phenomena. If we were to employ the language of causation in a suggestive manner, the image would be that of reciprocal causation, each category influencing and helping to form the other, indeed each essential to and partly constitutive of the other.

At times a justification (defendant business ought to compensate because it is situated to spread accident costs among those benefiting from its activity) and related aspects of social vision (the many accidents stemming from that activity cause concentrated and tragic social loss) are so presented as to appear to constitute distinct elements of opinions. Their inherently different characters make them generally appear as separate. But at times, as in the opinions invalidating contractual disclaimers of liability, observations about, say, coercion of or free choice by the victims signing the disclaimers are indistinguishably justification and social vision. In such circumstances, the court's description of the parties and their bargaining context blends social empiricism (what happened, and within what socioeconomic structure) with moral evaluation.

Let us illustrate the distinct but interdependent and complementary nature of each of these elements of legal argument. Justification tends toward a more abstract expression and more formal structure. It speaks, as it were, in whole sentences or even paragraphs, and with the voice of reason. However terse or even aphoristic, it strikes us literally as argument, leading us by a more or less direct route to the court's decision. Justification seeks to explain why the rule declared by the court ought to be preferred to another. It means to persuade, to legitimate the result, to rescue the court from a charge of arbitrariness or mechanical jurisprudence or moral blindness.

Social vision, on the other hand, tends to appear within opinions as the selective portrayal of aspects of society that bear on the decision, as fragmentary observations rather than as elements of a coherent and organic view of social life. Perhaps such a view is there, but the observer must imaginatively construct it from a record of scattered and incomplete remarks.

On its face, the social vision expressed within accident law is meant merely to inform rather than to convince, to be descriptive rather than argumentative. In reality, its function is more subtle and complex. Social vision is charged with and is meant to support a court's views about law's and society's moral goals. Often it is as much evaluation and moral judgment as it is description. Surely the elements of social vision are radically different from matters of fact about which courts take judicial notice, and are hardly subject to the strict requirements for the taking of such notice. They enter opinions and permeate argument naturally, narratively, informally.

Social vision has to do then not with reasoned elaboration but with sight and insight, with a court's grasp of a situation. It tells us salient fragments of a story about the accident's origins, parties, consequences, and context. Its graphic and sometimes expressive nature is often captured in an adjective—in, say, the contemporary empathetic images of courts of a "hapless" consumer, "innocent" victim, "inescapable" risk, "grave" danger, "frightening" consequence, or "devastating" loss. It is true that on its face, legal argument generally emphasizes justification. But justification necessarily absorbs and is oriented by vision. Each implies and requires the other. Legal argument, as it were, thereby joins insight to reason, the narrative to the normative, the graphic to the abstract, the expressive to the formal.

Again we observe a trend rather than a dramatic transformation in the courts' perception of society. For example, empathy for the plight of the victim, characteristic of modern heightened liability, found expression in some nineteenth-century opinions.[3] Although many opinions will note—in passing, as it were—one or another aspect of social vision, my description of the trend owes much to the relatively few opinions that portray in some detail those features of social life to which the accident before them is related. Such opinions seem to speak for many others that attempt no such portrayal. They make explicit what often is only hinted toward. They draw out perceptions and assumptions buried within the ritualistically invoked justifications for heightened liability.

ELEMENTS OF SOCIAL VISION IN ACCIDENT LAW

In the setting of accident law, the social vision expressed in opinions can be sorted into four types of observations, sometimes distinct and sometimes blending into each other.

1. Descriptions of some aspects of social life are set forth in an objective and neutral manner. Within this type fall descriptions of the modern system of production and distribution of goods (the importance of standard form contracts, the technological complexity of many products that assertedly places them beyond the consumer's understanding), of the accident problem (its statistical significance, the role of private insurance), or of the corporation (its cost-rational management and its capacity to spread costs through the market).

2. Courts characterize the social actors or contexts in a way that blends facts with an evaluation of their significance. Such evaluative characterizations include findings like unequal bargaining power in a contract transaction, or the absence of voluntary choice by an employee injured in a job with a high perceived risk and charged by the employer with assumption of risk. Those findings may effectively decide the issue of liability. They may merge with the formal justifications for the decision. They are necessarily informed by some implicit normative framework, some ideal of social and legal relations that gives moral significance to the facts. The same facts within a different implicit framework would be differently characterized.

3. Some observations are ambivalently descriptions of or unshakable postulates about human nature and political organization. They may be significant or even crucial for the recurrent justifications for liability. They are in a sense starting points—premises, images of man and society, intuitions so deep as rarely to be made explicit in those justifications. Thus assertions about the instrumental rationality of individual or corporate actors and their tendency to act consistently with cost-benefit calculations may set forth a court's understanding of how social actors in fact behave or its ideal of how they ought to behave within an implicit normative theory or vision about human nature and economic organization. Views about the interrelatedness of social activities and actors, about the degree to which all are bound together within a social community and have duties toward others in that community, may underlie a theory of distributive fairness arguing for proportionality in the sharing of burdens and benefits. They may underlie sympathy for the accident victim. Such views again are ambivalently descriptions of or postulates about political and social life.

4. Courts opine about the society's political goals and ideology. Their comments may appear as objective statements of widely shared social aspirations or ideology, historical or contemporary. But they may also express a court's own ideals or its views of desirable social policy. Courts, for example, have interpreted the liability-restrictive aspects of the classical fault system as having been responsive to a social goal of spurring nascent industry.[4] They have viewed contemporary society as one more sensitive to the plight of the victim and to the maintenance of minimum welfare standards.[5]

This brief classification—descriptions of context, characterizations of interactions, postulates, ideologies—decomposes the concept of social vision within accident law. It underscores a threshold difficulty in that concept, namely its ambivalent character as both social fact and ideal, as both descriptive and normative. The notion of a bare description by courts of social institutions, individual behavior, or prevailing ideology suggests a view of courts as value-neutral photographers, capturing over time different images of a changing society. But neither photographers nor courts can be so understood. The photographic portrait, conceived in the photographer's mind, is as much a creation as a description of social reality.

And so with the social vision of courts. The social context or goals which a judge may describe will be differently depicted by other observers, including other judges. A radical portrait would emphasize facts, social mechanisms, and ideology that would escape a more conventional one. It would tell a different story, reveal a different society. Either portrait will influence the way others—lawyers, judges, social actors—understand and act within the world. Through the changing visions of society that they express, courts help to make and remake the world that they appear to be describing.

Descriptions forming a part of courts' social vision should then be understood in their relation to implicit normative premises which make certain "facts" relevant. Moral argument and social facts, justification and social vision are all bound up in a way of grasping the world. Courts may observe that a failure to compensate accident victims leads to serious and widespread social costs, or they may note that uncompensated victims could have protected themselves against loss concentration through health insurance but failed to do so. In a given accident case, both observations may be accurate. Emphasis on one or the other may stem from a prior view of which form of social ordering—loss spreading through heightened liability or through private insurance—is desirable. Such views may themselves be associated with deeper images of society and of its relation to social actors, images of collective responsibility and sharing or of self-reliant individualism.

Nonetheless, courts set forth their visions of society as if the selection of facts and evaluative characterizations were uncontentious. The moral outlooks and ideological premises influencing their perceptions become secreted, as it were, within apparently objective social commentary. Courts thereby avoid the elaboration of a framework for evalation and prescription against which their description could better be understood.

THE CONTENT OF MODERN SOCIAL VISION

We here examine substantive themes in the social vision informing the trend toward heightened liability. Some of the themes, though distinctive to a modern social vision, treat matters that have long been common features of American life. What explains their fresh appearance within opinions must then be a fresh perception of their significance for moral and legal norms. For example, courts refer to the capacity of corporate business to spread liability costs among several related communities, a capacity surely present decades ago through the normal mechanism of the market. They refer to the external effects of a victim's misfortune on family and other related persons. Such forms of relational injury were surely visible a century ago. And they refer to the complexity of many industrial-age products, which blocks consumers from understanding their quality and how they function, a phenomenon that was widespread by the early twentieth century, and that indeed affected many objects of commerce in a preindustrial age.

Other themes that are distinctive to a modern social vision treat new features of American life. For example, private institutions such as liability insurance[6] and governmental institutions such as welfare programs have grown appreciably over the last half-century. They have dramatically changed judicial perceptions of the accident problem. So have such intensified problems of modern life as industry-generated pollution or wastes, products posing risks of major disasters through their malfunction, or mass victims of diseases stemming from medical drugs or workplace hazards that have long latency periods.[7]

At first blush, such obvious changes in American life offer the least problematic explanation for a changing social vision. But even here, the question remains why these distinctively modern phenomena have become "significant" for the moral and legal thought of courts, whereas other features of modern American life (widespread first-party insurance) are less noticed. The concluding section of chapter 4 explores such questions.

Consider some prominent themes in the modern social vision of courts:

1. *The accident problem.* Courts increasingly understand accidents not as random events first linking a defendant and victim, but as a problem of systematic incidence. That understanding has influenced justifications based on modification of defendants' behavior through cost internalization and on spreading accident losses. Each responds to one aspect of an urgent problem: the effort to reduce the number of accidents and the social costs of accident victims.

Several phenomena appear to explain this heightened awareness of the volume and toll of accidents.[8] Some opinions indicate a statistical understanding of the dimension of the problem, one surely influenced by scholarly research, debates and crises over insurance rates, legislative investigations, and accident schemes.[9] Moreover, cases in fields such as pollution, medical drugs, or design defects increasingly involve mass victims, a phenomenon brought to the court's attention whether only one plaintiff, a group of plaintiffs (joinder), or a class action is before it.[10]

Accidents are understood not only as massive in number but in the gross as predictable, on the basis of a particular defendant's or a general activity's experience. This actuarial appreciation of the accident problem, vividly illustrated through insurance ratings, underlies the rationales for both behavior modification and loss spreading. Business firms can predict and plan responsively.

Moreover, accidents grow particularly out of a few major activities—industrial pollution, hazardous wastes, product defects, medical drugs or malpractice, autos, the workplace.[11] It is therefore no surprise that heightened liability within the common law and insurer's or no-fault liability in legislative programs both tend to be defined in terms of particular types

of activities—in contrast with the negligence system's development of norms generally applicable to accidents.

The courts also pay more attention to the private and social
costs of accidents. They no longer assume "inevitable" accident
to be a cost of living for victims to bear, to be their "misfortune," but rather view it as a predictable social problem that is
properly alleviated through law. That view grows partly out of
a greater empathy with the suddenly worsened or indeed
tragic circumstances of the accident victim.[12] No doubt several
decades of welfare legislation responding to the problem of
concentration of loss, stressing both the external costs of concentration and the social benefits of loss spreading, contribute
to this heightened sensitivity.[13]

2. *Spreading mechanisms: insurance and the market.* Loss
spreading as a justification for heightened liability depends on
perceptions of insurance and market mechanisms that were
vital to early legislative programs such as workers' compensation. Those mechanisms are now highly visible in litigation as
well. A business firm's liability insurer, for example, pays the
victim in accordance with the judgment or settlement and the
policy. That payment comes out of a pool of premiums that
spreads the costs of accidents among the community of insureds. Further spreading occurs as the insureds manage their
premium charges through product or service pricing and other
routes to market spreading.

Numerous opinions emphasize the possibilities for legal
ordering that liability insurance opens through transfers of risk
from insureds to the insurer and related loss spreading.[14] The
availability of insurance has quieted the judicial concern expressed by the older negative justifications that accident costs
might ruin a defendant as well as a victim.[15] Indeed, doubt that
a given defendant is insured for liability has restrained courts
from imposing liability.[16] On the other hand, judges have cautioned that expansion of liability because of insurance may
generate intolerable costs, a perception that would today find

support in the recurrent crises over both rates and availability of insurance in a growing number of activities.[17]

More is at issue than a special awareness of business defendants' access to liability insurance. The influence of insurance reaches more broadly. Outside business settings, the middle classes have developed a consciousness about its vital role. Risk of sudden and severe loss is no longer viewed as a cost of living to which all are inescapably subject. Such risk can be transferred, as insureds pay premiums related to the risk that they generate or to which they are subject in order to acquire relative financial certainty.[18] Harm—to others in the case of liability insurance, to the insured in the case of loss insurance—will be covered within the policy limits by the insurer. First-party medical protection through individual or workplace-related plans as well as personal liability insurance in activities like driving become ordinary prudence.

Through accident plans, through property and medical and life insurance, through liability insurance, and through social insurance programs as well, risks are hedged as a matter of course. That hedging becomes part of the fabric of middle-class life, to the point where unmanaged risk of dramatic loss is viewed as an unacceptable threat to personal security. Surely that pervasive consciousness of insurance, of spreading loss over time and among many social actors through the periodic payment of premiums, influences the reaction to accident costs of judges who themselves are dominantly of middle-class origin and sensibility.

It is significant that courts have barely noted the availability of first-party medical protection for potential accident victims as an argument against heightened liability. Its availability, either through individual purchase or through employee-benefit programs that grow out of collective bargaining, weakens the justification for loss spreading through tort law, since the victim's own precautions could suffice for spreading.[19] Such forms of private insurance as well as welfare programs like

Medicare or Medicaid have figured in opinions treating the collateral-source rule, although thus far they have led only to slight qualifications of that rule.[20] In any event, the issue there goes to the amount of damages—whether relief from collateral sources should, to its extent, reduce defendant's liability—rather than to liability itself.

The courts' failure to consider the implications of such programs for tort liability may stem from the limited relief that they provide compared with tort law. First-party insurance for injury to property may equal or at least approach tort damages. But for personal injury it generally covers only medical costs, and often only a stated percentage of them. Workplace-related private insurance and rarer forms of personal insurance may cover percentages of other costs of injuries, such as lost wages or disability. Moreover, insurance markets are imperfect, and insurance protection is often of a technical and legal complexity that makes fully informed purchases difficult to achieve. Transaction costs in the acquisition of insurance by (all) potential victims would be high.

Courts may well doubt that many individuals will take adequate precautions because of their tendency to discount low-level risks (a broadly shared tendency) or because of their poverty (not all victims are middle class or included in the workplaces' insurance schemes). It is also the case that reliance by courts on first-party protection or welfare programs to spread at least medical costs would undermine that justification for strict liability which stresses the potential modification of defendants' behavior through internalization of accident costs. Whatever the explanation, the omission from most opinions of this important institutional fact underscores the selectivity of social vision. It suggests the range of moral beliefs and postulates about social behavior that influence that selection.

3. *Characteristics of parties.* Contemporary opinions frequently express a judicial empathy with (or, depending on one's perspective, disparagement of) potential accident victims. Courts question the capacity of the individual for intel-

ligent self-protection—cost-benefit prudence in avoiding accidents, acquiring insurance to protect against concentrated loss from accidents, and understanding and assessing contractual provisions before agreeing to them. Such views about individuals' knowledge, perception, and instrumental rationality bear directly on the tort doctrine creating heightened liability. They are, for example, relevant to the decision whether fault-based defenses survive in a strict-liability action, or whether manufacturers are under a duty to anticipate through design the carelessness of product users. They also influence courts' judgments about the validity of contractual disclaimers of liability.

Numerous opinions now view the victim as unable to grasp products' technological complexity.[21] Such opinions assume that many of the pervasive risks of modern society, such as injuries from pollution or defective autos, are controllable to only a small degree through the potential victim's care. In contrast, courts invest the business defendant with a bureaucratic, cost-benefit rationality that is applied to the goal of maximizing profits. Given the proper legal incentives, corporate bureaucracy will plan intelligently for behavior modification as well as for the spreading of liability costs that cannot be avoided.

Moreover, courts view corporate defendants not as atomistic and autonomous business units, isolated from their economic environments and each other, but rather as funnels to the linked communities of consumers, shareholders, and employees. Corporations are the formal rather than effective bearers of liability. Earlier tort opinions implicitly assumed all social actors to be more or less fungible. It did not appear relevant within the fault system's neutral embrace of all social actors whether defendant was an individual or a business. The difference is striking between the two categories within a modern social vision.

4. *Social relationships and structures.* Opinions express courts' perceptions of the patterns of social interaction that

lead to accidents. The tendency in recent decades is for courts to understand and refer to the parties to an accident less in personal or individualized ways and more in general, abstract, and categorical terms. Product manufacturers and consumers, polluters and farmers, employers and employees are the categories that inhabit decisions. Particular firms or individuals are relevant to the development of tort doctrine not because of their distinctive characteristics, but because of the general characteristics of the types of social actors into which they are assimilated.[22] These broad types engage in predictable, structured, and occasionally harmful interaction. Liability rules grow out of such predictable harm.

In opinions involving contractual disclaimers of liability in the context of, say, consumer purchases or apartment leases, courts comment on recurrent forms of transactions and characteristic market structures: form contracts with standard clauses to define liabilities, "shortages" that diminish the power of the individual to negotiate terms, domination of a market by a few producers offering their product or service on similar terms.[23] They again direct attention as much to structured patterns of interaction as to the individualized circumstances or characteristics of the events and parties.

5. *Views of society's goals and moral aspirations.* Courts here are at their most impressionistic. Their remarks create a general political or moral atmosphere within which the larger issues of utility and fairness can be resolved. An ambiguity permeates such remarks—whether they are meant to be objective, empirical statements about prevailing ideologies manifested in political and legislative processes, or whether they represent the view of a given judge about the nation's condition and ideals.

The classic nineteenth-century cases expressing so grand a social vision emphasized the need for growth and were wary of thwarting material progress by burdening entrepreneurs. Law was complicit with and instrumental to that growth. Such a vision of society was captured within the negative justifications for the fault system, which also expressed an individualistic, antipaternalist ideology.[24] The price of progress may have been high for those injured en route, but in the end all would benefit. The price could not be "withheld."[25] Such opinions expressed a sense of manifest destiny, of historical forces not to be checked for the relief of individual misfortune.

More recent opinions rarely expound at so majestic a level. Insofar as they express broad views about society, they emphasize two different themes. Both tend to contradict the earlier vision, either by finding its concerns no longer relevant because of changed conditions, or simply by proceeding from different moral and ideological premises.

First, some courts discount the earlier functional justifications for the negligence system—the need for the common law to foster industrial growth in preference to other goals—that they attribute to nineteenth-century courts. Industry is seen as strong enough to bear additional liability costs, a view fortified by the assumption of spreading rather than shifting loss.[26] Second, courts have absorbed the goals and premises of regulatory and welfare programs. If social security, unemployment insurance, Medicare and Medicaid, or workers' compensation recognize a need for security and minimum wellbeing, and some degree of social responsibility for the unfortunate, it is not astonishing that courts also move toward a sense of collective responsibility which takes individual misfortune seriously.

The justifications for loss spreading, whether within the idiom of utilitarian or right-fairness thought, express some such outlook. The underlying vision is one of interdependency, collective concern and sharing rather than an atomistic fragmentation of social actors. It links the victim closely to a broader community. It suggests moral bonds among citizens rather than radical autonomy, and a close nexus between individual welfare and social welfare.[27] Some of the opinions invalidating contractual disclaimers can also be understood as favoring (more) collective over (more) individualistic premises. A conception of the public good expressed through the rules of tort law prevails over principles of party autonomy and free will in private ordering.

Three Characteristics of Modern Social Vision

Several ideas that appeared within my descriptions of modern justifications and social vision here reappear, no longer subordinate to other themes but as the organizing and central concepts. They signal the distinctive characteristics of the trend toward heightened liability.

These ideas or phenomena, bearing particularly on social vision, are organized within three sets of contrasts: dyadic-systemic, individual-group, and unique-statistical. My argument is that the classical fault system is more amenable to characterization by the first of the contrasting ideas within each pair, whereas the social vision in modern heightened liability, and hence modern justifications, can better be characterized by the second. I therefore characterize social vision within modern accident law, including both expansion of fault liability and movement toward strict liability, as systemic-group-statistical. Of course my characterization speaks to tendencies toward, not location at, one or the other pole.

My argument is not one of a jurisprudentially or politically necessary correspondence between a given liability system such as modern heightened liability and a particular characterization of social vision. Nor is it that one logically entails the other. Rather, it is a historical assertion that certain correspondences have developed. Hence, I test it by applying these contrasting characterizations to the content of modern social vision and justifications.

The contrasting ideas within each of the three sets do not necessarily point in a particular moral or doctrinal direction, any more than do the abstract structures or logic of utilitarian or right-fairness arguments. As suggested by the following illustrations, a dyadic social vision might rest on individualistic or altruistic premises. A systemic vision might rest on atomistic and market-oriented premises or premises of collective concern. Two justifications, one embodying a dyadic and the other a systemic vision of the accident problem, might conceivably yield the same liability rules; two justifications each embodying a systemic social vision might yield different rules. But as I here employ these three sets and apply them to the recent, concrete historical progression from the classical fault system to modern heightened liability, the distinctions within them do take on a particular content and have some ideological connotation.

DYADIC-SYSTEMIC

The Nature of the Distinction

By a dyad I mean the dictionary definition: two units regarded as a pair. Within this essay's themes, the two units of the dyad are the parties to an accident, and paired by it. "Pair" implies no continuing, significant relationship between them. On the contrary, as used herein a dyadic perception of accidents is one of unexpected and random interactions, even if the parties had some prior contractual or status relationship. Dyads are formed by the accident and then dissolve, except as a pair continue to be bound for some period through liability claims growing out of the interaction.

By a systemic perception I mean one that grasps many different elements as interrelated parts of a larger scheme. The world is experienced or visualized as connected rather than as fragmented. The observer perceives interdependencies and cause-and-effect relationships among the elements of social life.[28]

Within this essay, the base elements are accidents, the parties to them, their social effects, and social mechanisms for avoiding accidents or alleviating those effects. A systemic perception locates those elements within broader social trends and structures and patterns of social interaction.[29] It links them more intricately to social institutions like insurance or the market and to the public ordering of social life.

These definitions suggest a threshold ambiguity in the contrast of dyadic with systemic. All interaction necessarily occurs within a social context. By hypothesis and definition, a social context reveals structural characteristics and recurrent patterns of interaction, whether the patterns are simple or complex. Hence, all perceptions of interactions (accidents) must be rooted in some systemic framework.

My working distinction between dyadic and systemic cannot then mean the absence or presence of social-systemic contexts for accidents and their parties. It is a distinction between perceptions of such contexts, between ways of grasping events within them. What is at issue is the degree to which the systemic framework emphasizing the remoter causes and effects of accidents informs the opinions of courts. Relative to a systemic vision, a dyadic one blinks much of this schematic framework. The vision is myopic. The court imagines isolated, discrete events. It does not look to connections among apparently disparate phenomena.

My description of the content and implications of a systemic vision treats such a vision not in the large, not in all contexts, but in the context of this essay. As the classical system gave way to modern heightened liability, that vision came to bear an affinity to the ideology and institutional structure of the regulatory-welfare state, particularly to its legislative-administrative expressions. The socioeconomic system is seen more readily as a whole. The management of the socioeconomic system becomes a characteristic goal of legal ordering. The regulatory-welfare state becomes the managerial state. Modern tort law, whether aiming at the reduction of accidents

or the spreading of their costs, expresses this vision of interrelatedness and complexity, of causes and effects among social
phenomena that are subject to legal control. The workings of
complex institutions such as the market are explicitly absorbed
by courts into their decision making. Tort accident law, too,
assumes a more managerial, system-oriented character.

Viewed in the abstract, a systemic perception as such need
not have fostered the trend toward heightened liability. Liability for fault was explained partly in systemic terms, most
explicitly through the justification expressed by the Hand Formula. Negative justifications for the fault system made explicit
that accident costs were understood in their relationship to
national goals. Thus nineteenth-century opinions expounding
a grand vision of the country's growth and stressing its need
for a legal system supportive of that growth had intrinsically a
systemic character.[30]

Conversely, it is not only systemic perceptions that support
heightened liability. Justifications for the enclaves of a formal
strict liability within the older common law sometimes expressed a dyadic vision of social interaction. For example, the
maxim "between two innocents, who caused the harm should
pay" rested on an intuition of fairness between discrete social
actors involved in a discrete interaction, rather than on a larger
social and systemic conception of accident avoidance or distributive justice. Nevertheless, in the historical context here
considered, and given the attributes of system that modern
opinions stress, it is a systemic vision that has favored heightened liability.

Illustrations
These illustrations of the trend from a dyadic to systemic perception of accidents involve indistinguishably social vision and
justification.

1. *Externalities.* Modern justification responds to a systemic vision of the social costs of accidents. The victim is but
the first in a chain of those harmed, a chain of interdependen-

cies linking the victim to the family, the workplace, or indeed to welfare programs through which the victim may ultimately transfer the accident costs to the general public. Courts employ doctrines such as proximate cause or no duty to cut the chain reaction at some point and arrest liabilities to all who may be derivatively or relationally harmed through the accident victim. But whether or not part of the measure of legal damages, the perceived costs of those indirectly harmed serve to heighten the sense of accidents' seriousness and thus to fortify the case both for rules encouraging accident reduction and for compensation.

2. *Behavior modification.* The Hand Formula, the prime example of utilitarian justification for fault liability, has the systemic character of all collective utilitarianism. The social vision informing it transcends merely dyadic interactions. Its goal, after all, is to maximize *social* welfare, and the instrument (rules) to realize it must draw on social systems like the market. Like the analogous modern justification for strict liability, the fault liability that the Hand Formula expressed was meant to have a prospective effect on behavior. It would reach beyond the mere resolution of a historical dispute to spur cost-justified reductions in accidents. What courts and juries found to be wrongful behavior would become widely known and would influence decisions of like-situated social actors.

Nonetheless, the fault standard, as applied, looked to specific historical conduct, to the fragment of a defendant's activity that was causally linked to the accident. The court or jury viewed that conduct in its relation to the dyadic interaction before the court. "Unreasonable behavior" is, after all, a contextual finding about the particular conduct of a particular defendant. Perhaps others can extrapolate from the context and conduct (railroad crossings must have protective guards) and change particular behavior. But "unreasonable" is characteristically an *ad hoc* conclusion rather than general and prospective in its implications.

Behavior modification in contemporary justification rests on a more complex and systemic perception of the accident problem. Justification slights the significance of the dyadic context for the accident by stressing the broad activity, and indeed views the corporate defendant as a miniature social system capable of research and development and of structural reform to bring accident costs down. The defendant is seen whole rather than as a cluster of discrete acts, some of which occasionally cause accidents. The court and the legal norm address the activity, whether blasting or manufacturing products or generating pollution, rather than specific conduct. Of course, to the extent that fault-based defenses figure in strict-liability actions, courts return to an *ad hoc* and dyadic investigation of the parties' conduct rather than work out the full implications of a categorical and systemic perception of accidents.

3. *Compensation and loss spreading.* Let us compare some justifications for compensation. The postulate of equal respect that supports the right to compensation under the fault system concerns relations among members of society acting within a social system. But the vision within that postulate is personal and dyadic rather than social and systemic. The moral fault underlying liability speaks to personal rather than collective morals. A member of society violates the right of another to be free of an interference and is therefore obligated as a matter of justice to make good the loss. Within such a dyadic image, judicial concern quite naturally touches compensation as such, payment to the victim by the morally faulty defendant, whether or not the spreading of liability costs will follow. The same observation applies to such traditional justifications for strict liability as *sic utere*, or "between two innocents, who caused the loss should pay."

At times, modern social vision expresses a collective image of a society characterized by strong bonds of social interdependence.[31] So does the modern fairness justification for heightened liability that rests on proportionality in the sharing of the benefits and burdens from an activity. Society is a collectivity rather than an aggregation of unrelated individuals. The activity at issue benefits many in some small way. Even when conducted without fault, it randomly and seriously burdens a few. Compensation by the defendant is but a prelude to spreading to the benefited communities. Broad communities related to the activity, rather than simply a dyadic interaction involving a violation of the victim's rights, form the framework for moral and legal decision. Collective rather than personal morals are at issue.

It is as critical to the utilitarian justification for loss spreading through strict liability that the initial liability bearer be viewed as a funnel to a larger social system. The very theoretical justification for loss spreading—a minor burden for many adds up to a smaller welfare loss than a severe burden on a few—implicates the entire social system in the victim's recovery.

Surely the prevalence of liability insurance nourishes a systemic as well as group-related and statistical vision of accidents. From the start, the private insurance industry is implicated in the accident. Indeed, by statute or by decisional law, the insurer may be sued directly by the victim and thus be literally before a court.[32] Whether or not a party, the insurance company displaces the defendant to the extent of managing the defense and if necessary compensating the victim out of pooled premiums contributed by a group of insureds. The court cannot readily imagine the consequences of the accident or judgment of liability in dyadic terms.

4. *Contractual derogations from tort liabilities.* The point was earlier made that contemporary opinions tend to look to the broader context of the contract transaction, to recurrent features of standard contracts, to market structures within which the transaction developed—in brief, to systemic and structural influences on the quality of bargain and choice. All this stands in contrast to a narrower, more dyadic view of the contract transaction, one inattentive to its linkages to a larger social system.

INDIVIDUAL-GROUP

The Nature of the Distinction

The contrast of individual-group offers a related perspective on the character of modern social vision. The question posed is how the court imagines the litigants. Does it view the defendant and the accident victim as individuated and unique social actors? Or do courts understand them primarily as participants in, or even representatives of, groups of social actors that are themselves in some sense the litigants? To the extent that the second interpretation is accurate, the nature of accident law changes. The court visualizes interaction between groups, and tort norms regulate group conflict.

The notion of a group within this individual-group polarity can best be explained by distinguishing it from three bordering notions. First, the common law has long included doctrines whose reach is defined in terms of groups: status groups of an ascriptive character deriving from political and social order; groups that individuals can choose to enter and leave (married women); or groups defined in terms of physical and mental characteristics (minors, mentally incompetent). Tort law employs several of these categories to vary the duties and rights of group members from those normally prevailing—the relaxed negligence standard for children, the special duties of innkeepers, and so on.

But the "groups" within the individual-group contrast here relevant—mass-accident victims, typical consumers, business defendants within a common industry—are not subjected to formal legal classification or distinctively regulated by the common law. They do not figure in the black letter law of Restatements. Their presence in litigation does not itself point to the application of one or another legal rule. Rather, they more

generally form a part of the social vision of courts. They influence or are regulated by doctrine in less explicit ways.

Second, the individual-group contrast differs from the lit-
eral phenomenon of the group in structural-reform litigation.
Suits brought by prisoners or the mentally ill may seek injunctive relief that would benefit the entire group defined by
the relevant institution, whether the action is brought by a few
plaintiffs or on behalf of a class within the institution. An
analogous situation arises in desegregation or employment-
discrimination suits, for the injunctive relief and the norm
underlying it benefit many individuals within groups defined
in racial, gender, or related terms. In such suits, the conflict
before the court is explicitly between a group and a specific
institution or a more general social practice.[33]

Accident law differs. The victim characteristically seeks
damages rather than an injunction. Moreover, the party structure of the litigation is generally simple and traditional. Multiple joinder or the use of class actions for damages has been
historically rare. Hence, tort litigation generally lacks the concrete phenomena of a group's presence and collective relief. In
this sense, a tort claim for money damages and relief for the
accident victim (who must prove an individual causal link)
remain personal rather than group-oriented and collective.
Nonetheless, affinities are now developing between structural
reform litigation and tort actions, as multiple joinder and class
actions in claims for money damages grow in frequency.[34]

Third, the idea of group here employed has some similarity
to political interest groups. To some extent, contemporary interest groups and the groups relevant to accident law overlap.
Consumers and environmentalists mobilize politically to
achieve greater product safety or control of pollution; victims
of product defects and pollution may be visualized as groups in
tort litigation.

Nonetheless, the notion of group within the social vision of
courts developing accident law has a more amorphous expression in social life. Political interest groups are formed and enter

the political process to achieve purposes, which may change over time. The groups figuring in accident law, with their less tangible identity, draw their character from the system of the production, distribution, and consumption of goods and services, including within that system the external accident costs that it generates. They do not form and dissolve at will for specific reasons. They have, as it were, a natural identity within the economic system. They inhere in that system.

For example, much accident litigation involves parties who can readily be characterized in terms of groups: product manufacturers and consumers, industrial polluters and farmers, landlords and tenants, retailers and customers. Typically individuals (the victim-plaintiffs in litigation) form part of many groups of changing membership (consumers, tenants) in their different roles or activities. Accidents may strike individuals within any of these typical roles and interactions. Hence, any one of them may be relevant to accident litigation.

This notion of group corresponds to a systemic social vision. Courts that understand social interaction in a more structured and systemic way often appear to view the relevant interaction as between groups. The relevant "system" amounts to recurrent patterns or structures of group conduct: product producers and purchasers, polluters and nearby residents.

This tendency of courts to see harmful interaction in terms of groups has some affinity to broader characteristics of the modern state. Groups or activities are indeed the typical categories of thought of the regulatory and welfare state. Its statutory rules tend to be defined in such terms rather than as abstract and universal norms. Groups or categories characterize legislative revision or displacement of the common law of accidents. Auto plans predominantly involve interaction within a group and a system of auto drivers, although outsiders such as pedestrians are also affected. Workers' compensation plans, product-safety regulations, and the regulation of hazardous wastes involve interaction between (a) groups of producers, and (b) groups of employees, or consumers, or residents near the sources of pollution.

Illustrations

Three distinct themes in contemporary opinions illustrate this notion of groups.

1. *Parties invested with group characteristics.* Consider first contemporary courts' understanding of the accident victim. Within the fault system, courts examined conduct concretely and contextually. Nonetheless, they generally saw victims as undifferentiated individuals, abstract and universal. It mattered not whether the victim was a consumer or an employee injured by a defective machine, a pedestrian crossing the tracks or an auto driver. Victims had the same general characteristics, and the defendant was held to a constant standard of care. By and large, that standard did not impose on a defendant a duty to anticipate the carelessness of potential victims. Apart from legal regimes for especially protected groups like children, defenses such as contributory fault or assumption of risk were meant to be evenhandedly applied to all such individual victims.

Contemporary courts imposing heightened liability tend to describe a defendant's conduct or activity more abstractly and less contextually. Nonetheless, they tend to define the characteristics of accident victims more contextually and in more detail. The consumer before the court is understood as one among consumers in general and is invested with the characteristics of that larger group with respect to knowledge, capacity, and behavioral rationality.

This tendency spurs two observations. First, because understood as one of many within a relevant group, the individual victim is not unique. Second, the individual is nonetheless seen more concretely than within the fault system, since the characteristics of victims are not universal but specific to the relevant group. The context examined is not the unique conduct or characteristics of the victim. It is social and structural.

2. *Mass victims.* The phenomenon of mass victims has become more common in tort litigation, particularly for claims involving design defects, medical drugs, radiation, or contamination from hazardous wastes and other forms of pollution.[35] Even when victims seek money damages rather than an injunction, courts tend to view the plight of the individual plaintiff as but an instance of a tragedy for a group.

This phenomenon is starting to influence the party structure of litigation. When a court certifies a class action for victims, a group is literally and not just figuratively before it. Tort law is explicitly transformed from one of dyadic interaction to one involving a group of victims—and, as noted below, sometimes a group of defendants as well. Relief through damages affects the group, although the requirement of proof of individual damages by each member of the class generally remains. Even when suit is brought by one plaintiff or a small number through joinder, information about the mass and group character of the accident is before the court, through background statistics and through knowledge that many similar suits are pending.

3. *Business groups.* Business defendants as well as victims may be perceived as part of a group. From one perspective such a view of defendants inheres in the tendency accompanying strict liability to stress that liability attaches to a broad activity rather than stems from unique conduct. That activity will be engaged in by many businesses similarly situated to the defendant. But my argument is more specific. Through the joinder of several producers (of medical drugs or pollution) the court sees graphically their multiple contributions to the harm suffered and the systemic relationships among them. The victims may indeed claim a joint rather than several liability of the producers.[36]

Joint liability may stem from the inseparable nature of the harm traceable to several defendants and suffered by the victim(s), or from a finding of concerted activity among the defendants even though the harm suffered by an individual victim can be traced to only one among them. When a claim of concerted activity of the defendants underlies a joint liability, proof of a causal link between a victim and a particular defendant is no longer necessary. Each defendant is treated as part of the group with which the victim can prove the necessary cause-in-fact relationship. The collective nature of the defendants' activity is emphasized through a judgment effectively addressing a group.[37]

Recent decisions treating problems of proof of a causal nexus between a victim's harm and a defendant's activity have heightened the perception of litigation as opposing group to group. For example, several defendants, interrelated through their practices within the drug industry, were viewed as subject to a several liability in proportion to their market shares of the drug causing the injury. Such market-share liability eliminated the need for an individual plaintiff to prove a causal link with a given defendant, such as the purchase of the drug from it.[38] That litigation also involved a plaintiff class action. Opposing groups were formally before the court. In tort litigation, a group of risk victims now confronts a group of risk generators.

UNIQUE-STATISTICAL

The Nature of the Distinction

To view a phenomenon or event—a risk, an accident—as unique is to view it as random, occasional, and understandable only within a closely defined causal context. Thus it escapes prediction. A statistical vision, on the other hand, addresses not the particular phenomenon but general and aggregated phenomena. It understands such matters abstractly rather than anecdotally, as recurrent and systemic, as subject in the aggregate to prediction. This is the chill vision of the actuary which underlies the institution of insurance.[39] Through the predictions that it yields the statistical vision holds open the possibility of planning for and managing risk and accidents.

The following sets, referring to risk and accidents, summarize the two visions. They suggest the close relationships among the systemic, group, and statistical characterizations of modern social vision.

unique	statistical
individual, personal	category, impersonal
concrete, anecdotal	generalized, purged of detail
occasional, random	recurrent, systemic
isolated conduct	part of an activity
unforeseeable (in the particular)	actuarially predictable (in the aggregate)
wait and see, fatalism	manageable, planning through insurance and regulation

The statistical vision permeates the economic and legal ordering of the regulatory and welfare state. It becomes the ideology, or science, of professional managers, private or public. The economy is symbolically captured in a mass of systematically gathered statistics that serve as the basis for (often contradictory) predictions and official policies. Individuals are subsumed within categories. Insurance, whose pervasive influence was earlier noted, becomes not simply an industry, but almost a mentality or form of consciousness. The wealth of statistical information nourishes the sense or illusion of managerial capacity, and of the ability of corporate or governmental bureaucracies to plan for and affect social phenomena.

Again, public law most graphically expresses this statistical vision. Regulatory and welfare programs rest on a statistical grasp of the problems occasioning the legislation—market shares of companies, supply and demand for low-income housing, the number of the indigent or aged. Legislative programs dealing with the reduction of or compensation for accidental injuries require the calculation of accident risks and costs, and in some cases calculation of the costs of reducing those risks as well—safety regulations within OSHA, the containment of hazardous wastes within various regulatory schemes, insurance rates within workers' compensation or auto plans. The programs deal with the statistical person, statistical risk, statistical damages. Courts developing the common law inevitably absorb this spirit of the many regulatory and compensatory schemes that they understand both as citizens and as judges in the context of applying statutes.

Illustrations
The statistical vision influencing common-law adjudication dominates courts' understanding of the accident problem.

　　1. *Statistical perception and behavior modification.* Strict liability justifications vividly express this statistical perception. The goal of behavior modification rests on an assumption of the cost-benefit rationality of potential defendants. Such calculations within a firm or activity rest in turn on the ability to predict risk and loss—not simply risk that the common law might view as unreasonable and hence condemn under the negligence standard, but all risk of injury, however reasonably imposed. That prediction grows principally out of experience within the firm's or industry's activity. Risk can be reduced as firms sponsor research for cost-justified precautions. To the extent that courts doubt the assumptions of this statistical vision, some of the arguments for strict liability weaken—as in drug cases where a court may consider the injuries caused by a pioneering drug to have escaped statistical prediction.[40]

　　2. *Statistical perception and loss spreading.* Conceptions of statistical risk also inform the loss-spreading justifications.[41] Even though not reducible beyond a certain point through cost-benefit calculations, risk can be accounted for and managed through self-insurance or liability insurance, product pricing, dividend or wage policy, and so on. This predictability informs even the fairness justifications for strict liability. The certainty that a number of people closely approximated by a statistical prediction will be injured through an ongoing activity strengthens the argument that their burdens should in fairness be shared by those benefiting from the activity. Such advance knowledge by the defendant-activity of the certainty of victims appears to support courts' references to intentional tort in strict-liability cases, and to strengthen the sense of an imposition requiring compensation.

The relevance of a statistical vision to fairness justifications for loss spreading suggests a paradox or even contradiction that inheres in some contemporary justification. From one perspective, the approach is abstract, scientific, impersonal, bureaucratic. From another perspective, the spirit may be understood as one of collective, even communitarian, concern and sharing. The expression of empathy for the victim, the sense of bonds uniting that victim to a larger community which ought to come to the rescue, the perception of market and insurance mechanisms for spreading, the actuarial vision through which the firm can plan and protect itself—all such phenomena form, as it were, a complex vision and justification, at once abstract and concrete, statistical and personal, bureaucratic and communitarian. These are the very paradoxes and contradictions of the regulatory and welfare state whose spirit has infused modern tort law.

3. *Statistical perception and causation.* Several types of accidents of growing statistical significance raise distinctive problems of causation. Some solutions brought to those problems have rested on statistical proofs. The common illustration involves harm that may be traceable to many sources, only one of which is represented by the defendant before the court—cancers that may be caused by hazardous wastes or asbestos for which the defendant is responsible, as well as by air-borne carcinogens or smoking. The problems posed by such multiple-cause accidents include not simply a selection of one among several distinct probable causes, but also a recognition of the synergistic effect of several causes, all of which contributed to a given injury. To resolve such problems, some legislation and legislative proposals validate the use of statistical information about the probabilities of different causes of the harm, and develop criteria for recovery that draw either solely on such information or on presumptions built on them.[42]

Courts considering statistical proof of causation have yet to employ a concept of pro rata or proportionate causation that might, for example, charge the defendant for the percentage of the accident cost that corresponds to the statistical probability (perhaps 0.1, perhaps 0.7) that the defendant's activity was the cause.[43] But shy of such innovative doctrine, a few courts have drawn on or permitted juries to draw on abstract statistical proof of the likelihood of a causal link to support a judgment of liability.[44]

Alternatively, issues of causation arise with respect to a group of defendants each of which manufactures the identical product known to cause plaintiff's injury, when the plaintiff is unable to identify which defendant manufactured the responsible product. As earlier noted, a recent doctrinal development authorizes the use of statistics about market shares to apportion liability severally among a group of such defendants.[45] The group generates a risk through production of a common product. Thus, each bears a liability proportionate (through market share) to the risk generated by it.[46] The vision is systemic-group-statistical.

Sources of Social Vision in Tort Accident Law: Public Law as a Mediating Category

Exploration of the many sources of or reasons for the social vision now informing accident law lies beyond the ambition of this essay. Historical trends in economic organization, political conflict and the emergence of powerful interest groups (such as consumers or environmentalists) advancing the cause of victims or of accident avoidance, a changing political ideology about governmental regulation and provision of welfare needs, novel risks bred by new technology, self-identification by a judge with one or another expression of American life or ideals, movements in jurisprudence or social thought (such as legal realism or welfare economics)—the catalog is as unhelpful as it is extensive.

But my subject is not accident law in the large. Since this essay treats common-law adjudication rather than legislation, considerations distinctive to courts limit the range and sources of social vision. Hence, a discussion of sources must be attentive to what is generally thought to be appropriate within a reigning judicial style, to what courts traditionally acknowledge as the limits on what they can achieve and hence on what they should utter.

Thus far I have suggested that several developing phenomena contributed to the changing judicial perception of accidents—for example, the modern sensibility about private insurance. My purpose now is to stress the role of public law in influencing those perceptions. I treat public law as a mediating category, as an institutional filter through which courts acquire an empirical knowledge about accidents in American society as well as an appreciation of goals in accident law to which the society has made some political commitment.[47] Here again the term "public law" serves only to classify legal norms in a formal institutional sense. It refers simply to legislative and administrative schemes rather than common law, and is not meant to carry the ideological connotation inherent in the jurisprudential and political distinction of public from private in legal and social ordering.[48]

Legislation, with its administrative creations, has become the articulate voice and formal instrument of the modern state, the medium through which regulatory goals and conceptions of social justice are best realized. Hammered out among interest groups, in legislative committees and debates, it captures a given social vision or illuminates conflict between social visions in a particularly explicit way. Statutory and administrative schemes reveal more vividly than common-law doctrine the trend within the liberal tradition from the ideology of the framework state to that of the regulatory-welfare state. That shift in ideology implies more resort to centralized decisionmaking to regulate social problems, a greater prominence of paternalistic premises to legal ordering, and heightened use of the rhetoric of redistribution.

It is a commonplace that legislation now permeates the common law. It affects tort accident law both tangentially and structurally. So does the social vision that it expresses. Consider first the different ways in which these formal and structural influences come about.

1. Legislation may selectively reform accident law. For well over a century, statutes have modified common-law doctrines to expand or confine liability. Illustrations reach from the nineteenth-century statutes imposing a strict liability for fires caused by railroads or abolishing employers' defenses to negligence actions, to contemporary statutes instituting comparative fault, imposing restrictions on recovery for product liability, restructuring traditional categories of landowners' liability, modifying the collateral-source rule, or limiting the use of *res ipsa loquitur*.[49] This category of legislative influence might be expanded to include the common-law doctrine of "negligence per se," under which safety standards (enforced through injunctive and criminal sanctions but not creating private rights of action) fill out the negligence standard and thereby merge the common law with regulatory legislation.[50]

2. Legislation restructures or displaces the common law. It may insert administrative processes between the plaintiff and the courts (recent medical malpractice statutes), and simultaneously limit recovery.[51] More significantly, legislative schemes eliminate common-law actions in broadly defined fields of activity. They relegate the accident victim to administrative processes, as well as to distinct bases and measures for recovery (workers' compensation plans, black lung and other occupational-disease legislation). Or they displace common-law actions only in part, the boundary being defined in terms of types of injury or amount of damages (no-fault auto plans).[52]

3. Within the familiar notion of statutory radiations,[53] the influence of legislation is by analogy. Although a statute may have no formal bearing on tort litigation, it may nonetheless give direction to common-law change by the force and political acceptance of its example. Its animating spirit and purposes are absorbed into tort law. Opinions expanding vicarious liability by analogy to the justifications for loss spreading that underlie workers' compensation plans offer a familiar illustration.[54] So do those drawing on principles in the Uniform Sales Act or the Uniform Commercial Code to construct strict product liability out of notions of implied warranty,[55] or those deciding nuisance actions in the light of public-health or environmental legislation.[56]

4. These three categories contribute to a fourth and critical one for understanding the mediating function of public law. It refers not to the relatively specific substantive influence of particular legislation, as do the prior three, but to the empirical data, understandings of social life, moral goals, and formal justifications that give rise to accident-directed legislation. What is vital within this fourth category is the social vision expressed within a broad corpus of public law that includes not only accident-directed legislation but also social insurance and welfare programs which incidentally aid accident victims. It is that vision which deeply influences judicial approaches to accident law.

Courts' attitudes toward accident cases are charged with the empirical findings and moral sentiments informing much legislation from workers' compensation plans to the present. The goals of modifying behavior of business firms through cost internalization and of loss spreading are endemic to that legislation.[57] Loss-spreading justifications advanced to support some administrative schemes resemble those of the courts in their conceptions of both welfare and fairness. Legislative programs express a systemic-group-statistical understanding of many problems. Surely the courts building modern accident law have done so with a deeper sense of the legitimacy of their enterprise because of the modern justifications' and vision's sympathetic relationship to programs that have grown out of and survived political battles to be confirmed in public law.

5   Reflections

These concluding thoughts treat familiar as well as new themes. The first section expands on some ideas earlier developed about the nature of legal argument. The second section departs from the essay's principal purpose of illuminating characteristics of legal argument through the recent trends in tort law. There I offer my evaluation of the changes here portrayed in accident law, both within and beyond the law of tort.

Themes in Retrospect

The earlier chapters, concentrating on each of the three elements of legal argument, explored a number of themes that proved to be common to them—themes like judicial choice or constraint, coherence or contradiction within each element of argument, and reasons for the described trends. Now those themes are at the center of a discussion suggesting their broader relevance for legal argument.

1. *Private and public law, adjudication and legislation.* Here I treat not the formal, institutional distinction that I have employed between common law and public (statutory and administrative) law, but rather the ideological conception of common law as private law and of adjudication as a neutral legal process, in contrast with a "public" legislative realm of law and politics.

That conception defines the "private" component of law as

consisting of a neutral and facilitative framework for individual choice and action, as nonregulatory and noninstrumentalist in design and spirit, as expressing general and stable principles, and thus as quintessentially legal rather than political. Often the "private" is associated with the common law, particularly with contract and property, as well as with the conception of a neutral, apolitical technique of adjudication. In contrast, public law is classically expressed through regulatory legislation. It expresses contingent notions of public policy, has an instrumentalist and coercive character, intervenes in and regulates the private sphere of action, and is quintessentially collective and political in spirit.[1]

This distinction between private and public law expresses part of a broader vision or ideology of the separateness of private and public spheres within the liberal political tradition. That complex vision suggests a sphere of private life and action (such as the market, organized by principles of property and contract) independent of the public sector or state. To some degree that sphere is protected against interference by the state. The protection derives from tradition or from a constitution, as well as from judicial adherence to notions of the rule of law, including notions of legality associated with a particular adjudicatory technique.[2]

My premise has been that common-law argument and adjudication are informed and structured by collective justification as well as social vision. Tort adjudication is in this root sense inescapably "public," rather than a neutral and apolitical technique for resolving disputes. Within the common law, the classical fault system and the judicial opinions that developed it are not more private or public, not more or less distanced from political beliefs, not more or less neutral or principled, than modern heightened liability. They are simply different. They rest on different moral and political premises and are associated with different social visions.

Common-law adjudication and legislative processes grow out of different self-conceptions or ideologies of judges and legislators about their range of competence and role in the American polity. They employ different methods. They confront different problems of legitimacy as well as different practical and institutional constraints. Nonetheless, the two constitute realizations, however different, of a larger political process.

If modern heightened liability proclaims the public and political character of tort law more explicitly and forcefully than did negligence liability, the explanation may lie in its closer correspondence with the developing legislative-administrative law bearing on accidents. Social vision and justifications that are now prevalent in tort law have found powerful expression, sometimes their earlier expression, in legislative and administrative processes. There is different emphasis within but no discontinuity between justifications and visions now prevalent in tort law and in these other institutional contexts. It is more difficult today to conceive adjudication as law—characterized by precedent, stable principled decisions, neutral and autonomous technique—and, by way of contrast, to conceive legislation as politics—characterized by contradictions in goals and principles, conflicting interests, choice.

2. *Continuity and change, constraint and choice.* Certain elements of continuity in tort accident law inform this study. Basic justificatory principles and characteristic social visions recur over time, sometimes in almost patterned ways. Ideals of accident law stand in continuing tension, and thereby give a sense of stability to the debates within the common law. But this is not a continuity of the same dominant justification or vision. It is not a continuity of dominant tort rules and principles. Rather, it is the continuity of similarly structured conflicts.[3]

Within accident law, the repeated conflicts are not difficult to identify. We have observed, for example, the recurring intuitions of justice that point to polar doctrinal conclusions: "liability is unfairly imposed absent a breach of moral duty to others," *or* "between two innocents, who caused the harm should pay." We have observed the conflicting views about the rationality and behavior of typical categories of accident victims. With such pairs of principle and counterprinciple or vision and countervision there will over time be tilt. One or the other may become dominant in a given period. But the dominance is unstable.

Even the sense of continuity stemming from the opposition of high-level justificatory principles fades as we examine the more specific, fleshed-out theories of justification. As very general principles or policies become historically contextualized and informed by a changing social vision, the justifications expressing them take on novel characteristics. They are not quite the same over time. Despite its important links with a similar ideal within the classical negligence system, behavior modification today involves different goals and assumptions. Loss spreading as a justification for heightened liability differs significantly from earlier justifications which stressed the right of accident victims to compensation.

Surely, then, the image of the common law underlying my description of accident law is at odds with the notion of a body of autonomous and stable principles. This essay denies the presence within the common law of one dominant logic or ideal, immanent or manifest, which over time embraces most doctrine within one coherent justificatory framework.[4]

Rather, the essay stresses the historical contingency of tort law's doctrines and justifications. That sense of contingency underscores the important degree of judicial choice in lawmaking. Other themes in this essay heighten this awareness of choice. For example, the earlier discussion of both doctrine and justifications emphasized their indeterminacy, their susceptibility to divergent interpretations and applications.

I have not, however, argued that the common law lacks any coherence and resists any degree of prediction—that, for example, at any one time or at all times it is subject to characterization as highly indeterminate, equally open to important contradictory choices, internally incoherent, deeply unstable.[5] Rather the essay has described patterned ways in which choice has been exercised, within limited types of justifications and social visions. Although my portrait of tort adjudication surely stresses indeterminacy in the decision of an individual case, it also underscores the more-or-less structured resolution in the large of the problem of indeterminacy. That is, at a given time, it may be apparent that particular cases offer courts considerable choice, and outcomes may individually be difficult to predict. The general course of opinions at that time, however, may be reasonably predictable, in view of reigning doctrine and the prevalence of one or another set of justifications and of a given social vision. But that reign and prevalence are unstable. Times change.

In brief, my description has been both of historical boundaries and of freedom within those boundaries. The essay has sought to identify themes at levels higher than the formal expression of law through rules, levels which give meaning and direction to doctrine. At that higher level we can identify not one coherent system of older and contemporary tort law, but recurrent choice, some structured tensions or contradictions. And we can identify changes in those structures, as one or another ideal or vision gains prominence and different ideals and visions emerge. However much the essay qualifies the notion of a trend, however frequently it points to the contradictions and ambiguities within it, a trend there has been which has made possible this sketch of tort accident law's changing character.

3. *Causation and configuration.* My description of the relationships among doctrine, justification, and social vision stressed the influence of the latter two upon doctrine. It stressed as well the importance of doctrine in capturing those two elements, in rendering them concrete through their embodiment in rules, in projecting them forward in time.

It is possible to imagine different moral ideals and social visions that could have supported modern heightened liability, with or without the related notions of loss spreading. The powerful contemporary justifications do have redistribu-

tional goals, but limited ones. A different redistributional goal
such as a strong "deep pocket" theory, for example, might rest
explicitly on the goal of reforming the existing distribution of
wealth and power and work changes not only in liability rules
but also in the measure of damages—perhaps limitations on
recovery for lost earnings.[6]

A modern system of heightened liability could then have
rested on other justifications and social visions. Nonetheless,
the historical trend here described reveals a particular configuration among doctrine, justification, and social vision. The
three stand in a distinctive complementary association that
characterizes an important part of accident law. It is that configuration or complementary association, neither logically necessary nor historically inevitable, which lends the modern tort
law of accidents such coherence as it has.

Why then did this configuration develop? Surely my argument denies that courts have simply responded to or adapted
tort law to objective social circumstances. Rather, it has depicted how courts have perceived and in this sense helped to
construct different social realities over time. Nonetheless, the
task remains of explaining why the particular picture here described has been drawn.

That task of causal explanation, that formidable and perhaps impossible task, lies beyond this essay. It could implicate
matters as complex and little touched on herein as gradual
changes in courts' perceptions of their institutional role. My
more modest undertaking has been to explore the phenomenon of common-law change and the related structures of
legal argument. Such change and argument have not been
portrayed as distinctive or "internal" to law, as autonomous in
any rigorous sense of that word. Rather, this essay relates the
work and argument of the courts to the "outside" world, to
social structures and institutions, to moral and political discourse, to ideologies about this country's experience and
goals. These relationships were captured in my description of

the mutually dependent and complementary phenomena of moral justification and social vision.

My earlier comments suggested some of the difficulties in attempting a historical explanation of the changes in these ingredients of argument leading to their present configuration. An effort at explanation would include consideration of the influence on judges and lawyers of academic writing within the tradition of legal realism that exposed the shaky premises and contradictions within the common law and thereby freed minds and institutions for change. It would allow for the more immediate and confined influence of contemporary scholars seeking to unify doctrine within one or another moral theory. It would speculate about the effect on legislators and judges of developing social theory and inquiry, such as the welfare economics that inspired the law-and-economics scholarship, or the empirical analyses of social institutions within the law-and-society and other movements. It would explore the effects on courts of political and public interest groups advancing moral and political claims relevant to heightened liability, to the point where those claims have become common currency on the American political scene, partially recognized and legitimated through political processes.

That is, the justifications and vision characteristic of the modern tort law of accidents were in a sense "there"—in academia, in programs of interest groups, in public law and legislative debate, in the broad ideology of the managerial-regulatory-welfare state. If not inevitable, neither is it surprising that tort accident law found support and direction in those sources. The ideas were not only available, they had also become relatively conventional. None of the justifications or views of society on which courts drew were likely to be seen as radical or threatening to established beliefs.

The Course of Accident Law

Trends may be reversed and movement may be cyclical. Administrative regulation is under attack, nowhere more sharply than in its tort-related expressions: safety and environmental legislation. The redistributive impulse within welfare legislation is weakening. The rhetoric within the national administration is one of less government and more freedom of choice in production and consumption, of self-reliance over collective protection.

This shift in political mood, emphasizing concern for business activity relative to concern for accident victims, provokes the question whether the resurgence of a less regulatory, protective, paternalistic, and collective ideology may arrest the liability-prone trend in tort law. The recurrent "crises" over the rates and availability of liability insurance make that question the more relevant, for they inform much discussion of tort law in the mid-1980s and inspire statutory changes or proposals that to some extent reverse the common law's doctrinal thrust toward heightened liability.[7]

These changes and proposals represent in their totality a substantial assault on the developing tort law. Some among them place caps on damages (either for pain and suffering, or total recovery), reintroduce contributory fault, restrict the occasions for joint and several liability, reverse the collateral-source rule, and limit lawyers' fees. Such liability-restrictive measures depart radically from characteristic legislative interventions in tort law in earlier periods, which expanded liability or which aided potential victims while subjecting them to additional limitations. Workers' compensation laws, for example, gave no-fault recovery but limited its amount. The contemporary statutes do not offset their restrictions on recovery with provisions favoring accident victims.

It is then possible that a different set of justifications informed by a different social vision could affect the judicial process as well as the executive and legislative branches, partly through the influence of changing legislative agendas and partly through appointments or elections to the bench affecting state as well as federal courts. Narrower boundaries could be defined for heightened liability, and doctrines now on the wane such as assumption of risk could regain some of their former vitality.

Thus, we speculate about how much is likely foreclosed and how much remains open in the way of reversing the direction of several decades of tort law. But arrest in the development or even reduction in the strength of such related legislative programs as compensation systems or regulatory schemes is not likely to persuade the common law to dramatic or rapid change. It took many decades of ideological, institutional, and legislative changes before tort accident law experienced its transformation of the last few decades. Those changes can no longer be seen as fragile departures from the classical negligence system, as dubious excursions from mainstream doctrine that, with legislative encouragement, are subject to rapid erosion. Heightened liability is now imbedded in important fields of tort accident law. If enacted, the pending statutory proposals will surely have their bite, but they amount to something less than systemic change.

Moreover, the current arrested development or reduced strength of regulatory and compensatory programs is not tantamount to their abolition. Accident plans, safety regulation, and social insurance or welfare programs have definitively changed the political landscape. Other vital sources of a modern social vision, such as the role of liability insurance or the toll in mass victims of a defendant's pollution or drug or other product, will continue to inform the common-law justifications.

Of course, even independently of new legislation, the pace of change within the common law may subside. Surely the doctrinal movements will be irregular, even turbulent, at the margin. But much of that turbulence will stem less from the influence of broader political changes than from problems internal to contemporary tort accident law. The very growth and prominence of the justifications for heightened liability have underscored those problems.

Some problems are endemic to any effort to expand liability beyond the classical fault system. Courts will find it increasingly difficult to explain why certain activities are subject to strict liability whereas others remain governed by negligence law. Those difficulties will likely produce continuing interstitial change about such matters as what constitutes an abnormally dangerous activity, or about the bases for liability of those employing independent contractors. In some instances, the power of modern justifications and social vision will overwhelm earlier distinctions as courts develop one or another route to heightened liability.

Surely there will be no uniform direction of doctrinal change. The undercurrents are not unidirectional. In important ways the ideals informing justifications for heightened liability conflict with each other. They may point in opposite directions within tort law, or point beyond tort law. The goal of behavior modification, for example, may suggest that some defenses based on victims' conduct should be allowed. Liability would thereby be reduced. But the goal of spreading accident costs, insofar as it is not met by the availability of loss insurance, suggests not simply heightened liability but also compensation schemes that go beyond tort law. Or the ideal of a fair distribution of losses may suggest that funding for compensating victims be sought more broadly than through the defendant causally related to a tort action.

Other problems calling into question the adequacy of tort law as the dominant response to the accident problem stem from the phenomena that any modern system of accident law must address. The developing nature of and sensibility about accidents put increasing strain on the tort system. That system struggles to adapt itself to higher costs and greater delays in litigation. It struggles to respond to such modern and widespread phenomena as latent and slowly developing diseases from products and pollution, and systemic risks or episodic disasters producing mass victims.[8] Its adaptive mechanisms, as earlier noted, include resort to class actions and modification of requirements of proof of actual causation.

Such innovations in the structure of litigation and in doctrine have served vital purposes. The imagination of the bar and the inventiveness of judges have helped to avoid injustice to victims lacking other routes to recovery. These new forms of tort litigation have also served as a powerful medium for bringing to the attention of the general public and legislatures the incidence of serious and mass injuries and continuing threats to health and life. The tragedy of asbestos disease and the related conduct of the asbestos industry offer a vivid example of such litigation's functions of education and publicity. By dramatizing problems and provoking discussion, mass tort litigation has spurred thought about other ways in which tort law can grow.

Nonetheless, such adaptive mechanisms have their limits. It is not simply that they may render litigation highly complex. They place constant demands on lawyers' imagination and judges' willingness to experiment in order to devise appropriate modes of trial or settlement. New incidents of systemic risk imposition and mass disasters will doubtless pose distinctive problems requiring *ad hoc* solutions. Despite their achievements, the recently developed approaches to trial and settlement may constitute more a necessary strategy of transition to a different accident-relief system than a viable long-term solution for the modern accident problem. In good part, that solution will likely lie elsewhere.

For over a century we have observed legislative intervention into tort law. That intervention has become more commonplace and significant. Today it extends from discrete and focused provisions to broad and embracive changes. Selective legislation ranges from regulation of the use of *res ipsa loquitur,*[9] or imposition of comparative fault,[10] to the present liability-restrictive changes and proposals. We see increasing resort to more extensive planlike reforms interacting with the common law, such as the legislation regulating medical malpractice suits with respect to damages and procedures,[11] or proposals for the periodic payment of damages for projected future costs.[12] Of course, the full-fledged plan in activities like driving restructures an entire field of accident law.

This legislatively created accident law, briefly sketched in my introductory chapter, has both cut bolder and more radical paths and developed more promising responses to the accident problem. Such legislative innovations have led to a growing awareness of the substantial gap between the probability and measure of victims' relief, as well as the cost in money and time of obtaining relief, within the tort system and, say, under accident plans to the extent that they displace tort law. In fields like automobile accidents, it was largely the court delays and the high percentage of the insurance dollar going to lawyers' fees that stimulated ideas for a plan lowering such transaction costs. The gap between the common law and the plans becomes the more puzzling as one considers the similarity in the experience and suffering of victims following one or the other route to recovery.

Part of the explanation for the inventiveness of the statutory schemes lies in their freedom from the institutional or structural constraints to which courts have viewed themselves subject, constraints equally applicable to the classical fault system and modern heightened liability. Consider, for example, the fundamental requirement of causation-in-fact, and its implications for party structure. Courts have reformed liability rules only within the framework of the case and parties before them, even if damages are then spread through market mechanisms. With rare exceptions, the courts have insisted that the defendant(s) must be (more likely than not) related to the accident within the meaning of but-for causation.

In redistributing costs from the victim, courts have then assumed that they were confined to assigning them to the defendant whose general activity or conduct gave rise to the accident—indeed, one of the paths toward achieving behavior modification. Thus, manufacturers or retailers must initially bear the costs of product-related accidents, industrial producers must initially bear the costs of pollution, and so on. Obviously, legislative reforms can infuse new institutional structures with new principles of financial contribution that break these causal links between parties within the common law of tort. Funds for compensating victims may be secured from all participants in a broadly defined activity, or indeed from the general public.

Other constraints on the judicial reconstruction of accident law are less deeply implanted in the judicial imagination, but are nonetheless the legacies of a strong doctrinal tradition. Compensation, for example, would appear open to substantial judicial rethinking, perhaps with respect to ceilings on recovery or control of damages for pain and suffering or distinctions between damages for types of liability (say, fault and strict liability).[13] Each of these possibilities poses practical and conceptual problems for courts. Even if they could be overcome and manageable doctrine developed, it is doubtful that the judiciary would consider such changes to be within its, rather than the legislature's, competence. In fact, such types of changes have generally been legislative. Courts have reshaped damages only indirectly: redefining the interests given legal protection, adopting comparative-fault principles, developing criteria for punitive damages, rethinking the role of discount rates or of inflation in computing the present value of future costs.[14]

A further consideration suggests that deep changes in the structure of accident law are not likely to be the judiciary's work. The courts developing tort accident law tend not to explore the cosmos. As the earlier descriptions of judicial argument suggest, appellate opinions in this field speak at a relatively modest level of rhetoric, of ideals and visions. Of course the questions before courts in these accident cases are significant. They raise some of the basic issues and dilemmas of the modern regulatory and welfare state. But the large themes of moral and political order which inhere in those questions—an individualistic orientation stressing self-reliance and risk-taking, or a collective orientation emphasizing social protection and sharing; an atomistic or communitarian view of social life; and so on—rarely figure explicitly in appellate argument. They are embraced and even secreted within the more conventional discourse about doctrine and justification.

Judges express themselves in tort cases less broadly and majestically than they do in fields like constitutional law when addressing the nature of American history or ideals. In tort opinions, they rarely debate concepts as basic as freedom or equality or due process, evocative concepts open to such radically different understandings that they can generate deep criticisms of society leading to basic doctrinal change.[15] To the contrary, the ideals explicitly advanced by courts in tort law through some blend of justificatory theory and social vision are not likely to challenge basic premises of the society's current approaches to resolving the accident problem.

For such reasons—the boundaries to judicial imagination, the power of traditional ideas imbedded in doctrine, the relatively modest level of normative discourse—a significant restructuring of accident law is likely to be achieved only through the free invention of legislation.[16] Consider in this respect the role of the no-fault accident plans, principally workers' compensation and auto plans, as well as legislative proposals for other fields such as hazardous wastes.[17] In their present incarnations, such plans do not represent, from almost any observer's perspective, an ideal response to the accident problem. We witness ongoing battles for their reform with respect to matters like the measure of compensation. Nonetheless, they continue to stand as a challenge to tort accident law, as an invitation to further experimentation.

That invitation stems from the plans' creativity. By transforming a body of accident law in design and content, each plan reveals how much of tort law may be open to reconsideration. The plans express more dramatically than does change within the common law how contingent our historical or present arrangements are, how open they are to rethinking and revision.

Each plan reconstructs four basic aspects of the tort accident law preceding its creation: the legal basis of recovery, the compensation or other benefits to be afforded victims, the means of funding or financing such benefits, and the institutional processes for making decisions. Each detail—the precise rule for attributing accident costs to an activity, limitations on damages or criteria for damages based on victims' needs, compulsory financial contributions through participants' insurance premiums or other payments to funds, periodic payments to victims, and so on—contrasts dramatically with the common law.

Accident schemes, for example, can mandate financial contributions of all those participating in an activity. Schemes like no-fault auto plans can break the direct link between a risk generator and victim that characterizes both the common law and a plan like workers' compensation. Recent and proposed legislation on hazardous wastes exacts contributions from companies that are chemical feedstock producers, only indirectly related to the immediate accidents (perhaps stemming from manufacturing operations utilizing the feedstocks) and thus unlikely to have been parties to any tort litigation.[18]

In achieving their novel design and character, the plans express in the full sense a systemic and statistical vision of accidents. Each of the four aspects of the plans contrasting with the common law involves the others. Developing criteria for the levels of compensation, of course, implicates financing, as indeed does a goal of behavior modification. The legal basis for recovery implicates both compensation and financing. Proposals for distributing benefits and collecting funds may find a necessary or better home in administrative processes. The plan must be seen as a whole.

Some of the ideals shaping modern tort law could then find a fuller realization in plans that are free of the boundaries set by traditional common-law thinking and free of the traditional constraints on what courts can achieve. One scholarly proposal, building on a scheme realized in New Zealand, looks to the progressive displacement of tort accident law by ever more inclusive, society-wide accident plans. The financial burden of accidents of every description would be relieved up to stated amounts by payments from a central fund, which would not be associated with any one industry or activity. Nonetheless, the moneys necessary for accident relief would be provided by industry, for the fund would allocate its costs among industrial activities in proportion to their assumed gross causal responsibility.[19]

Whether through activity-specific or society-wide plans, paths would then be opened to the more direct pursuit of one or another ideal. Goals for compensation and contributions, though necessarily related to each other in gross amounts, could be implemented independently. A combination of accident plans and direct safety regulation backed by criminal sanctions would permit selective aims to be more or less separately pursued: the desired level of cost internalization to an activity, the degree of centralized control over specific risks.

Despite these differences, despite the example in plans of innovative experiment, it is important to note that modern tort law and accident plans have much in common. They occupy different points on a rather limited spectrum. Like the classical fault system and modern heightened liability, accident plans merge compensatory and regulatory functions. That is, tort law and the plans regulate behavior indirectly, through cost internalization to business activities. We can term all such accident systems, common law and statutory, "reparation systems"—that is, systems that merge compensatory and regulatory functions, that both give relief to victims and stimulate behavior modification by charging the accident costs to a causally related activity.[20]

A different but just as vital characteristic further binds tort law and accident plans. I noted earlier the ambivalent nature of a social vision linked to modern heightened liability and its goal of loss spreading.[21] On the one hand, it spoke to caring, sharing, compassion, collective concern. On the other, it implied impersonal business bureaucracies, the absorption of individuals within statistical categories, and related abstraction and dehumanization.

A similar ambivalence affects our present discussion. Although modern heightened liability and the plans afford compensation where earlier tort law did not, they may by the same token subtly and covertly suggest the legitimacy as well as inevitability of accidents. By recognizing the systemic recurrence of accidents, the modern statistical social vision may tend to stabilize present arrangements. It may foster the view that ideals of fairness or utility have been satisfied when the costs of accidents are duly accounted for through internalization to actors or activities, even though victims may continue to suffer life-impairing injuries for which money damages can never fully compensate.

To that extent, the advances in accident law that have been made in recent decades may tend to forestall still larger and bolder advances. They may blunt criticism of the toll of accidents by stressing the degree to which behavior is indirectly regulated and the degree to which losses of victims are now spread among the beneficiaries of activities. But the relatively powerless, those without as much choice as others about field of work or location, remain subject to higher risks even as they receive increasing legal assurance that harm from these risks will bring some measure of compensation.[22]

The two powerful contrasts with reparation systems—both tort law and accident plans—are found precisely in those systems that separate the goal of compensation from that of regulation and pursue only one or the other.[23] Both types of systems, the compensatory and regulatory systems, strike radically different paths and indeed assert radically different ideals—to a limited extent in their present realizations, and surely in their potential. The charts in the appendix and their related text trace the basic relationships among these three types of systems.

Welfare programs for the needy or aged constitute our typical compensation systems that benefit accident victims incidentally through the medical or other assistance they receive. Those programs, innocent of the goal of curbing accidents and funded in whole or part from general tax revenues, make central the issues of a minimum welfare level or a fair distribution of wealth that escape, as I have suggested, the law of tort.[24]

The more significant contrast for our present discussion is afforded by the relatively new schemes of safety regulation. They are more flexible than the common law or the accident plans. Thus, they are open to more varied and effective means of indirect regulation (pollutant charges and so on) that do not mandate action but leave with the regulated industries the decisions about how much risk to generate. But the dramatic departure of such regulatory systems from tort law and accident plans lies in their reliance on direct regulation requiring or prohibiting particular conduct. Such systems, in their dramatic evolution over the last two decades,[25] constitute the boldest contemporary approach to the accident problem.

I earlier developed a comparison between negligence and strict liability by using an image in a nineteenth-century opinion of the meaning of the negligence standard—in effect, treat others as if their interests were your own.[26] My discussion suggested that strict liability was more faithful to that moral maxim than the negligence standard it was meant to justify. That is, strict liability requires an enterprise to bear otherwise external costs of its fault-free activity. The consequence is that the enterprise, at least from the point of view of compensation, does treat the victims as if they were a part of the enterprise itself. It now bears costs that would be borne if the victims' interests were indeed its own.

Even under strict liability, however, social actors are "free" to impose risk of harm, provided that they also compensate the victims of that risk. Victims are not—often cannot realistically be—consulted in advance to determine their willingness to be subject to risk provided that there is assurance of compensation. Occasions within tort law for injunctive relief against the risk imposer are rare, the more so in the absence of a defendant's negligence. Under strict liability, therefore, defendants can "take and pay," in the sense that they are free to impose what are viewed as reasonable risks of taking welfare from others, provided that they pay for (the legal measure of) victims' welfare losses.

Direct regulation can proceed more radically. Despite its well-known problems—bureaucratic inefficiency, risk of rigidity in setting standards that block innovation, inadequate enforcement, evasion of regulation and capture of regulators by the regulated industries, susceptibility to shifts in general political opinion, and so on[27]—it offers a great potential for restructuring practices. Safety regulation may terminate the choice to take and pay. Social actors may be directed by regulation not to "take" at all or to impose risks of harm only in specified ways. The implications for the level of risk to which potential victims (factory workers, product users, populations exposed to pollution) would be exposed are, of course, enormous. No longer will that level depend on the calculations of interest of social actors subject to one or another reparation system.

Through such direct regulation, conceptions of fairness could influence not simply the extent of an obligation to compensate, as they now do within tort law or workers' compensation. The conceptions could also suggest which types of impositions were initially permissible, the types of risks to which workers or consumers or the general population should be subject. Of course, the degree of difference between systems of direct regulation and tort law or accident plans would depend on the methodology—one or another version of a cost-benefit standard, or a feasibility standard, for example—that statutes and judicial decisions instruct the agencies to use to develop safety regulations, as well as on the types of sanctions for violation of these regulations (injunction, fine, imprisonment) and the seriousness of enforcement.[28]

Such are the diverse possibilities opened by the decades of extraordinary growth of which the doctrinal trend in tort law and the development of liability and loss insurance form only a part. Heightened liability in tort, a greater resort to activity-specific plans with the possibility of a broader society-wide accident plan, compensation systems divorced from regulation, and administrative imposition of direct and indirect regulation have all achieved an important role in responding to the accident problem. The boldness and creativity, the fuller realization of ideals nourishing modern heightened liability, the more adequate solutions to the contemporary accident problem will all likely continue to lie beyond the law of tort.

Appendix

Notes

Index

Appendix

In several parts of this essay, particularly in chapter 5, I compared aspects of tort accident law with other institutions, schemes, and programs that also bear on the accident problem. Those comparisons included private institutions like liability or loss insurance, and legislative-administrative schemes such as accident plans, welfare programs, and direct regulation. I presented a few relationships among these contemporary approaches, in part alternative to each other and in part complementary, to handling the accident problem.

This appendix expands on and systematizes such observations. Its two charts do not attempt a complete representation of all institutions that now bear on accidents by way of compensation and regulation. Rather, they aim at a clear statement of relationships among the varied institutions that have figured in this essay. Chart 1 portrays the components of accident law relevant to this essay in formal, institutional terms. Chart 2 reorganizes those components to stress substantive concepts basic to the accident problem.

Chart 1

Chart 1 includes within its formal arrangement all accident-related institutions to which the essay has referred. Some are common law, some are statutory and administrative, and some are private. My comments below explain a few terms that fig-

152

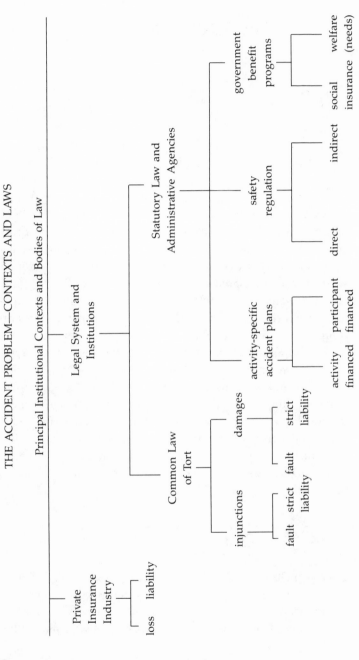

CHART 1
THE ACCIDENT PROBLEM—CONTEXTS AND LAWS

Principal Institutional Contexts and Bodies of Law

ured only briefly in the essay and sketch some relationships relevant to the essay among the varied components of the chart.

TERMS

Activity-specific accident plans
I refer to plans that displace the common law in whole or part with respect to accidents growing out of a specified activity. The essay has referred both to workers' compensation and to no-fault auto-accident plans. Such plans provide compensation to victims and charge the costs of compensation to the activity generating the risk. Of the two plans, workers' compensation is *activity financed,* in the sense that employers are required to contribute to the insurance fund, whereas the no-fault auto-accident plans are *participant financed,* in the sense that drivers are required to purchase insurance as a condition to car registration. The alternative to activity-specific accident plans would be one society-wide plan covering accidents from a broad range of activities. Several versions of such a plan are found in the readings cited in note 19 to chapter 5.

Government benefit programs
I refer to the kinds of public compensation systems that are noted in the essay. Some, the *social insurance* programs, are specially funded through payroll taxes or other particular charges rather than financed out of general tax revenues. Characteristically, the criteria of eligibility for benefits under such programs (social security payments or unemployment compensation) are independent of the general financial need of recipients. Other *welfare* programs such as Medicaid tend to be funded out of general tax revenues and to make their benefits available only to those meeting some criterion of financial need. Both types of benefit programs may afford relief, in (medical) services or in cash, to accident victims.

RELATIONSHIPS

Insurance and tort law or accident plans
The essay has stressed the pervasive influence of insurance on heightened liability in tort law, at the levels of doctrine, justification, and social vision. Principles of liability and loss insurance also underlie the accident plans.

Government benefit programs and tort law
Such programs influence tort doctrine concretely in several ways, including the collateral-source rule. The essay has suggested their relevance to the developing attention of the courts to the situation of accident victims—that is, to social vision.

Direct (safety) regulation and tort law
Schemes of direct regulation in fields like worker or product safety, or control of pollution, influence tort doctrine concretely in several ways, including negligence per se and preemption. They influence courts in less determinate ways through their demonstration of a political, legislative concern with the accident problem in general or with problems in a given field—that is, an influence on courts' justifications and social vision. Like accident plans, direct regulation expresses a systemic, group, and statistical vision of the accident problem.

Accident plans and tort law
There are concrete doctrinal problems, such as working out the degree to which a plan displaces tort law. In a less precise way, plans like workers' compensation have influenced courts' justifications for heightened liability.

Chart 2

Chart 2 reorganizes the components of chart 1 within the three types of systems that are relevant to the accident problem—the

CHART 2

THE ACCIDENT PROBLEM—REPARATION, REGULATION, COMPENSATION

Systems of Reparation, Regulation, and Compensation

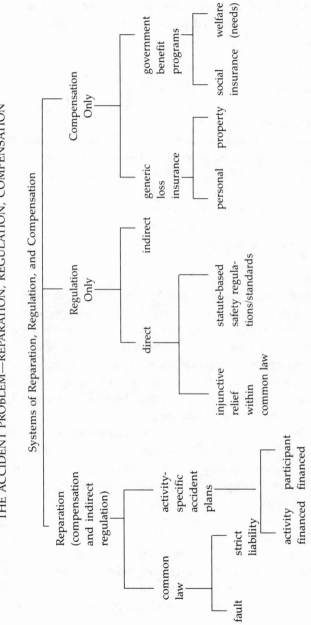

systems of reparation, regulation, and compensation that figured in chapter 5's discussion. My notes build on that discussion.

TERMS

Compensation
Relief for the accident victim is usually monetary (tort damages) but sometimes consists of in-kind services (medical care under Medicaid). Some compensation systems (tort law, accident plans) secure funds for accident victims by charging a causally related actor or activity. Others, such as social security or Medicaid, secure funds for compensation from other sources such as payroll taxes or general tax revenues.

Regulation
Regulatory systems seek to control the generation of risk of accidents. Statutory-administrative "direct" regulation, such as safety standards, requires or prohibits specified ways of engaging in an activity. "Indirect" regulation, rather than requiring or prohibiting conduct, imposes certain (accident) costs on the actor or activity and thereby relies on market incentives to persuade actors to modify their behavior to reduce (bring to a more nearly optimum level) accident-related risk and harm. Thus, indirect regulation involves systems as different as the common law and accident plans (both of which also give compensation), as well as such administrative regulation as the imposition of pollutant taxes on industry (regulation that does not involve compensation).

Reparation
Reparation systems give compensation to victims *and* charge the accident costs to a causally related actor or activity. Thus, they blend compensation with indirect regulation. Tort law and the activity-specific accident plans are classic examples of

compensation systems that are also reparation systems. (The compensation will generally be paid by an actor's liability insurer or be paid out of an insurance fund collected from participants in the activity.) On the other hand, compensation systems like Medicaid do not involve any regulation, and administrative schemes of indirect regulation (imposition of pollutant tax on manufacturer) need not involve any compensation. Hence, neither of those examples would constitute a reparation system.

OBSERVATIONS

1. All reparation systems involve compensation, but not all compensation systems constitute reparation. Types and amounts of compensation vary among these systems.

2. All reparation systems involve (generally indirect) regulation, but not all regulatory systems constitute reparation.

3. Systems of direct regulation generally do not provide for the compensation of victims. They may do so, as by creating a private statutory action for accident victims seeking compensation from violators of safety standards. Violation of such standards may also figure in tort litigation through the doctrine of negligence per se.

4. Injunctions in tort (nuisance) actions and direct regulation systems are similar in that both prohibit or require stated conduct. But there are important differences. For example, the safety standard has general prospective application to all participants in the relevant activity, whereas the injunction usually affects particular actors and grows out of a more contextual examination of a dispute. Generally, a standard will be more specific in defining how an activity may be performed. Standards and injunctions are enforced in different ways.

5. Generic loss insurance does not involve regulation. By "generic," I mean health plans or disability insurance that are not specific to any activity—that is, that cover health or disability needs stemming from any activity or natural illness.

Loss insurance that is activity specific, such as no-fault auto plans or airplane disaster insurance, is "costed" to the particular activity involved and thus achieves some indirect regulation of behavior. At a minimum, it may affect how much or whether one engages in the activity.

Notes

CHAPTER 1. PURPOSES

1 Note 1 (chapter 4), infra, compares my definition and use of the concept of social vision with the work of other scholars exploring judicial opinions, work employing concepts such as "ideal pictures" of the world or "political vision."

2 The definition underscores that this essay does not treat the law of tort in the large, including fields unrelated to unintended physical injury such as defamation or misrepresentation or invasion of privacy. Such diverse fields, conventionally grouped in teaching and treatise-writing under the formal classification of tort law, implicate distinct phenomena and pose distinct problems of doctrine, justification, and social vision. Particular observations that I make herein about liability trends in tort accident law—the character thereof and reasons therefore—may or may not prove to be valid for one or more of these other fields. That is not my interest. Accident law and the accident problem are my subject, not "tort law" in the large with its historical diversity of concerns.

3 In its discussion of the tort (common) law of accidents, this essay stresses doctrine, justification, and social vision related to liability for money damages. That is, it treats tort accident law with respect to compensation rather than injunctive relief. In fact, occasions for injunctions in tort accident law are rare, since most accidents are "one shot," done and over before a lawsuit. Those occasions arise dominantly in land cases, particularly nuisance actions involving continuing interferences. For characteristic discussions of the choice between injunction and damages in such

settings, see *Madison* v. *Ducktown Sulphur, Copper & Iron Co. Ltd.*, 113 Tenn. 331, 83 S.W. 658 (1904), and *Boomer* v. *Atlantic Cement Co.*, 26 N.Y.2d 219, 257 N.E.2d 870 (1970).

In recent years, plaintiffs in a growing number of class actions have sought forms of injunctive relief in addition to declaratory judgments and awards of damages—relief, for example, ordering a defendant to notify designated categories of the population of the dangers in a widespread product, or to establish free clinics for examining all members of a class action, or to establish insurance funds to cover class members suffering harm after the litigation. See, e.g., note 3 in *Payton* v. *Abbott Labs*, 83 F.R.D. 382, 389 (D. Mass. 1979), a conditional certification of a plaintiff class, certification later vacated in *Payton* v. *Abbott Labs*, 100 F.R.D. 336 (D. Mass. 1983).

4 A. Larson, *The Law of Workmen's Compensation* (1952), Vol. I, §§1.00–5.30, describes the typical structures and features of workers' compensation acts. Those acts are reviewed and critically appraised in the Report of the National Commission on State Workmen's Compensation Laws (1972). Auto no-fault plans—based on compulsory loss insurance rather than, as in workers' compensation plans, liability insurance—are categorized and described in Henderson, "No-Fault Insurance for Automobile Accidents: Status and Effect in the United States," 56 *Ore. L. Rev.* 287 (1977). Workers' compensation plans typically are intended to displace completely the common law of tort, whereas auto no-fault plans typically are intended to do so only in part.

5 The relevant administrative agencies of the federal government are the Consumer Product Safety Commission, the Occupational Safety and Health Administration, and the Environmental Protection Agency. For a description of the recent growth of such agencies and their regulatory programs, see Vogel, "The 'New' Social Regulation in Historical and Comparative Perspective," in T. McCraw, ed., *Regulation in Perspective: Historical Essays* 155 (1981).

6 E.g., §2072 of the Consumer Product Safety Act, 15 U.S.C. §§2051 et seq., enacted in 1972.

7 See, e.g., *Union Pacific Railroad Co.* v. *McDonald*, 152 U.S. 262 (1894).

8 For a recent summary of programs that may be relevant to accident victims, see the section of chapter 7 entitled "The Structure of American Welfare Provisions," N. Furniss and T. Tilton, *The Case for the Welfare State* (1979).

9 For cases considering the relevance of private or social insurance or welfare programs to the collateral source rule (the rule that payments to the victim from insurance and related programs will not reduce tort recovery), see *Helfend* v. *Southern California Rapid Transit District*, 2 Cal. 3d 1, 465 P.2d 61 (1970); *Reid* v. *District of Columbia*, 391 A.2d 776 (D.C. App. 1978).

10 The related but distinct contrast between "private" law and "public" law, a contrast with important political and ideological connotations, figures in chapter 5's reflections about themes in this essay. For the bulk of this essay, the distinction between common law and public law is a purely formal classification without political or ideological significance.

CHAPTER 2. DOCTRINE

1 These doctrinal distinctions—the standard of care for negligence, the criteria for strict liability—are fundamental to a plaintiff's chances for recovery. But they need not be decisive. As stressed in Rabin, "The Historical Development of the Fault Principle: A Reinterpretation," 15 *Ga. L. Rev.* 925, 928–33 (1981), a liability system such as the "fault system" defies easy description, for it involves varying relationships among many aspects of doctrine, including actual (but-for) and legal causation, defenses, immunities, and limited or no duties in particular contexts. Such other aspects of tort doctrine may expand or contract liability independently of the basic standard of liability. In its description of the trend toward heightened liability, this essay relates some of these other doctrinal changes—defenses, immunities, landowners' duties—to the change in the basic liability standard. It does not attempt to account for changes in other aspects of tort doctrine, such as concepts of legal causation, which exercise an important if less visible and definable influence on the nature and effect of tort liabilities. Nor does this essay take account of trends in the measurement of compensatory and punitive damages or in the availability of the latter.

2 *Blyth* v. *Birmingham Waterworks Co.*, 11 Exchequer 781, 156 Eng. Rep. 1047 (1856) (negligence standard); *George Foltis, Inc.* v. *City of New York*, 287 N.Y. 108, 38 N.E.2d 455 (1941) (*res ipsa loquitur* charge); *Lubin* v. *Iowa City*, 257 Iowa 383, 131 N.W.2d 765 (1965) (beyond-fault liability).

3 *MacPherson* v. *Buick Motor Co.*, 217 N.Y. 382, 111 N.E. 1050 (1916) (liability for negligent manufacture); *Goldberg* v. *Kollsman Instrument Corp.*, 12 N.Y.2d 432, 191 N.E.2d 81 (1963) (liability for breach of implied warranty, or strict liability).

4 The many textual illustrations in chapter 2 of doctrinal change will each be accompanied by one or two case citations. The customary and convenient first reference for a description of the relevant doctrine and its changes would today be P. Keeton, D. Dobbs, R. Keeton, and D. Owen, *Prosser and Keeton on the Law of Torts* (5th ed. 1984).

5 The trend has, of course, been uneven. A few states such as California and New Jersey have been the pacesetters. The prominent role of the California Supreme Court is recounted in Ursin, "Judicial Creativity and Tort Law," 49 *Geo. Wash. L. Rev.* 229 (1981). Tort doctrine in such states has moved more dramatically to heighten liability, and the opinions of courts in these leading states have been much cited and used as models in other states. See, for example, *Ramirez* v. *Amsted Industries, Inc.*, 171 N.J. Super. 261, 274–76, 408 A.2d 818, 825–26 (1979); *Cook* v. *Salishan Properties, Inc.*, 279 Or. 333, 339–40, 569 P.2d 1033, 1035–36 (1977). Nonetheless, the trend described in this essay has been nationwide. The illustrative excerpts from opinions and citations in the notes that follow are drawn representatively from a wide variety of states.

6 The interesting and important thesis is developed in Rabin, "The Historical Development of the Fault Principle: A Reinterpretation," 15 *Ga. L. Rev.* 925 (1981), that the nineteenth century is better understood as a period of slow development of a liability-expanding negligence system, eroding significant limiting doctrines and areas of no duty, than as a period in which negligence law cut back liability (thereby aiding or subsidizing nascent industry) in relation to an earlier assumed strict liability that it progressively displaced. In its characterization of the older and modern liability principles, my essay uses a later period as a starting and dividing point, the mid-twentieth century. It does, however, share with Rabin's analysis (of the prior century) the view that expansion of liability within the framework of the negligence system itself has played an important part in the expansion of tort liability—in my essay, the *contemporary* expansion. See also R. Keeton, *Venturing to Do Justice* 3–10, 54–63, 151 (1969); Schwartz, "The Vitality of Negligence and the Ethics of Strict Liability," 15 *Ga. L. Rev.* 963, 964–77 (1981).

7 See L. Friedman, *A History of American Law* 470–84 (2d ed. 1985).

8 The classic case is *MacPherson* v. *Buick Motor Co.*, 217 N.Y. 382, 111 N.E. 1050 (1916), bringing to their culmination in terms of a general principle a number of New York cases commencing with *Thomas* v. *Winchester*, 6 N.Y. 397, 57 Am. Dec. 455 (1852). The comparable trend toward making providers of services (such as builders) liable to third parties injured because of negligent construction, without attention to privity of contract, is signaled by the progression from *Curtin* v. *Somerset*, 140 Pa. 70, 21 A. 244 (1891), to *Totten* v. *Gruzen*, 52 N.J. 202, 245 A.2d 1 (1968).

9 *Titus* v. *Bradford, Bordell & Kinzua Railroad Co.*, 136 Pa. 618, 20 A. 517 (1890), applies custom rigorously in the context of a railroad accident. The defendant met his duty by furnishing appliances "of ordinary character and reasonable safety. . . . '[R]easonably safe' means safe according to the usages, habits, and ordinary risks of the business. . . . No man is held by law to a higher degree of skill than the fair average of his profession or trade. . . . [N]o jury can be permitted to say that the usual and ordinary way, commonly adopted by those in the same business, is a negligent way, for which liability shall be imposed." Id. at 626, 20 A. at 518. *Northwest Airlines, Inc.* v. *Glenn L. Martin Co.*, 224 F.2d 120 (6th Cir. 1955), a case involving the question whether a plane that crashed ought to have been equipped with radar to avoid a thunderstorm, sets forth the more relaxed and liability-prone use of custom. "[T]he fact that Northwest conformed to the practice of other airlines failing to equip [the plane] . . . with radar did not establish its exercise of ordinary care as a matter of law. Customary practice is not ordinary care; it is but evidence of ordinary care." Id. at 129.

10 The test derives its name from the opinion of Judge Learned Hand in *United States* v. *Carroll Towing Co.*, 159 F.2d 169, 173 (2d Cir. 1947).

11 In *Osborne* v. *Montgomery*, 203 Wis. 223, 234 N.W. 372 (1931), the court said that, in determining liability for wrongful acts, there was need for judicial "balancing of the social interests involved in the case. . . ." A defendant carefully driving a car through a populated area on a rainy day would not be liable to a plaintiff on whom muddy water was thereby thrown, "because the benefit of allowing people to travel under such circumstances so far outweighs the probable injury to bystanders that such conduct is not disapproved." The court compared driving a fire truck through a populated area over the speed limit but with the care appropriate

to the circumstances, and noted that (in the event of an accident) "society weighing the benefits against the probabilities of damage . . . justifies the risk and holds [the driver] not liable." Id. at 232–33, 234 N.W. at 376. Judicial concern for excessive hampering of the retail trade through liability rules is expressed in *Van Skike* v. *Zussman*, 22 Ill. App. 3d 1039, 318 N.E.2d 244 (1974).

12 See, e.g., *Martin* v. *Herzog*, 228 N.Y. 164, 126 N.E. 814 (1920).

13 In a product-liability case involving elements of negligence and strict liability, *Heaton* v. *Ford Motor Co.*, 248 Or. 467, 435 P.2d 806 (1967), the court stated that where there was no evidence of a precise flaw in a tire, "the plaintiff may nonetheless be able to establish his right to recover, by proving that the product did not perform in keeping with the reasonable expectations of the user. . . . [A product] should be strong enough to perform as the ordinary consumer expects. . . . The jury is supposed to determine the basically factual question of what reasonable consumers do expect from the product." Id. at 471–74, 435, P.2d at 808–9.

14 In *Ciofalo* v. *Vic Tanney Gyms, Inc.*, 10 N.Y.2d 294, 177 N.E.2d 925 (1961), the court upheld an exculpatory clause in a contract between a gym and a user thereof. Outside special categories of contracts, and "where the public interest [was not] directly involved, a provision absolving a party from his own negligent acts will be given effect." Id. at 297, 177 N.E.2d at 926. See the discussion at pp. 86–90, infra.

15 Compare *Titus* v. *Bradford, Bordell & Kinzua Railroad Co.*, 136 Pa. 618, 20 A. 517 (1890), with *Saglimbeni* v. *West End Brewing Co.*, 274 A.D. 201, 80 N.Y.S.2d 635 (1948), aff'd 298 N.Y. 875, 84 N.E.2d 638 (1949).

16 See, e.g., *The T. J. Hooper*, 60 F.2d 737 (2d Cir. 1932); *Helling* v. *Carey*, 83 Wash. 2d 514, 519 P.2d 981 (1974).

17 See generally, E. Mishan, *Economics for Social Decisions: Elements of Cost-Benefit Analysis* (1973); Tribe, "Policy Science: Analysis or Ideology," 2 *Phil. & Pub. Aff.* 66 (1972); and works cited in note 15 (chapter 3), infra. For judicial comments on cost-benefit and feasibility analysis in the context of a regulatory statute, see *American Textile Manufacturers Institute* v. *Donovan*, 452 U.S. 490, 506–36 (1981).

18 For acknowledgment of such indeterminate aspects of the Hand Formula in judicial opinions, see note 31 (chapter 3), infra. See the writings on policy and cost-benefit analysis cited in note 17 (chapter 2), supra.

19 See, e.g., *Spalding* v. *Waxler*, 2 Ohio St. 2d 1, 205 N.E.2d 890 (1965).

20 See, e.g., O. W. Holmes, *The Common Law* 85–87 (M. D. Howe ed. 1963); R. Pound, *An Introduction to the Philosophy of Law* 90–91 (rev. ed. 1954). Cf. *Jolley* v. *Powell*, 299 So. 2d 647 (Fla. App. 1974) in its discussion of tort liability for negligence of the insane: "It is surely not unusual in tort law nor indeed is it unfair that persons may be held responsible for failing to live up to a standard which, as a matter of fact, they cannot meet. . . . So liability without subjective fault . . . is one price men pay for membership in society." Id. at 648.

21 Schwartz, "Tort Law and the Economy in Nineteenth-Century America: A Reinterpretation," 90 *Yale L. J.* 1717 (1981), criticizes interpretations of nineteenth-century tort law which have viewed that law as restricting liability to aid or subsidize nascent industry. He explores the case law of two states, California and New Hampshire, in which he finds evidence of strict application of negligence criteria against business defendants in suits by strangers and relatively lenient application of contributory-fault criteria. Both judges and juries made such applications. Nonetheless, it is my contention, notwithstanding earlier liability-prone tendencies in one or another state and field of accident law, that it is the last few decades which have witnessed a broad trend to expand liability throughout accident law.

22 E.g., *Pierce* v. *Yakima Valley Memorial Hospital Ass'n*, 43 Wash. 2d 162, 260 P.2d 765 (1953); *Li* v. *Yellow Cab Company of California*, 13 Cal. 3d 804, 532 P.2d 1226 (1975).

23 Cf. R. Keeton, *Venturing to Do Justice* (1969), where the author summarizes recent judicial trends in tort law (such as abolishing immunities and moving toward comparative fault) and states (p. 151): "Many current trends toward broader liability represent no deviation from the theme of fault but rather a movement toward closer adherence to it."

24 E.g., *McConville* v. *State Farm Mutual Automobile Insurance Co.*, 15 Wis. 2d 374, 113 N.W.2d 14 (1962).

25 See, e.g., *Ybarra* v. *Spangard*, 25 Cal. 2d 486, 489–91, 154 P.2d 687, 689–90 (1944); *Escola* v. *Coca-Cola Bottling Co. of Fresno* (concurring opinion), 24 Cal. 2d 453, 462–63, 150 P.2d 436, 441 (1944).

26 E.g., *Landers* v. *East Texas Salt Water Disposal Co.*, 151 Tex. 251, 248 S.W.2d 731 (1952).

27 E.g., *Sindell* v. *Abbott Laboratories*, 26 Cal. 3d 588, 607 P.2d 924 (1980). See pp. 120 and 124, infra.

28 E.g., *Canterbury* v. *Spence*, 464 F.2d 772 (D.C. Cir. 1972).

29 E.g., *Brown* v. *Merlo*, 8 Cal. 3d 855, 506 P.2d 212 (1973).

30 E.g., *Basso* v. *Miller*, 40 N.Y.2d 233, 352 N.E.2d 868 (1976)

31 See A. Larson, *The Law of Workmen's Compensation* (1952), vol. I, §6.00, "The Five Lines of Interpretation of 'Arising' [Out of Employment]."

32 See, e.g., *Losee* v. *Clute*, 51 N.Y. 494, 10 Am. Rep. 638 (1873) (no duty of boiler manufacturer to victim of explosion of boiler located in paper mill of the vendee of manufacturer); *Shipley* v. *Fifty Associates*, 106 Mass. 194 (1870) (imposing strict liability, following *Rylands* v. *Fletcher*, 19 L.R. 220, 3 H.L. 330 [1868]). For a brief summary of statutory pockets of strict liability, such as liability for harm caused by fires, see L. Friedman, *A History of American Law*, 478–79 (2d ed. 1985).

33 This is not to say that judicial perception, or at least judicial rhetoric, was consistent about the breadth or dominance of one or another liability system. Compare *Losee* v. *Buchanan*, 51 N.Y. 476, 491 (1873) ("[T]he rule is, at least in this country, a universal one . . . that no one can be made liable for injuries to the person or property of another without some fault or negligence on his part") with *Exner* v. *Sherman Power Construction Co.*, 54 F.2d 510, 514 (2d Cir. 1931) ("The solution of the problem in each particular case has never been dependent upon any universal criterion of liability (such as 'fault') applicable to all situations. If damage is inflicted, there ordinarily is liability, in the absence of excuse").

34 For characteristic judicial discussions of the liability principles expressed through the writs of trespass and trespass on the case, see *Brown* v. *Kendall*, 60 Mass. (6 Cush.) 292, 295–96 (1850); *Fowler* v. *Lanning* [1959] 1 Q.B. 426, 1 All E.R. 290. See generally, M. Horwitz, *The Transformation of American Law, 1780–1860*, 85–94 (1977).

35 All these maxims were in contest in *Losee* v. *Buchanan*, 51 N.Y. 476 (1873). The opinion, stating that the rule of no liability "without some fault or negligence" was "universal," concluded that the maxim, "where one of two innocent parties must suffer, he who puts in motion the cause of the injury must bear the loss," had "no application whatever to a case like this" (boiler explosion in paper mill of defendant injuring unrelated plaintiff). It also observed that the maxim *sic utere tuo* "has many exceptions and limitations, made necessary by the exigencies of business and society." Id. at 490–91, 480.

36 See *Ira S. Bushey & Sons, Inc.* v. *United States*, 398 F.2d 167 (2d Cir. 1968); *Konick* v. *Berke, Moore Co.*, 355 Mass. 463, 245 N.E.2d 750 (1969); *Becker* v. *Interstate Properties*, 569 F.2d 1203 (3d Cir. 1977).

37 *Fletcher* v. *Rylands*, 14 L.R. 523, 1 Exch. 265 (1866), aff'd in *Rylands* v. *Fletcher*, 19 L.R. 220, 3 H.L. 330 (1868).

38 See *Yommer* v. *McKenzie*, 255 Md. 220, 257 A.2d 138 (1969); *McLane* v. *Northwest Natural Gas Co.*, 255 Or. 324, 467 P.2d 635 (1970); *Langan* v. *Valicopters, Inc.*, 88 Wash. 2d 855, 567 P.2d 218 (1977); *Siegler* v. *Kuhlman*, 81 Wash. 2d 448, 502 P.2d 1181 (1972).

39 *Jost* v. *Dairyland Power Cooperative*, 45 Wis. 2d 164, 172 N.W.2d 647 (1969); *Boomer* v. *Atlantic Cement Co.*, 26 N.Y.2d 219, 257 N.E.2d 870 (1970). But, cf. *Copart Industries, Inc.* v. *Consolidated Edison Co. of New York, Inc.*, 41 N.Y.2d 564, 362 N.E.2d 968 (1977).

40 See pp. 31–32, infra.

41 See *McLane* v. *Northwest Natural Gas Co.*, 255 Or. 324, 327–33, 467 P.2d 635, 637–39 (1970); *Langan* v. *Valicopters, Inc.*, 88 Wash. 2d 855, 859–65, 567 P.2d 218, 221–23 (1977).

42 See *Barker* v. *Lull Engineering Co., Inc.*, 20 Cal. 3d 413, 430–32, 573 P.2d 443, 455–56 (1978).

43 See two cases involving suits by an employee, injured in an industrial setting, against a product manufacturer: *Cepeda* v. *Cumberland Engineering Co., Inc.*, 76 N.J. 152, 182–92, 386 A.2d 816, 831–36 (1978); *Suter* v. *San Angelo Foundry and Machine Co.*, 81 N.J. 150, 406 A.2d 140 (1979) (overruling Cepeda and not allowing defense of contributory negligence).

44 For examples of courts drawing on justifications from other fields of strict liability, see note 40 (chapter 3), infra.

45 Restatement (Second) of Agency (1957); Restatement (Second) of Torts (vols. 1 and 2, 1965; vol. 3, 1977; vol. 4, 1979). Relevant provisions on vicarious liability appear in §§ 212–49 of the Restatement of Agency. Relevant provisions in the Restatement of Torts on abnormally dangerous activities, nuisance, and product liability are set forth in the text and notes below.

46 Restatement (Second) of Torts §519 comment d (1977).

47 Restatement (Second) of Torts §520 (1977). Some courts have mechanically applied the six factors to reach a decision, although noting that not all factors weigh evenly. See, e.g., *Langan* v. *Valicopters, Inc.*, 88 Wash. 2d 855, 567 P.2d 218 (1977). Others have applied primarily one of the factors in a given case, e.g., *Yommer* v. *McKenzie*, 255 Md. 220, 257 A.2d 138 (1969). At least one court has characterized the "Restatement approach" as suggesting a negligence standard. *Yukon Equipment, Inc.* v. *Fireman's Fund Insurance Co.*, 585 P.2d 1206, 1211 (Alaska 1978).

48 See *Richman* v. *Charter Arms Corp.*, 571 F. Supp. 192, 200–9 (E.D. La. 1983) for a classic instance of a court's carefully rehearsing

each of the criteria of §520, there to determine whether the marketing of handguns constitutes an abnormally dangerous activity. The court of appeals, referring to Louisiana law, concluded that it did not and ordered judgment entered for the manufacturer. For its discussion of the complex criteria under Louisiana law for "ultrahazardous activities," see *Richman* v. *Charter Arms Corp.*, 762 F.2d 1250, 1254–69 (5th Cir. 1985).

49 See Restatement (Second) of Torts §§822–31 (1979).

50 For judicial discussions of this economic ingredient in feasibility analysis, see *United Steelworkers of America* v. *Marshall*, 647 F.2d 1189, 1265–73, 1281–82 (D.C. Cir. 1980), and *American Textile Manufacturers Institute, Inc.* v. *Donovan*, 452 U.S. 490, 530–36 (1981).

51 Restatement (Second) of Torts §822 comment g (1979). See §829A.

52 See, e.g., *Phillips* v. *Kimwood Machine Co.*, 269 Or. 485, 525 P.2d 1033 (1974) (design defect, unreasonable danger); *Beshada* v. *Johns-Manville Products Corp.*, 90 N.J. 191, 447 A.2d 539 (1982) (state-of-the-art defense).

53 See *Fruit* v. *Schreiner*, 502 P.2d 133, 141 (Alaska 1972).

CHAPTER 3. JUSTIFICATION

1 See, e.g., G. Calabresi, *The Costs of Accidents* (1970), and R. Posner, *Economic Analysis of Law* (2d ed. 1977), particularly chapter 6. See note 17 (chapter 2), supra and note 15 (chapter 3), infra.

2 Fletcher, "Fairness and Utility in Tort Theory," 85 *Harv. L. Rev.* 537 (1972).

3 See Keeton, "Conditional Fault in the Law of Torts," 72 *Harv. L. Rev.* 401, 407–9, 441–43 (1959).

4 Epstein, "A Theory of Strict Liability," 2 *J. Legal Stud.* 151 (1973); Epstein, "Defenses and Subsequent Pleas in a System of Strict Liability," 3 *J. Legal Stud.* 165 (1974); Epstein, "Causation and Corrective Justice, A Reply to Two Critics," 8 *J. Legal Stud.* 477 (1979).

5 See Fletcher, "Fairness and Utility in Tort Theory," 85 *Harv. L. Rev.* 537 (1972); C. Fried, *Contract as Promise: A Theory of Contractual Obligation* (1981); Posner, "A Theory of Negligence," 1 *J. Legal Stud.* 29 (1972).

6 See Landes and Posner, "The Positive Economic Theory of Tort Law," 15 *Ga. L. Rev.* 851 (1981). Compare with my observation in the text the comments about the "descriptive claim that the common law never wavers" in its pursuit of efficiency, in Epstein, "The Static Conception of the Common Law," 9 *J. Legal Stud.* 253, 269 (1980).

7 Although I ground my observations in what courts have said, in this essay's numerous descriptions of and quotations from opinions, it should be clear that I cannot document all observations in the same way that I can support statements about tort doctrine in chapter 2. Less detailed citation is possible. Much in the way of inference and extrapolation is necessary when courts have been sparse in their justifications, suggestive rather than elaborate. My observations attempt to spell out some of the unstated premises to and further implications of what courts say. See note 2 (chapter 4), infra, for comments on supporting my observations about social vision.

8 Holmes, "Path of the Law," 10 *Harv. L. Rev.* 457, 466 (1897). See also Dewey, "Logical Method and Law," 10 *Cornell L. Q.* 17 (1924).

9 It is, of course, rare that judges self-consciously compose opinions within one or the other tradition of moral thought. Opinions are not methodologically consistent. Classification of justifications for fault or heightened liability within utilitarian or right-fairness thought is a means of ordering opinions, an ordering consistent with standard distinctions in moral theory and jurisprudence. See note 10 (chapter 3), infra. The purpose of that ordering is to look beneath the surface of opinions to clarify the premises—sometimes inconsistent or contradictory premises—of justificatory argument.

10 The descriptions that follow are drawn from a number of classical and contemporary sources. For either analysis or advocacy of utilitarianism: B. Barry, *Political Argument* (1965); J. Bentham, *The Theory of Legislation* (Ogden ed. 1789, Hildreth trans. 1931); A. Dicey, *Lectures on the Relation between Law and Public Opinion in England during the Nineteenth Century* (2d ed. 1914); H. L. A. Hart, "Utilitarianism and Natural Rights," 53 *Tul. L. Rev.* 663 (1979); J. S. Mill, *Utilitarianism,* in 10 *Collected Works of John Stuart Mill* 203 (J. Robson ed. 1969) (Dolphin Books, 1961). For development and criticism of theories of right and fairness: R. Dworkin, *Taking Rights Seriously* (1977); C. Fried, *Right and Wrong* (1978); I. Kant, *Groundwork of the Metaphysics of Morals*

(H. J. Paton trans. 1956); J. Locke, *Two Treatises of Government*
(Laslett ed. 1960); J. Rawls, *A Theory of Justice* (1971).

11 My usage is similar to the distinction drawn between a *concept* of
fairness and a *conception* of fairness in R. Dworkin, *Taking Rights
Seriously* 134–35 (1977).

12 See, generally, E. Mishan, *Economics for Social Decision: Elements
of Cost-Benefit Analysis,* 18–24, 101–10 (1973). For illustrations of
the difficulties of quantification in a regulatory context, see M.
Baram, "Cost-Benefit Analysis: An Inadequate Basis for Health,
Safety, and Environmental Regulatory Decisionmaking," 8 *Ecol-
ogy L. Q.* 473 (1980); National Highway Traffic Safety Administration, *Societal Costs of Motor Vehicle Accidents* (1975).

13 Distributional concerns, perhaps some notion of a minimum
personal welfare or an egalitarian orientation, could inform such
calculations. But they do so as elements of a conception of aggregate welfare (social welfare will be maximized by assuring all
of a minimum standard of living), rather than as imperatives of
one or another ideal of distributive justice. No such ideal—perhaps a fair distribution of entitlements or a fair sharing of the
burdens and benefits of social life—constrains this goal of maximizing welfare.

14 See the discussion in B. Barry, *Political Argument* 43–47 (1965).

15 The often-cited, perhaps seminal article in the voluminous writings of recent decades about law and economics—writings by
both professors of economics and of law—is Coase, "The Problem of Social Cost," 3 *J. L. & Econ.* 1 (1960). Economic analysis
has figured importantly in the writings of several legal scholars
that have been cited in this essay, particularly books by Guido
Calabresi and Richard Posner, note 1 (chapter 3), supra. Texts by
economists have been directed to the study of law, e.g., A. M.
Polinsky, *An Introduction to Law and Economics* (1983). The "law
and economics" movement has gained academic adherents and
has been subjected to criticism from conceptual-technical and
ideological perspectives. Two recent publications contain articles of theoreticians and/or practitioners of this approach and of
critics: "Symposium on Efficiency as a Legal Concern," 8 *Hofstra
L. Rev.* 485–770, 811–972 (1980). "The Place of Economics in
Legal Education," 33 *J. Legal Educ.* 183–368 (1983). Leading critical articles include Baker, "The Ideology of the Economic Analysis of Law," 5 *Phil. & Pub. Aff.* 3 (1975); Horwitz, "Law and
Economics: Science or Politics?," 8 *Hofstra L. Rev.* 905 (1980);

Kennedy, "Cost-Benefit Analysis of Entitlement Problems: A Critique," 33 *Stan. L. Rev.* 387 (1981).

16 The few graphic exceptions underscore the general observation. For two opinions attempting to apply a "law and economics" methodology to decide on liability in the context of physical accidents, see *Union Oil Co.* v. *Oppen*, 501 F. 2d 558, 569 (9th Cir. 1974), and *Brody* v. *Overlook Hospital*, 121 N.J. Super. 299, 296 A.2d 668 (1972), rev'd, 127 N.J. Super. 331, 317 A.2d 392 (1974), aff'd, 66 N.J. 448, 332 A.2d 596 (1975).

17 R. Dworkin, *Taking Rights Seriously* 22–23, 94–100 (1977) contrasts principles and policies. There, unlike the argument of this essay, the contrast is meant to stress the distinctive role of principles in adjudication, in the reasoning of courts.

18 For a discussion of intuitionism in its classic and modern forms, see H. J. McCloskey, *Meta Ethics and Normative Ethics* (1969) and J. Rawls, *A Theory of Justice* 34–40 (1971). The classic exposition of the theological foundation of law and morals is found in the *Summa Theologica* of St. Thomas Aquinas. Abstract reason and natural law both permeate the contractarian tradition. Classic works within these traditions include I. Kant, *The Metaphysical Elements of Justice* (J. Ladd trans. 1965); J. Locke, *Two Treatises of Government* (Laslett ed. 1960); J. Rawls, *A Theory of Justice* (1971).

19 The literature within the spirit of critical legal studies is rich in the demonstration of the indeterminacy of norms and normative theories. For a discussion of the contradictory uses to which justificatory theories of right and utility (or social welfare) have been put, see Kennedy, "The Structure of Blackstone's Commentaries," 28 *Buffalo L. Rev.* 205, 354–64 (1979).

20 The growth of welfare economics and of a law-review literature starting with articles like that of Terry, "Negligence," 29 *Harv. L. Rev.* 40 (1915) surely contributed to the judicial resort to such economic justifications for liability rules.

21 This systematization of affirmative and negative justifications is distinct from the pairings of opposite maxims (i.e., "who causes the harm ought to pay," as opposed to "no liability without fault") which have become conventional in legal scholarship, at least since the writings of the legal realists. As the text will indicate, affirmative and negative justifications are meant to be complementary and consistent rather than opposed in their premises and implications. For a brief statement of a related analytic framework involving three "principles of compensation" and their "negative application," see the new Sec. 85 of

P. Keeton, D. Dobbs, R. Keeton, and D. Owen, *Prosser and Keeton on the Law of Torts* (5th ed., 1984), particularly pp. 613–14.

22 See, e.g., *Losee* v. *Clute*, 51 N.Y. 494, 10 Am. Rep. 638 (1873); *Union Pacific Rwy. Co.* v. *Cappier*, 66 Kan. 649, 72 P. 281 (1903).

23 See, e.g., *Fisher* v. *Carrousel Motor Hotel, Inc.*, 424 S.W.2d 627 (Tex. 1967). *Beach* v. *Hancock*, 27 N.H. 223 (1853), involving an assault, justifies liability (and punitive damages) on several grounds. The court said in part: "One of the most important objects to be attained by the enactment of laws and the institutions of civilized society is, each of us shall feel secure against unlawful assaults. . . . We have a right to live in society without being put in fear of personal harm." Id. at 229. Compare Restatement (Second) of Torts §18 comment c (1965), referring to offensive contacts constituting a battery: "Since the essence of the plaintiff's grievance consists in the offense to the dignity involved in the unpermitted and intentional invasion of the inviolability of his person and not in any physical harm done to his body, it is not necessary that the plaintiff's actual body be disturbed." Compare the concept of negative rights in C. Fried, *Right and Wrong* 110–14 (1978).

24 Compare *Dobson* v. *Camden*, 705 F.2d 759 (5th Cir. 1983), a decision involving 42 U.S.C. §1983 (1979). In discussing the role of §1983 in curbing official misconduct through damage awards to the misconduct's victim, the court referred to two general goals of tort law, compensation and deterrence. Compensation, "concerned with fairness," was "backward-looking." "The reason for compensating a plaintiff under this theory, the reason Congress and the courts went to the effort of providing a remedy, is that it seems *wrong* for someone to suffer harm from a lawless action. That person deserves, in some moral sense, to be made whole." Id. at 764. The court characterizes this reasoning as "fairness theory."

25 See the discussion at p. 22, supra.

26 See note 10 (chapter 2), supra.

27 See the related discussion at pp. 73–75, infra. Compare the suggestion of a relation between the methodology of the Hand Formula and "concrete rights" (which take into account competing rights) in R. Dworkin, *Taking Rights Seriously* 98–99 (1977). "In certain kinds of cases the argument from competing abstract principles to a concrete right can be made in the language of economics." Id. at 98. The Hand Formula "[does] not subordinate an individual right to some collective goal, but provide[s] a

mechanism for compromising competing claims about right." Id. at 100.

28 Compare *Dobson* v. *Camden*, 705 F.2d 759 (5th Cir. 1983), a decision involving 42 U.S.C. §1983 (1979). In discussing the role of damages in cases involving official misconduct, the court said: "The 'science' of economics can provide us with some insight as to how to reach the correct level of deterrence. Each activity produces costs and benefits. An action is appropriate, from this economic point of view, when the benefits outweigh the costs. . . . Cost internalization provides us with a mechanism for reaching the correct level of deterrence for official misconduct." Id. at 765.

29 The Hand Formula was anticipated in scholarly writing such as Terry, "Negligence," 29 *Harv. L. Rev.* 40 (1915). It was first explicated in the scholarly literature in such a way as to make it broadly applicable to tort liability, historical and contemporary, in Posner, "A Theory of Negligence," 1 *J. Legal Stud.* 29 (1972). The theory was further developed in R. Posner, *An Economic Analysis of Law* 122–42 (2d ed. 1977). The Hand Formula has since figured in much of the literature on law and economics, whether written by economists or law teachers.

30 In *Harrell* v. *Travelers Indemnity Co.*, 279 Or. 199, 567 P.2d 1013 (1977), the court construed the insurance policy before it to cover punitive damages awarded against the insured defendant for reckless driving after drinking. It held that such coverage would not violate "public policy," at least when applied to reckless rather than intentional conduct. It said: "It has long been recognized that there is no empirical evidence that contracts of insurance to protect against liability for negligent conduct are invalid, as a matter of public policy, because of any 'evil tendency' to make negligent conduct 'more probable' or because there is any 'substantial relationship' between the fact of insurance and such negligent conduct." Nor did it find such evidence with respect to punitive (as opposed to compensatory) damages. Id. at 207, 567 P.2d at 1017. A dissenting opinion observed: "The court's frequent statements that punitive damages are meant to deter are true of any sanction in the sense that society would prefer avoidance of the harmful conduct and hopes the sanction will discourage it. . . . [C]ompensatory damages based on fault similarly rest on deterrence of harmful conduct; yet arguments against liability insurance on that ground were long since rejected." Id. at 231–32, 567 P.2d at 1029.

31 Some courts, however, have evidenced their sensitivity to the difficulties in application of the Hand Formula. In a later opinion, Judge Learned Hand commented on the problems in defining negligence that "arise from the necessity of applying a quantitative test to an incommensurable subject-matter. . . ." All attempts at quantification of the components of the Hand Formula "are illusory, and, if serviceable at all, are so only to center attention upon which one of the factors may be determinative in any given situation." *Moisan* v. *Loftus*, 178 F.2d 148, 149 (2d Cir. 1949).

Indeed, in an earlier opinion treating a maritime tort, Judge Hand commented on the problem of foreseeability as a test for liability. That test "is more equivocal than appears on the surface. It ignores the excuses for much conduct which is likely to involve damage to others; for we are not bound to take thought for all that the morrow may bring, even when we should foresee it. Our duties are a resultant not only of what we should forecast, but of the propriety of disregarding so much of it as our own interests justify us in putting at risk. It must be confessed therefore that the standard so fixed scarcely advances the solution in a concrete case; it only eliminates the egregious, leaving the tribunal a free hand to do as it thinks best. But that is inevitable unless liability is to be determined by a manual, mythically prolix, and fantastically impractical." *Sinram* v. *Pennsylvania R. Co.*, 61 F.2d 767, 771 (2d Cir. 1932). Cf. *Hall* v. *E. I. DuPont De Nemours & Co.*, 345 F. Supp. 353, 366 (E.D.N.Y. 1972).

32 For a general discussion of the difficulties inhering in such cost-benefit analysis, whether within the common law or in the development of safety standards, see *American Textile Manufacturers Institute* v. *Donovan*, 452 U.S. 490, 506–40 (1981), particularly notes 26 and 27 at pp. 506–8.

33 This theme in the opinions is deep, implicit. The Nitro-Glycerine Case [*Parrot* v. *Wells, Fargo & Co.*], 82 U.S. (15 Wall.) 524 (1872) is here typical. In denying liability without fault for trespass, the Court stressed that defendants were not "responsible" absent proof of violation of some duty. The theme figures in the scholarly literature. In Lecture III of O. W. Holmes, *The Common Law* 77–78 (M. D. Howe ed. 1963), the author states: "The undertaking to redistribute losses simply on the ground that they resulted from the defendant's act would . . . be open . . . to the still graver [objection] of offending the sense of justice. Unless . . . under the circumstances a prudent man would have

foreseen the possibility of harm, it is no more justifiable to make me indemnify my neighbor against the consequences, than to . . . compel me to insure him against lightning." Cf. the argument in Thayer, "Liability without Fault," 29 *Harv. L. Rev.* 801 (1916).

34 In attacking the strict liability principles of *Rylands* v. *Fletcher,* the court in *Brown* v. *Collins* 53 N.H. 442, 16 Amer. Rep. 372 (1873), warned that such principles would throw "an obstacle in the way of progress and improvement." It went on to observe that the United States had "settled down to those modern, progressive, industrial pursuits" which the common law, adapted to the new society, "encourages and defends." Many of the common law's "rational rules" responded to the growth of trade and "productive enterprise." Id. at 448, 450, 16 Amer. Rep. at 379, 381. In *Losee* v. *Buchanan,* 51 N.Y. 476 (1873), the court concluded that a factory at which a boiler had exploded was not liable for resulting harm to a nearby property owner. "We must have factories, machinery, dams, canals and railroads. They are demanded by the manifold wants of mankind, and lay at the basis of all our civilization." Such productive activities were not responsible for damage "accidentally and unavoidably" caused neighbors. Most property rights in society "are not absolute but relative, and they must be so arranged and modified, not unnecessarily infringing upon natural rights, as upon the whole to promote the general welfare." Id. at 484–85. See Gordon, "Critical Legal Histories," 36 *Stan. L. Rev.* 57, 64–65, 75–81 (1984), for a review and assessment of historians' functionalist interpretation of common-law change, including the development of nineteenth-century tort law. Compare the interpretation of the growth of negligence law in M. Horwitz, *The Transformation of American Law,* 1780–1860, 97–101 (1977).

35 The way in which this conclusion is expressed in the text is of course contemporary. Nineteenth-century courts were more likely to conclude that beyond-fault liability would violate "policy."

36 In a case involving the extent of liability of a railroad for a fire that spread from property to property, the court noted that an unlimited liability in these circumstances "would be the destruction of all civilized society." *Ryan* v. *New York Central Railway Co.,* 35 N.Y. 210, 217 (1866). The Ryan case signals the degree to which doctrines like legal or proximate cause that restricted liability were informed by the same concerns and justifications that

courts expressed when dealing, say, with the choice between negligence and strict liability. See Horwitz, "The Doctrine of Objective Causation," in D. Kairys (ed.), *The Politics of Law* 201 (1982). In *Beatty* v. *Central Iowa R. Co.*, 58 Iowa 242, 12 N.W. 332 (1882), the court concluded that defendant railroad had not been negligent in its construction of a crossing. It observed that the increased danger in use of the highways "is necessarily incident to and attendant upon this improved mode of transportation. . . . The price of progress cannot be withheld." Id. at 247–48, 12 N.W. at 334.

37 Compare the views of Holmes, set forth in the 1881 publication of *The Common Law,* about the development of tort law during the nineteenth century. In criticizing strict or insurer's liability and justifying the negligence system, Holmes says at different points in Lecture III of *The Common Law* (M. D. Howe ed. 1963): "The general principle of our law is that loss from accident must lie where it falls. . . . A man need not, it is true, do this or that act . . . but he must act somehow. Furthermore, the public generally profits by individual activity. As action cannot be avoided, and tends to the public good, there is obviously no policy in throwing the hazard of what is at once desirable and inevitable upon the actor." Id. at 76–77. In justifying an external standard of due care, Holmes points to the difficulties of "nicely measuring a man's powers and limitations. . . . But a more satisfactory explanation is that, when men live in society, a certain average of conduct, a sacrifice of individual peculiarities going beyond a certain point, is necessary to the general welfare." Id. at 86. The negligence system, as it were, assures some minimum level of security that is necessary for society's work to get done, while avoiding the excessive deterrence of action likely to result from strict liability.

See Schwartz, "Tort Law and the Economy in Nineteenth-Century America: A Reinterpretation," 90 *Yale L. J.* 1717 (1981), for the view based on an examination of appellate opinions of California and New Hampshire that the nineteenth-century courts, "in implementing the negligence system, were solicitous of victim welfare and generally bold in the liability burdens they were willing to impose on corporate defendants." Id. at 1774. Of course, a liability-prone application of the classical negligence system's rules remains distinct from the changes in rules within that system and the growth of strict liability rules with their distinctive justifications. See pp. 20–25, supra.

38 See, e.g., *Losee* v. *Buchanan*, 51 N.Y. 476, 484–85, 487 (1873).
39 Such ideas are implicit in opinions like *Beatty* v. *Central Iowa Railway Co.*, 58 Iowa 242, 247, 12 N.W. 332, 334 (1882) (no liability in railroad accident): "All persons must accept the advantages of this mode of intercommunication with the danger and inconveniences which necessarily attend it."
40 *Rodgers* v. *Kemper Construction Co.*, 50 Cal. App. 3d 608, 124 Cal. Rptr. 143 (Ct. App. 1975) observed in a vicarious-liability case that the employer could best spread the risk through pricing and liability insurance. "In some respects this rationale is akin to that underlying the modern doctrine of strict tort liability for defective products." Id. at 618, 124 Cal. Rptr. at 148. *Becker* v. *Interstate Properties*, 569 F.2d 1203 (3d Cir. 1977) involved the independent contractor exception to vicarious liability. The court turned to New Jersey law and drew from many fields within it, principally product liability, to ascertain the principles underlying innovative tort claims and recoveries. From those fields it developed three principal concerns of tort law that were viewed as relevant to the decision. Id. at 1209–14. *Chavez* v. *Southern Pacific Transportation Co.*, 413 F. Supp. 1203 (E.D. Cal. 1976) drew on opinions treating strict product liability to support a liability for abnormally dangerous activities. Id. at 1208–9.
41 Compare the inquiry into "what is the cost of what" in G. Calabresi, *The Costs of Accidents* 135–73 (1970). That inquiry, within a welfare-maximizing framework, suggests that liability be assigned to activities within a set of criteria aiming at the best or "cheapest" accident avoidance. Earlier writings of a systematic character sought to develop criteria by which courts could decide on assignment of costs in fields of beyond-fault liability such as vicarious liability. See, e.g., the discussion of the relevance to the frolic-detour distinction of goals such as risk avoidance or risk distribution in Douglas," Vicarious Liability and Administration of Risk," 38 *Yale L. J.* 584, 720 (1929), particularly pp. 585–94. Numerous appellate opinions refer to such writings, particularly to Calabresi, in their discussion of the appropriate limit to liability.
42 The court stated in *Butaud* v. *Suburban Marine & Sporting Goods, Inc.*, 543 P.2d 209 (Alaska 1975), that in product defect cases, the "purpose of strict liability is to overcome the difficulty of proof inherent in negligent and warranty theories, thereby insuring that the costs of physical injuries are borne by those who market defective products." Id. at 214. *Siegler* v. *Kuhlman*, 81 Wash. 2d

448, 502 P.2d 1181 (1972) imposed strict liability for harm stemming from a collision with a truck transporting flammable fuel
and the resulting fire. The court, noting several justifications for
strict liability, included an observation about "the likely destruction of cogent evidence from which negligence or want of it may
be proved or disproved." Id. at 454, 502 P.2d at 1185.

43 A characteristic contemporary statement of the general principle
underlying the assignment of liability appears in *Becker* v. *Interstate Properties*, 569 F.2d 1203 (3d Cir. 1977). "[I]t is a well-recog-
nized principle of tort law that, where feasible, liability for an
accident should be allocated to those in the best position to control the factors leading to such accidents." Id. at 1211.

44 The elements of behavior-modification justifications set forth below and drawn from the judicial opinions were anticipated in
some of the scholarly literature on tort law that was widely
known by judges and cited in opinions. See, e.g., 2 F. Harper
and F. James, *The Law of Torts* 755–57 (1956), for its discussion of
the advantage, from the perspective of deterrence, of placing
strict liability on large business or governmental units that are in
better positions than individuals to rationalize operations and
introduce systemic changes. See also note 41 (chapter 3), supra.

45 See, e.g., *Beshada* v. *Johns-Manville Products Corp.*, 90 N.J. 191, 447
A.2d 539 (1982).

46 In *Day* v. *Trans World Airlines, Inc.*, 528 F.2d 31 (2d Cir. 1975), the
court construed broadly the coverage of provisions of the War-
saw Convention governing international air travel, so that passengers subjected in an airport to an attack by terrorists were
within their terms and thus able to benefit from the Convention's strict liability principles. The court construed the Convention broadly "in harmony with modern theories of accident
cost allocation. . . . The airlines, in marked contrast to individual passengers, are in a better posture to persuade, pressure or,
if need be, compensate airport managers to adopt more strin-
gent security measures against terrorist attacks. . . . If necessary, the airlines can hire their own security guards. And, the
companies operate under circumstances more conducive to in-
vestigating the conditions at the airports they regularly serve
than do their passengers. Moreover, they can better assess the
probabilities of accidents, and balance the reduction in risk to be
gained by any given preventive measure against its cost." Id. at
34.

47 In *Ira S. Bushey & Sons, Inc.* v. *United States*, 398 F.2d 167 (2d Cir.
1968), the court cites and agrees with authorities to the effect
that what is meant by reasonably foreseeable risk in a vicarious
(strict) liability setting differs from what is meant by foreseeable
unreasonable risk in negligence cases. The foresight relevant to
strict-liability cases was closer to the meaning of that concept in
workers' compensation plans—namely, that an employer
should anticipate risks (whether or not unreasonable) arising
out of the course of employment. Id. at 171–72. *Rodgers* v. *Kemper Construction Co.*, 50 Cal. App. 3d 608, 124 Cal. Rptr. 143 (Ct.
App. 1975), another vicarious liability case, distinguished foresight in a fault setting (a level of probability inducing an actor to
undertake a burden of precaution) from vicarious or strict liability settings. There, foresight as a test meant only that an
event "is not so unusual or startling that it would seem unfair to
include the loss resulting from it among other costs of the employer's business." Id. at 619, 124 Cal. Rptr. at 148–49. *Hall* v.
E. I. DuPont De Nemours & Co., Inc., 345 F. Supp. 353 (E.D.N.Y.
1972) referred to an interplay between concepts of foresight in
negligence and strict-liability settings, all in the context of a
product-defect case. It referred to a view of strict liability in
which accidents and injuries "are seen as an inevitable and statistically foreseeable 'cost' of the product's consumption or use."
Id. at 368. Noting that a broad concept of foreseeability had been
used in negligence cases, it pointed out that under strict liability,
risk was not situational and contextual but related to foreseeability of kinds of risks that an enterprise was likely to generate. Id. at 369.
48 The famous concurrence of Justice Traynor in *Escola* v. *Coca-Cola
Bottling Co. of Fresno*, 24 Cal. 2d 453, 461, 150 P.2d 436, 440 (1944)
set the tone for many later judicial statements. "Public policy"
required that liability be placed "wherever it will most effectively
reduce the hazards to life and health inherent in defective products that reach the market. . . . [A] manufacturer can anticipate
some hazards and guard against the recurrence of others, as the
public cannot." Id. at 462, 150 P.2d at 440–41. Nonetheless, other
courts have expressed doubt, at least in the particular circumstances before them, that heightened liability will lead institutional defendants to modify their behavior. Thus, in a vicarious
liability case, *Ira S. Bushey & Sons, Inc.* v. *United States*, 398 F.2d
167 (2d Cir. 1968), the court said (on p. 170) that a "more efficient
allocation" of resources could be expected to follow from height-

ened liability only if "there is some reason to believe that imposing a particular cost on the enterprise will lead it to consider
whether steps should be taken to prevent a recurrence of the
accident." It concluded that there was little reason to believe that
vicarious liability would there lead the defendant to a better
screening of employees.

49 In *Sindell* v. *Abbott Laboratories*, 26 Cal. 3d 588, 607 P.2d 924
(1980), a drug-defect case, the court described the manufacturer
as "in the best position to discover and guard against defects in
its products and to warn of harmful effects; thus, holding it liable for defects and failure to warn of harmful effects will provide
an incentive to product safety." With respect to medical drugs,
"the consumer is virtually helpless to protect himself from serious, sometimes permanent, sometimes fatal, injuries caused
by deleterious drugs." Id. at 611, 607 P.2d at 936. See generally
pp. 104–5, infra.

50 This type of reasoning, characteristic of opinions imposing a
strict liability, also permeates some opinions on negligence law.
In *Banks* v. *Hyatt Corp.*, 722 F.2d 214 (5th Cir. 1984), the court
considered the liability for negligence of an innkeeper whose
guest was shot outside the hotel. The question was one of a
special relational duty to warn or protect guests. "Tort law has
become increasingly concerned with placing liability upon the
party that is best able to determine the cost-justified level of
accident prevention [citations to writings of G. Calabresi and
R. Posner]." Thus holding the innkeeper liable for an assault by
a third party "is sensible, not because of some abstract conceptual notion about the risk arising within 'the course of the
relation,' but because the innkeeper is able to identify and carry
out cost-justified ('reasonable') preventive measures on the
premises." As between the innkeeper and the guest, the innkeeper is the only one in a position "to take the reasonably necessary acts to guard against the predictable risk of assaults." Id.
at 226–27.

51 The court in *Beshada* v. *Johns-Manville Products Corp.*, 90 N.J. 191,
447 A.2d 539 (1982) considered the problem of an earlier apparently unknowable risk from asbestos. It noted accident avoidance as a goal of strict product liability. In response to the
defendants' argument that such a goal was irrelevant where a
hazard was undiscoverable, the court noted that the defendants
"have treated the level of technological knowledge at a given
time as an independent variable not affected by defendants' con-

duct." The defendants, however, ignored "the important role of industry in product safety research. . . . By imposing on manufacturers the costs of failure to discover hazards, we create an incentive for them to invest more actively in safety research." Id. at 207, 447 A.2d at 548. In *Jordan* v. *Sunnyslope Appliance Propane & Plumbing Supplies Co.*, 135 Ariz. 309, 660 P.2d 1236 (Ct. App. 1983), the court considered whether a dealer in used products could be held strictly liable for harm from the unreasonably dangerous condition of a product that it sold. The court noted several arguments against strict liability: the dealer was outside the regular chain of distribution, could not readily communicate with the manufacturer to suggest that certain defects be eliminated, and so on. Nonetheless, the court observed that the dealer "is an integral part of the marketing system. At any rate, imposing strict liability on the commercial dealer of used products should result in increased maintenance and inspection of such products before they are offered for sale." Id. at 313, 660 P.2d at 1240.

52 See Shavell, "Strict Liability versus Negligence," 9 *J. Legal Stud.* 1, 2–3, 6–8 (1980).

53 In a case involving vicarious liability, the court addressed the resource-allocational justifications for increasing liability, and pointed out that in given circumstances a plaintiff may be better situated to guard more cheaply against an accident. One cannot always automatically assume the defendant to be in a better position. *Ira S. Bushey & Sons, Inc.* v. *United States*, 398 F.2d 167, 170–71 (2d Cir. 1968).

54 The issue of the plaintiff's conduct arose indirectly in *Campos* v. *Firestone Tire & Rubber Co.*, 192 N.J. Super. 251, 469 A.2d 943 (Super. Ct. App. Div. 1983). The court vacated a judgment for the plaintiff based on the ground that the defendant had failed to warn adequately of the potential danger in use of a machine. It argued that reasons for product liability would not here be served, for "in the case before us only the plaintiff's impulsive act in the face of obvious danger caused the accident. . . . Nor does the 'accident avoidance' policy prong support plaintiff's position. Even his own expert conceded that a pictorial warning on the rims or elsewhere was not 'going to be very effective' to restrain him from doing what he did." Id. at 261, 469 A.2d at 949. (That court's judgment for the defendant was reversed in *Campos* v. *Firestone Tire & Rubber Co.*, 98 N.J. 198, 485 A.2d 305

(1984), and remanded for a new trial to include different jury instructions on related issues, including proximate cause.)

55 In *Cepeda* v. *Cumberland Engineering Co., Inc.*, 76 N.J. 152, 386 A.2d 816 (1978), the court concluded that, until adoption of comparative fault in strict liability cases, continuing to permit "unreasonable voluntary exposure of oneself to a known danger" as a defense to a strict-liability claim "seems a fair balance of justice and policy in this area." Id. at 189–90, 386 A.2d at 834. The case involved a claim by an employee, injured in an industrial setting, against a product manufacturer. *Cepeda* was overruled in a case arising in a similar context involving a claim of a design defect, *Suter* v. *San Angelo Foundry and Machine Co.*, 81 N.J. 150, 406 A.2d 140 (1979). In applying comparative fault principles to reduce a plaintiff's recovery, the court in *Daly* v. *General Motors Corp.*, 20 Cal. 3d 725, 737, 575 P.2d 1162, 1169 (1978) concluded that there was no reason to charge the defendant with a share of the plaintiff's damages "which flows from his own fault." Such reduction in damages would not lessen the incentives on the defendant to produce safe products, for only a portion of the damages were avoided. In making safety decisions, the defendant-manufacturer could not assume that plaintiffs would be negligent.

56 Resources are more efficiently allocated "when the actual costs of goods and services (including the losses they entail) are reflected in their price to the consumer." *Chavez* v. *Southern Pacific Transportation Co.*, 413 F. Supp. 1203, 1209 (E.D. Cal. 1976).

57 In *Carpenter* v. *Double R Cattle Co., Inc.*, 105 Idaho 320, 669 P.2d 643 (Idaho App. 1983), the court discussed favorably the provisions in the Restatement (Second) of Torts, which imposed liability for nuisance without fault. "However, our view is not based simply upon general notions of fairness; it is also grounded in economics. The Second Restatement deals effectively with the problem of 'externalities.' . . . Where an enterprise externalizes some burdens upon its neighbors, without compensation, our market system does not reflect the true cost of products or services provided by that enterprise. Externalities distort the price signals essential to the proper functioning of the market. . . . The market system best serves the goal of efficiency when prices reflect true costs; and the goal of distributive justice is best achieved when benefits are explicitly identified to the correlative costs." Id. at 330, 669 P.2d at 653. (This judgment of the court of appeals from which the quotation was taken was

vacated, and the district court's judgment for defendants rein-
stated, in an appeal to the state supreme court in *Carpenter* v.
Double R Cattle Co., Inc., 108 Idaho 602, 701 P.2d 222 (1985). The
supreme court did not refer specifically to the quoted observations of the court of appeal. It disapproved that court's adoption
of the Restatement (Second) of Torts provisions on nuisance,
particularly the provision that a defendant could be held liable
in nuisance regardless of the utility of its conduct if the harm
was "serious" and the payment of damages "feasible.")

58 In *Murray* v. *Fairbanks Morse*, 610 F.2d 149 (3d Cir. 1979), the
court points out the problem in not accounting for plaintiff's
fault (there, in the context of comparative fault) in a product-
liability suit. If such fault is not accounted for, the manufacturer
would pay for and spread costs attributable not to the defect but
to plaintiff's conduct. As a consequence, "the future cost of the
manufacturer's product will be artificially inflated and will not
accurately represent the actual risk posed by the defective product. . . . [T]he consuming public at large may be adversely affected. If the future cost of a product does not accurately reflect
the risk posed, then consumers may actually choose cheaper,
less safe products because the cost of the manufacturer's product is artificially high. See generally G. Calabresi, The Costs of
Accidents (1970)." Id. at 161.

59 The distinction here made can be illustrated, for example, by a
comparison between a justification for fault liability based on the
victim's right not to be interfered with (p. 50, supra) and a justification for strict liability based on the fairness of spreading burdens of an activity among those who benefit from it (p. 70,
infra). The distinction bears some relation to the use within tort
law of concepts of corrective and distributive justice, a theme
developed in England, "The System Builders: A Critical Appraisal of Modern American Tort Theory," 9 *J. Legal Stud.* 27
(1980). Cf. the discussion in 2 F. Harper and F. James, *The Law of
Torts* 761–64 (1956).

The distinction between shifting and spreading is brought
out clearly in a number of opinions. See, for example, *Martin* v.
Harrington and Richardson, Inc., 743 F.2d 1200 (7th Cir. 1984), in
which the court, referring to applicable Illinois law, concluded
that the sale of handguns to the public was not an ultrahazardous activity imposing strict liability on the manufacturer for
injuries stemming from the illegal use of a handgun. A concurring opinion agreed that "[w]hatever may be said for or

against this approach . . . it is not now the law of Illinois." It observed that analysis of the problem would be "incomplete, however, if we lose sight of the fact that . . . death and injury from bullet wounds are an external cost of handgun manufacture and sale, imposed on gun victims or on society as a whole. The central reality is that these costs exist in fact, and the only question is who should bear them. The imposition of strict liability on the manufacturer or seller of handguns should not be viewed as an attempt to drive handguns from the market—for the courts, an improper goal. Rather, it is an effort to place the costs inherent in handguns on the users rather than on the victims. Strict liability . . . places the costs of injury on a party who is able to spread those costs widely among all users through higher prices," 743 F.2d at 1206–7.

60 The different expressions and theories of a moral duty are captured in the opinions in *Rylands* v. *Fletcher,* the case that served as the point of departure for discussion in many American cases (from 1868 on) of the choice between strict liability or liability only for negligence. In the Court of Exchequer Chamber, Blackburn, J., in imposing liability without fault for damage caused plaintiffs' coal mines by water flowing into them from a reservoir constructed by defendants, stated that the general rule on which he relied "seems on principle just. The person . . . whose mine is flooded by the water from his neighbour's reservoir . . . is damnified without any fault of his own; and it seems but reasonable and just that the neighbour, who has brought something on his own property which was not naturally there . . . which he knows will be mischievous if it gets on his neighbour's, should be obliged to make good the damage. . . ." *Fletcher* v. *Rylands,* 14 L.R. 523, 526, 1 Exch. 265, 280 (1866). In the House of Lords (which affirmed the judgment of the Exchequer Chamber), Lord Cranworth expressed a related conception of fairness, closer to the maxim, "between two innocents. . . ." He stated: "In considering whether a defendant is liable to a plaintiff for damage which the plaintiff may have sustained, the question in general is not whether the defendant has acted with due care and caution, but whether his acts have occasioned the damage. . . . For when one person, in managing his own affairs, causes, however innocently, damage to another, it is obviously only just that he should be the party to suffer. He is bound *sic uti suo ut non loedat alienum.*" *Rylands* v. *Fletcher,* 19 L.R. 220, 222, 2 H.L. 330, 341 (1868).

61 Thus, *Brown* v. *Collins*, 53 N.H. 442, 16 Amer. Rep. 372 (1873), a case hostile to strict liability and rejecting a *Rylands*-style liability, referred to early English cases in which the judges appeared to look only to the hardship of the victims. But such an approach "disregards the question whether, by transferring the hardship to the other party, anything more will be done than substitute one suffering party for another. . . ." Id. at 446, 16 Amer. Rep. at 376.

62 Of course, many recent opinions imposing a strict liability continue to justify liability without reference to loss spreading. See *Berg* v. *Reaction Motors Div., Thiokol Chemical Corp.*, 37 N.J. 396, 181 A.2d 487 (1962), which imposes liability for damage caused nearby landowners by the testing of rocket engines. The court asserted that "every consideration of fairness and justness dictates that the defendant at least make its neighbors whole for the structural damage it caused." Id. at 406, 181 A.2d at 492. It cited in support of its holding the older cases imposing strict liability for injury stemming from blasting operations, cases which "embody current notions as to what is right and just." Although socially useful and carefully executed, blasting "nonetheless is an ultrahazardous activity which introduces an unusual danger into the community and should pay its own way in the event it actually causes damage to others." Id. at 410, 181 A.2d at 494.

63 In *Hicks* v. *State of New Mexico*, 88 N.M. 588, 544 P.2d 1153 (1975), the court abolished sovereign immunity of the state in a negligence suit. It pointed out that, given the availability of liability insurance, there would be no "intolerable financial burden upon the State. . . . In addition, it would appear that placing the financial burden upon the State, which is able to distribute its losses throughout the populace, is more just and equitable than forcing the individual who is injured to bear the entire burden alone." Id. at 590, 544 P.2d at 1155.

64 The textual discussion in this section and the illustrations in notes make clear that courts are terse in their use of a utilitarian justification for loss spreading, and often ambiguous about the character of the justification. The explication in text draws, to the extent possible, on the appellate opinions. In teasing out the premises to judicial argument, the text also draws on the description of secondary costs (dislocation costs of accidents) in G. Calabresi, *The Costs of Accidents* 39–67 (1970). Earlier scholarly works much cited by the courts also developed utilitarian justifications for loss spreading. See, e.g., 2 F. Harper and F. James,

The Law of Torts 762–63 (1954); Douglas, "Vicarious Liability and Administration of Risk," 38 *Yale L. J.* 584, 720 (1929), particularly pp. 592, 599–601, 724–27, dealing with risk shifting and risk distribution.

65 The court in *Chavez* v. *Southern Pacific Transportation Co.*, 413 F. Supp. 1203 (E.D. Cal. 1976) discussed strict liability in the context of abnormally dangerous activities. "The harsh impact of inevitable disasters is softened by spreading the cost among a greater population and over a larger time period." Id. at 1214.

66 Restatement (Second) of Torts, §402a, comment c (1965), refers in the context of product liability to treating accidental injury as a product cost for which manufacturers can obtain liability insurance. Typical observations appear in *Becker* v. *Interstate Properties*, 569 F.2d 1203 (3d Cir. 1977). The court (referring to New Jersey law) describes that law's concern in formulating tort doctrine "that the burden of accidental loss be shifted to those best able to bear and distribute that loss. . . . [Where the defendant-contractee] is a substantial entrepreneur and a member of an industry that carries large liability insurance policies as a matter of course, there is little question but that he is in the better position to bear the costs of such an accident. Moreover, the developer can spread the increased costs of insurance or liability to ultimate users of the project. It is only in rare circumstances that a victim will have a similar option." Id. at 1209–10.

In *Ross* v. *Ross*, 294 Minn. 115, 200 N.W.2d 149 (1972), the court interpreted a Dramshop Act to impose civil liability on every violator of the Act (whether or not in the liquor business, thus including social hosts). The case involved a noncommercial provider of liquor to a minor whose intoxication then led to the plaintiff's injury. In his concurring opinion, Justice Rogosheske stated that he could not endorse language of the opinion implying that the "strict liability" imposed by the Act "upon a commercial seller of liquor can, with equal justification, be imposed upon a social host even though he may or may not carry either the type of, or sufficient, liability insurance to protect against the risk of such liability." The purpose of the statute was to provide damages to "an innocent person from a commercial activity which can best bear the burden of loss by insuring against it as a cost of engaging in a hazardous business for profit." Id. at 124–25, 200 N.W.2d at 154–55. *Kelly* v. *Gwinnell*, 96 N.J. 538, 476 A.2d 1219 (1984) imposed a common-law negligence liability on a social host providing liquor to a car driver who injured the plaintiff. The court suggested that such defendants would likely be covered by a homeowners policy, but recognized that they might be unprotected by insurance. The dissent was based partly on the view that social hosts were unlikely to be able to spread the loss through insurance. Id. at 550, 568–69, 476 A.2d at 1225, 1234–35.

Compare the early judicial understanding of the workers' compensation acts in *Ives* v. *South Buffalo Ry. Co.*, 201 N.Y. 271, 94 N.E. 431 (1911), where the court described the theory of the New York law to be that inherent employment risks "should in justice" be placed on the employer "who can protect himself against loss by insurance and by such an addition to the price of his wares as to cast the burden ultimately upon the consumer. . . ." Id. at 294, 94 N.E. at 439.

67 See, e.g., G. Calabresi, *The Costs of Accidents* 39–40 (1970). Some such theory may underlie the judicial observations set forth in note 65, supra. For a criticism of such a justification as applied to the spreading of accident costs through tort law, see R. Posner, *Economic Analysis of Law* 344–46 (2d ed. 1977). The justification is, of course, broadly relevant to contemporary regulation. For a criticism of its use in the context of tax policy, see Blum and Kalven, "The Uneasy Case for Progressive Taxation," 19 *U. Chi. L. Rev.* 417, 465–71 (1952).

68 See note 19 (chapter 4), infra. Some reasons for the rarity of judicial consideration of first-party insurance as a preferred path toward loss spreading are suggested at pp. 103–4, infra.

69 See, e.g., note 66 (chapter 3), supra.

70 Thus the court in *Siragusa* v. *Swedish Hospital*, 60 Wash. 2d 310, 373 P.2d 767 (1962), in holding that an employee was not to be charged with assumption of risk, said: "In almost all areas of industrial activity, social insurance has replaced the common law rules of liability and defenses which grew out of the judicial inclination to foster a growing economy. No longer can it be said that a judicially-imposed doctrine of assumption of risk is necessary or desirable to protect expanding industry from being crippled by employers' responsibility for tortious conduct towards their employees." Id. at 318, 373 P.2d at 773. Another court in a similar vein referred to the nineteenth-century rule against liability on warranty without privity of contract and observed: "It was an outgrowth of the beginning of the industrial revolution when it was thought it was necessary to protect struggling and unstable industry against an onslaught of disastrous claims."

Dippel v. *Sciano*, 37 Wis. 2d 443 at 450, 155 N.W.2d 55 at 58 (1967). The court in *Hoffman* v. *Jones*, 280 So. 2d 431 (Fla. 1973) adopted a comparative-negligence rule in lieu of contributory fault. It characterized the "historical justification" or "initial justification" for the displaced rule—protection of nascent industry—as "no longer valid. . . . Modern economic and social customs . . . favor the individual, not industry." Id. at 436–37.

71 Thus, the court in *Woodill* v. *Parke Davis & Co.*, 79 Ill. 2d 26, 402 N.E.2d 194 (1980) underscored the need to impose limits on strict liability in a drug case. Otherwise, the defendant drug company would become an insurer despite its lack of foreseeability of harm. "This court is acutely aware of the social desirability of encouraging the research and development of beneficial drugs." Id. at 37, 402 N.E.2d at 199. Similarly, in rejecting a proposed rule of market-share liability in lieu of individual proof of actual causation in a drug case, a court stated: "Public policy favors the development and marketing of new and more efficacious drugs. The Restatement (Second) of Torts recognizes this policy by rejecting strict liability in favor of negligence for drug related injuries. . . . Imposition of such broad liability could have a deleterious effect on the development and marketing of new drugs. . . ." *Payton* v. *Abbott Labs*, 386 Mass. 540, 573, 437 N.E.2d 171, 189–90 (1982).

Compare *Carpenter* v. *Double R Cattle Co., Inc.*, 108 Idaho 602, 701 P.2d 222 (1985), where the court rejected provisions on nuisance in the Restatement (Second) of Torts to the effect that a defendant could be held liable in damages regardless of the utility of its conduct if the harm were "serious" and if payment of damages were "feasible" without jeopardizing the continuance of the conduct. ". . . [I]n a nuisance action seeking damages the interests of the community, which would include the utility of the conduct, should be considered. . . . The State of Idaho is sparsely populated and its economy depends largely upon the benefits of agriculture, lumber, mining and industrial development. To eliminate the utility of conduct . . . from the criteria to be considered in determining whether a nuisance exists . . . would place an unreasonable burden upon these industries." 701 P.2d at 227–28.

72 See the excerpts from opinions in notes 76–79 (chapter 3), infra. As they also did with respect to utilitarian justifications for loss spreading, see note 64, supra, legal scholars stressed some of the powerful contemporary fairness justifications before they

became common in tort opinions. For example, Bohlen, "The Rule in Rylands V. Fletcher," 49 *U. Pa. L. Rev.* 298, 373, 423 (1911) develops on pp. 444–46 arguments based on *Rylands* that are close to contemporary benefit-burden justifications, p. 70, infra. Bohlen, referring to cases that reject the need for fault as a condition to liability, notes that during a transition period courts will either abandon such doctrine or will continue in a path to "work out some new principle for the distribution of loss, which will satisfy the more highly socialized modern sense of justice." Id. at 452–53. Cf. the analogous predictions, drawing on the experience of the new workers' compensation acts, in Smith, "Sequel to Workmen's Compensation Acts," 27 *Harv. L. Rev.* 235, 344 (1914), at 365–68. More recently, Keeton, "Conditional Fault in the Law of Torts," 72 *Harv. L. Rev.* 401 (1959), attacked the idea that a defendant's risk-spreading capacity alone could serve as a basis for strict liability, and developed fairness justifications for strict liability that draw on ideas of unjust enrichment and the spreading of loss in proportion to benefits received from an activity. Id. at 407–9, 441–43. Representative, widely read writings in contemporary scholarship developing right-fairness arguments for strict liability include Epstein, "A Theory of Strict Liability," 2 *J. Legal Stud.* 151 (1973), and related writings cited in note 4 (chapter 3), supra; Fletcher, "Fairness and Utility in Tort Theory," 85 *Harv. L. Rev.* 537 (1972).

73 In *Shipley* v. *Fifty Associates,* 106 Mass. 194 (1870), the court considered the liability without fault of a landowner for injury caused a pedestrian on neighboring land because of snow falling off a roof. "In such a case, the maxim *Sic utere tuo ut alienum non laedas* [use your own property so as not to injure that of others] would be applicable. . . ." The landowner must keep snow on the roof "at his peril. . . . He has no right to appropriate his neighbor's land in that manner for his own convenince. . . ." Landowners could not collect and retain snow on roofs until it fell "at the expense of their neighbor, or of the traveler, whose rights for this special purpose are as complete as those of an adjoining proprietor." Id. at 199–200. *Green* v. *General Petroleum Corp.,* 205 Cal. 328, 270 P. 952 (1928), involved a nonnegligent oil-well blowout. The court invoked the *sic utere* maxim, which it viewed as incorporated in the California Civil Code. It rejected the defendant's argument that an owner's use of land "is subject to and limited by the right of other property owners to develop the natural resources of their lands in a lawful and prudent man-

ner." Id. at 335, 270 P. at 955. For a negative view of the *sic utere* doctrine in a nuisance case applying a negligence rather than strict standard of liability, see *Rose* v. *Socony-Vacuum Corp.*, 54 R.I. 411, 416, 173 A. 627, 629 (1934).

74 The court in *Siegler* v. *Kuhlman*, 81 Wash. 2d 448, 502 P.2d 1181 (1972) observes: "The rule of strict liability rests not only upon the ultimate idea of rectifying a wrong and putting the burden where it should belong as a matter of abstract justice, that is, upon the one of the two innocent parties whose acts instigated or made the harm possible, but it also rests on the problems of proof. . . ." Id. at 455, 502 P.2d at 1185. The maxim is sometimes explicitly linked to the intentional character of the risk imposition. In *Chavez* v. *Southern Pacific Transportation Co.*, 413 F. Supp. 1203 (E.D. Cal. 1976), the court (applying California law) observed that intentionally engaging in ultrahazardous activity, even when doing so nonnegligently, "is sufficiently anti-social that, as between two innocents, the actor and not the injured should pay for mishaps." Id. at 1207. The maxim also figures in negligence cases which approach a strict liability, such as the liability of the insane for negligently inflicted harm. Thus the opinion in *Jolley* v. *Powell*, 299 So. 2d 647 (Fla. App. 1974), notes that even absent the "subjective fault" of the defendant, other principles point to liability, including "where one of two innocent persons must suffer a loss, it should be borne by the one who occasioned it." Id. at 649.

75 *McLane* v. *Northwest Natural Gas Co.*, 255 Or. 324, 467 P.2d 635 (1970) considered reasons for strict liability in the setting of injury related to the storage of natural gas, an abnormally dangerous activity. In engaging in a "weighing process" to determine who should bear the inherent risks of this activity, the court said: "The basis of the liability is the intentional behavior in exposing the community to the abnormal risk. . . . There is no reason why defendant's activity should not pay the cost of the additional risk of harm which arises from the activity's unusual nature. . . . It is not a normal risk which is mutually created and borne by all. . . . Undoubtedly, another factor which enters the picture is the feeling that where one of two innocent persons must suffer, the loss should fall upon the one who created the risk causing the harm." Id. at 327, 329–30, 467 P.2d at 637–38. *Berg* v. *Reaction Motors Div.*, *Thiokol Chemical Corp.*, 37 N.J. 396, 181 A.2d 487 (1962) notes in a characteristically terse way that an ultrahazardous activity "introduces

an unusual danger into the community and should pay its own way in the event it actually causes damage to others." Id. at 410, 181 A.2d at 494. Some of the acute problems in developing an adequate conception of what constitutes *reciprocal* or *non-reciprocal* risk imposition are explored in Fletcher, "Fairness and Utility in Tort Theory," 85 *Harv. L. Rev.* 537 (1972).

76 In *Jost* v. *Dairyland Power Cooperative*, 45 Wis. 2d 164, 172 N.W.2d 647 (1969), a utility was liable in damages for pollution injuring nearby farmland and houses. Considering several justifications for liability, the court stated: "In any event it is apparent that a continued invasion of a plaintiff's interests by non-negligent conduct, when the actor knows of the nature of the injury inflicted, is an intentional tort, and the fact the hurt is administered non-negligently is not a defense to liability. . . . To contend that a public utility, in the pursuit of its praiseworthy and legitimate enterprise, can, in effect, deprive others of the full use of their property without compensation, poses a theory unknown to the law of Wisconsin, and in our opinion would constitute the taking of property without due process of law." Id. at 173–77, 172 N.W. 2d at 652–54. Compare *Lubin* v. *City of Iowa*, 257 Iowa 383, 131 N.W.2d 765 (1965), holding the city liable for damage from a break in the water main. "It is neither just nor reasonable that the city . . . can deliberately and intentionally plan to leave a watermain underground beyond inspection and maintenance until a break occurs and escape liability. . . . When the expected and inevitable occurs, [the city or corporation so operating] should bear the loss and not the unfortunate individual whose property is damaged without fault of his own." Id. at 390–91, 131 N.W.2d at 770.

77 In *Richman* v. *Charter Arms Corp.*, 571 F. Supp. 192 (E.D. La. 1983), the court considered whether the manufacture and marketing of handguns should be characterized as an abnormally dangerous activity, thereby subjecting businesses in such activities to strict liability for harm to victims of the illegal use of such guns. "The people who benefit most from marketing practices like the defendant's are handgun manufacturers and handgun purchasers. Innocent victims rarely, if ever, are beneficiaries. Consequently, it hardly seems unfair to require manufacturers and purchasers, rather than innocent victims, to pay for the risks those practices entail." Id. at 203. (The district court expressed these views in the context of a discussion of the criteria in sec. 520 of the Restatement (Second) of Torts. The

court of appeals, after a close review of the applicable state law of Louisiana, concluded that the marketing of handguns did not constitute an "ultrahazardous activity" under such law, and ordered judgment entered for the defendant manufacturer. *Richman* v. *Charter Arms Corp.*, 762 F.2d 1250 (5th Cir. 1985).)

78 *Bridegeman-Russell Co.* v. *City of Duluth,* 158 Minn. 509, 197 N.W. 971 (1924) involved a water-main break in a municipal system. The court noted that the damage could ruin an individual and said: "[E]ven though negligence be absent, natural justice would seem to demand that the enterprise, or what really is the same thing, the whole community benefited by the enterprise, should stand the loss rather than the individual. It is too heavy a burden upon one." Id. at 511, 197 N.W. at 972. The case was drawn upon in *Lubin* v. *Iowa City,* 257 Iowa 383, 131 N.W.2d 765 (1965), where the court said: "The risks from such a method of operation should be borne by the water supplier who is in a position to spread the cost among the consumers who are in fact the true beneficiaries of this practice and of the resulting savings in inspection and maintenance costs." Id. at 391, 131 N.W.2d at 770. Note 76 (chapter 3), supra, contains further relevant excerpts from the *Lubin* case, treating the question of the "intentional" character of the conduct and harm.

In *Beshada* v. *Johns-Manville Products Corp.,* 90 N.J. 191, 447 A.2d 539 (1982), involving asbestos-related illness, the court referred to corporations' "risk spreading" by incorporating insurance costs into the price of the product so that the product costs "will be borne by those who profit from it: the manufacturers and distributors who profit from its sale and the buyers who profit from its use. . . . [S]preading the costs of injuries among all those who produce, distribute and purchase manufactured products is far preferable to imposing it on the innocent victims who suffer illnesses and disability from defective products. This basic normative premise is at the center of our strict liability rules. . . . The burden of illness from dangerous products such as asbestos should be placed upon those who profit from its production and, more generally, upon society at large, which reaps the benefits of the various products our economy manufactures. That burden should not be imposed exclusively on the innocent victim." Id. at 205–6, 209, 447 A.2d at 547, 549.

Analogous justifications stressing proportionality in burdens and benefits inform other bodies of law germane to accidents. See, e.g., *Hicks* v. *State of New Mexico,* 88 N.M. 588, 544 P.2d 1153

(1976) (abolishing immunity of the state from liability in a negligence suit). They have also long informed distinct bodies of law such as constitutional decisions under the takings clause. See, e.g., *Monongahela Navigation Co. v. United States*, 148 U.S. 312, 325 (1893). The right to compensation when private property is taken "prevents the public from loading upon one individual more than his just share of the burdens of government. . . ."

79 In *Bierman v. City of New York*, 60 Misc. 2d 497, 302 N.Y.S.2d 696 (Civ. Ct., City of N.Y. 1969), the court specifically noted that the victim of an accident caused by a ruptured water main benefited from the water-distribution system (including the possible benefit of lower water rates under a regime of negligence rather than strict liability) only as one among many and should not bear the whole burden of the accident, but rather only her fair share as a part of loss spreading.

80 See Ames, "Law and Morals," 22 *Harv. L. Rev.* 97 (1908): "So that today we may say that the old law has been radically transformed. The early law asked simply, 'Did the defendant do the physical act which damaged the plaintiff?' The law of today, except in certain cases based upon public policy, asks the further question, 'Was the act blameworthy?' The ethical standard of reasonable conduct has replaced the unmoral standard of acting at one's peril. . . . We have seen how in the law of crimes and torts the ethical quality of the defendant's act has become the measure of his liability instead of the mere physical act regardless of the motive or fault of the actor." Id. at 99–100. Compare the discussion of grounds for liability in chapter 1 of J. Salmond, *The Law of Torts* (7th ed. W. Stallybrass 1928), and the related "Excursus A: The General Principles of Liability," id. at 63–70.

81 See chapter 4 of R. Pound, *An Introduction to the Philosophy of Law* (rev. ed. 1954). Pound refers to law in the nineteenth century as a "realization of the idea of liberty. . . . Liberty was the free will in action. Hence it was the business of the legal order to give the widest effect to the declared will and to impose no duties except in order to effectuate the will or to reconcile the will of one with the will of others by a universal law. . . . Liability could flow only from culpable conduct or from assumed duties. . . . The bases of liability were culpable conduct and legal transaction, and these came down to an ultimate basis in will." Id. at 79–80. Pound then points to the difficulty of reconciling negligence law as it had developed with this idea of will, because of the promi-

nence of the objective standard of care. He criticizes current proposals to extend civil liability without fault, as by expanding vicarious liability or product liability. The "humanitarian" and "insurance" principles underlying such proposals were fallacious. It was not a universal proposition that manufacturers could stand losses better than the accident victims. It was unsatisfactory to achieve "high humanitarian purposes" by making others "involuntary" Good Samaritans. Pound coupled his attacks on such proposals with attacks on the welfare state and social insurance. "[O]ne may well feel that much, at least, of the laudable humanitarian program is beyond practical attainment by law." Id. at 100–104.

82 The Nitro-Glycerine Case [*Parrot* v. *Wells, Fargo & Co.*], 82 U.S. (15 Wall.) 524, 538 (1872).

83 See the discussion about the relationship between the Hand Formula and ideas of fairness or respect at p. 51 and note 27 (chapter 3), supra.

84 *Losee* v. *Buchanan*, 51 N.Y. 476 (1873), held that, in its circumstances, liability for injury to another's property depended on "some fault or negligence" of the defendant. It referred to the factories and machinery that the country "must have." "If I have any of these upon my lands, and they are not a nuisance and are not so managed as to become such, I am not responsible for any damage they accidentally and unavoidably do my neighbor. He receives his compensation for such damage by the general good, in which he shares, and the right which he has to place the same things upon his lands." Id. at 484–85.

85 See the quotations from R. Pound, *An Introduction to the Philosophy of Law* (rev. ed. 1954), in note 81 (chapter 3), supra. Scholarly literature critical of loss spreading through tort law, including criticism related to my observations in text, is gathered and commented on in Ursin, "Judicial Creativity and Tort Law," 49 *Geo. Wash. L. Rev.* 229, 295–304 (1981).

86 With respect to the first type of redistributive goal, wealth redistribution, compare the distinction between historical principles and end-result or patterned principles of distribution in R. Nozick, *Anarchy, State and Utopia* 153–160 (1974).

87 Nonetheless, some judges view loss-spreading justifications as a way of soaking the rich. Such was the argument of the dissenting opinion in *Sindell* v. *Abbott Laboratories*, 26 Cal. 3d 588, 607 P.2d 924 (1980), a case involving alleged drug defects and subjecting the defendant drug manufacturers to a several liability

based on their market shares rather than on proof of a causal link between each of them and the plaintiff. The dissenting justice attacked the majority's "deep pocket" theory of liability of the manufacturers, "presumably because they are rich. . . ." That a defendant had better "ability to bear the cost" had no pertinence to liability. A system of equal protection of the laws "does not flower" when liability "is determined by a defendant's wealth." Such a view leads to "two rules of law—one applicable to wealthy defendants, and another . . . to defendants who are poor or who have modest means." Id. at 618, 607 P.2d at 941.

88 Among contemporary writings in moral and political theory treating issues of (re)distribution, J. Rawls, *A Theory of Justice* (1971) has had a major academic influence. Rawls develops two lexically ordered principles of justice, the second of which applies to the distribution of income and wealth. He treats both principles as a special case of a more general conception of justice as fairness—that all social values (including self-respect, income, and wealth) are to be distributed equally unless an unequal distribution is to everyone's advantage. Rawls refers to the two principles as the "maximin solution to the problem of social justice," a solution involving the maximization of the minimum possible position. Liberty, income, and wealth are to be distributed equally "unless an unequal distribution . . . is to the advantage of the least favored." Id. at 152, 303. Legal scholars have developed moral-legal arguments that are relevant to ideals of the welfare state such as the satisfaction of minimum needs. See, e.g., Michelman, "On Protecting the Poor through the Fourteenth Amendment," 83 *Harv. L. Rev.* 7 (1969); Michelman, "Welfare Rights in a Constitutional Democracy," 1979 *Wash. U. L. Q.* 659. For a radically different (nonpatterned) conception of distributive justice, see R. Nozick, *Anarchy, State, and Utopia* (1974).

89 Compare the opinion in *Codling* v. *Paglia*, 32 N.Y.2d 330, 298 N.E.2d 622 (1973), which talks of the mass-production and distribution system for the widest availability of goods. "Justice and equity would dictate the apportionment across the system of all related costs—of production, of distribution, of postdistribution liability. . . . Whatever the total cost, it will then be borne by those in the system, the producer, the distributor and the customer." Id. at 341, 298 N.E.2d at 628.

90 Cf. Abel, "A Critique of American Tort Law," 8 *Brit. J. L. & Soc.* 199 (1981). The author observes that "remedial discrimination is

internal to the tort system: the quantum of damages preserves, and indeed amplifies, the present unequal distribution of wealth and income." Id. at 202. The author notes illustratively that in an accident between a poor individual and a rich individual, the rich party if defendant will pay little for lost earnings or, probably, property damages, whereas the poor party if defendant would pay more. "This inequality is exaggerated by the fact that damages for pain and suffering are often expressed as a multiple of the pecuniary damages. . . ." Ibid. "Tort law . . . offers symbolic support for inequality. . . . By preserving the income streams of those who suffer physical injury (and of their dependents), tort law affirms the legitimacy of the existing income distribution. . . . Tort law proclaims the class structure of capitalist society: you are what you own, what you earn, and what you do." Id. at 206–207.

91 The court in *Wights* v. *Staff Jennings, Inc.*, 241 Or. 301, 405 P.2d 624 (1965) expressed a concern that "enterprise liability" with its stress on risk and loss spreading through business defendants "proves too much." Such an argument would require strict liability in all cases "where the loss could be distributed." If enterprise liability were so extended, "there is a strong argument for limiting the victim's measure of recovery to some scheme of compensation similar to that employed in workmen's compensation." The legislature alone has the power to set up such a compensation scheme. Id. at 309–10, 405 P.2d at 628–29.

92 Such considerations have led courts to question whether public-law programs are not the better route toward loss spreading. In *Schofield* v. *Merrill*, 386 Mass. 244, 435 N.E.2d 339 (1982), a bare majority of the court held to the rule immunizing landowners, even where they had been negligent, from liability to adult trespassers injured on their land. The court observed that the "temptation to extend liability in favor of trespassers is born of a desire to permit a reallocation of the costs of serious injuries. . . . A source of this tendency in the law is the thought that the costs of serious injuries should, through the medium of insurance, be borne by society at large. It has been said that the tendency of modern tort law has been in the direction of a system of liability without fault. . . . But concerns [of compensating the accident victim] more properly should be the subject of some sort of universal accident insurance system. They cannot, for reasons too numerous to mention, be addressed by the courts

on a piecemeal basis in the context of negligence law." Id. at 253, 435 N.E.2d at 344–45.

93 In *Maloney* v. *Rath*, 69 Cal. 2d 442, 445 P.2d 513 (1968), the court considered the types of problems that might arise in a regime of strict liability governing auto accidents. It imagined diverse types of accidents involving colliding cars. "Who is to be strictly liable to whom in such cases? However imperfectly it operates, the law of negligence allocates the risks and determines who shall or shall not be compensated when persons simultaneously engaged in the common enterprise of using the streets and highways have accidents. . . . A rule of strict liability would require its own attendant coterie of rules to allocate risk and govern compensation among co-users of the streets and highways." Id. at 445–46, 445 P.2d at 515. In *Ferguson* v. *Northern States Power Co.*, 307 Minn. 26, 239 N.W.2d 190 (1976), the court considered whether to classify high-voltage transmission wires as part of an abnormally dangerous activity that would subject the defendant to strict liability. It refused to do so. The court did point out that "a convincing argument can be made for holding the utility strictly liable. Moreover, spreading the cost of serious injury over all consumers of electricity is equitably more appealing. However, the court is persuaded by the amicus briefs which detail the severe economic consequences which may be sustained by the many small electric utilities in the state by the abrupt imposition of such a rule." Id. at 32, 239 N.W.2d at 194. See also R. Keeton, "Compensation for Medical Accidents," 121 *U. Pa. L. Rev.* 590 (1973) (problems of causation in medical cases).

94 In *Phillips* v. *Kimwood Machine Co.*, 269 Or. 485, 525 P.2d 1033 (1974), plaintiff employee sued a manufacturer for injury from a product defect. The defendant argued that risk and loss distribution was the principal rationale for strict product liability, and here plaintiff's employer could as well spread the cost of injury through its product pricing. The court stated: "While the enterprise liability theory may be indifferent as to whether the defendant or plaintiff's employer should bear this loss, there are other theories which allow us to make a choice. Where a defendant's product is adjudged by a jury to be dangerously defective, imposition of liability on the manufacturer will cause him to take some steps (or at least make calculations) to improve his product. Although such inducement may not be any greater under a system of strict liability than under a system of negligence recovery, it is certainly greater than if the liability was imposed

on another party simply because that other party was a better risk distributor. We suspect that, in the final analysis, the imposition of liability has a beneficial effect on manufacturers of defective products both in the care they take and in the warning they give." Id. at 503–4, 525 P.2d at 1041–42.

95 The most influential and developed of the systemic conceptions of the goals of accident law is that in G. Calabresi, *The Costs of Accidents* (1970), with its description of the interrelationships among three types of accident costs—primary (accident impacts), secondary (dislocation costs from accidents), and tertiary (transaction costs)—and of systems of liability rules seeking to reduce these costs.

96 There are exceptions. *Tillman v. Vance Equipment Co.*, 286 Or. 747, 596 P.2d 1299 (1979) decided against imposing strict liability for product defects on sellers of used goods generally. The court identified three justifications for strict product liability: risk-spreading ability, the reasonable expectation of the purchaser, and risk reduction, or incentive to the manufacturer to produce a better product. Used-goods dealers could achieve spreading, but "we are not convinced that the other two considerations . . . weigh sufficiently" to justify strict liability. Id. at 754, 596 P.2d at 1303. *Becker v. Interstate Properties*, 569 F.2d 1203 (3d Cir. 1977) examined the independent-contractor exception to vicarious liability. It said: "The three concerns of tort law outlined above—spreading costs, minimizing losses, assuring that an activity's risks are borne by its beneficiaries—will not always point in one direction. Often trade-offs among those considerations will be necessary. . . . But the case before us presents no occasion to face such difficulties . . ." since the three objectives "are all served by a single doctrine. . . ." Id. at 1214.

97 For explications and criticism of that ideology that are relevant to the following discussion, see M. Rheinstein, *Max Weber on Law in Economy and Society* (E. Shils and M. Rheinstein, trans. 1954) 144–47, 188–91 (1954); Kessler, "Contracts of Adhesion—Some Thoughts about Freedom of Contract," 43 *Colum. L. Rev.* 629 (1943); Kennedy, "Distributive and Paternalist Motives in Contract and Tort Law, with Special Reference to Compulsory Terms and Unequal Bargaining Power," 41 *Md. L. Rev.* 563, 568–70, 577–83 (1982).

98 These ideas are systematically developed in the writings of F. A. Hayek. See, e.g., *The Constitution of Liberty* (1960). Hayek states that we avoid coercion "by enabling the individual to secure for

himself some private sphere where he is protected. . . ." For such protection against coercion by others or the state, we need private property, which is "serviceable in the achievement of our aims . . . due mainly to the enforcibility of contracts. The whole network of rights created by contracts is as important a part of our own protected sphere . . . as any property of our own." Id. at 139, 141.

99 See C. Fried, *Contract as Promise: A Theory of Contractual Obligation* (1981). The author describes the critical role of contract within a liberal individualistic conception of society. The contract paradigm of society stresses the will of the parties and neutral enforcement by the judiciary, whereas in tort the role of the community in resolving conflict "is particularly prominent," for these resolutions are "involuntary transactions." Id. at 4. The discussion later refers to "the more communitarian standards of tort law." Id. at 21. In referring to the recent growth of product liability, R. Epstein, *Modern Products Liability Law* 6 (1980) states that "the entire system cares much less for contractual models for setting liability and much more for public law models of regulation—judicial regulation to be sure, but regulation nonetheless." See the related comparisons between contract and tort in *Victorson v. Bock Laundry Machine Co.*, 37 N.Y.2d 395, 400–403, 335 N.E.2d 275, 277–78 (1975).

100 Numerous articles within the broad tradition of "law and economics" have stressed the need for tort liability rules when transaction costs are too high for contracts realistically to be made—perhaps contracts stating liability rules. See, e.g., Calabresi and Melamed, "Property Rules, Liability Rules, and Inalienability: One View of the Cathedral," 85 *Harv. L. Rev.* 1089, 1106–10 (1972); Posner, "Strict Liability: A Comment," 2 *J. Legal Stud.* 205, 219 (1973). For an early and classic judicial explication of the distinction between contractual obligation (between related parties) and tort obligation (running to strangers), see the opinion of Shaw, C. J., in *Farwell v. The Boston and Worcester Rail Road Corp.*, 45 Mass. (4 Metc.) 49 (1842). Cf. the discussion of contract and regulation in Coase, "The Problem of Social Cost," 3 *J. Law & Econ.* 1, 15–19 (1960).

101 Courts upholding contract provisions have been franker with respect to such phenomena as coercion and unequal bargaining power. In holding relevant statutory regulation unconstitutional and therefore leaving in effect provisions in an employment contract prohibiting union membership, the court said in *Cop-*

page v. *Kansas,* 236 U.S. 1, 17 (1915): "No doubt, wherever the right of private property exists, there must and will be inequalities of fortune; and thus it naturally happens that parties negotiating about a contract are not equally unhampered by circumstances. This applies to all contracts. . . . [W]herever the right of private property and the right of free contract co-exist, each party when contracting is inevitably more or less influenced by the question whether he has much property, or little, or none. . . . [I]t is from the nature of things impossible to uphold freedom of contract and the right of private property without at the same time recognizing as legitimate those inequalities of fortune that are the necessary result of the exercise of those rights."

102 See, e.g., R. Posner, *Economic Analysis of Law* 1–24, 65–69, 84–88 (2d ed. 1977).

103 See C. Fried, *Contract as Promise: A Theory of Contractual Obligation* 1–21 (1981).

104 Kessler, "Contracts of Adhesion—Some Thoughts about Freedom of Contract," 43 *Colum L. Rev.* 629 (1943).

105 Numbers of themes relevant to these comments and to the following discussion are captured in a decision invalidating an exculpatory clause referring to medical services at a hospital, *Tunkl* v. *Regents of University of California,* 60 Cal. 2d 92, 383 P.2d 441 (1963). The court said in summary that an invalid exculpatory clause "involves a transaction which exhibits some or all of the following characteristics. It concerns a business of a type generally thought suitable for public regulation. The party seeking exculpation is engaged in performing a service of great importance to the public, which is often a matter of practical necessity for some members of the public. The party holds himself out as willing to perform this service for any member of the public who seeks it. . . . As a result of the essential nature of the service, in the economic setting of the transaction, the party invoking exculpation possesses a decisive advantage of bargaining strength against any member of the public who seeks his services. In exercising a superior bargaining power the party confronts the public with a standardized adhesion contract of exculpation, and makes no provision whereby a purchaser may pay additional reasonable fees and obtain protection against negligence." Id. at 98–100, 383 P.2d at 445–46.

106 *Henningsen* v. *Bloomfield Motors, Inc.,* 32 N.J. 358, 161 A.2d 69 (1960) invalidated a disclaimer in a standard-form sales contract

of an implied warranty. The court asserted that "[t]he traditional contract is the result of free bargaining of parties who are brought together by the play of the market, and who meet each other on a footing of approximate economic equality. In such a society there is no danger that freedom of contract will be a threat to the social order as a whole. But in present-day commercial life the standardized mass contract has appeared. . . ." Id. at 389, 161 A.2d at 86.

107 See Kennedy, "Distributive and Paternalist Motives in Contract and Tort Law, with Special Reference to Compulsory Terms and Unequal Bargaining Power," 41 *Md. L. Rev.* 563 (1982), for an analysis of methods and motivations in the judicial imposition of compulsory terms—for example, the invalidation of a disclaimer of an implied warranty. The author illustrates the character, difficulties, and ambiguities of efficiency, distributive, and paternalist motives and effects, and argues, despite its problems, for explicit judicial resort to the last.

108 In *Henningsen* v. *Bloomfield Motors, Inc.*, 32 N.J. 358, 161 A.2d 69 (1960), in commenting on the wording and effect of the disclaimer in a standard-form contract of an implied warranty, the court said: "An instinctively felt sense of justice cries out against such a sharp bargain." Id. at 388, 161 A.2d at 85. *Trentacost* v. *Brussel*, 82 N.J. 214, 412 A.2d 436 (1980), commenting on a provision in a standard-form lease contract, noted that in a situation of a housing shortage and unequal bargaining power of landlord and tenant, the tenant "cannot realize his legitimate present-day demands for fair treatment in the economic forum." Id. at 226, 412 A.2d at 442.

109 *Henrioulle* v. *Marin Ventures*, 20 Cal. 3d 512, 573 P.2d 465 (1978), involving a residential lease during a period of a housing shortage, noted that "tenants are likely to be in a poor position to bargain with landlords." Id. at 519, 573 P.2d at 469. *Henningsen* v. *Bloomfield Motors, Inc.*, 32 N.J. 358, 161 A.2d 69 (1960), observed that the disputed warranty disclaimer was in "a standardized form designed for mass use. It is imposed upon the automobile consumer." Id. at 390, 161 A.2d at 87. The manufacturer could not use superior bargaining power to insulate itself from liability "and to impose on the ordinary buyer, who in effect has no real freedom of choice, the grave danger of injury to himself and others" from dangerous machines. Id. at 404, 161 A.2d at 95.

110 See cases cited in notes 105, 106, and 108 (chapter 3), supra; Rakoff, "Contracts of Adhesion: An Essay in Reconstruction," 96 *Harv. L. Rev.* 1173, 1176–97 (1983).

111 *Hunter* v. *American Rentals, Inc.*, 189 Kan. 615, 371 P.2d 131
    (1962), involved an exculpatory clause related to a car-rental
    agreement. The accident's cause involved violation of a safety
    statute by the defendant. In invalidating the clause, the court
    said: "Contracts for exemption for liability from negligence are
    not favored by the law. . . . The rule is unqualifiedly laid down
    by many decisions that one cannot avoid liability for negligence
    by contract." The clause in question violated "public policy." Id.
    at 617, 371 P.2d at 133. *McCutcheon* v. *United Homes Corp.*, 79
    Wash. 2d 443, 486 P.2d 1093 (1971) invalidated an exculpatory
    clause in a lease. If the clause were upheld, destroying the land-
    lord's obligation to exercise due care in maintenance of the com-
    mon areas, *"the standard ceases to exist.* In short, such a clause
    destroys the concept of negligence in the landlord-tenant rela-
    tionship." Such a clause "offends the public policy of the state"
    because it "contravenes long established common law rules of
    tort liability. . . ." Id. at 447–48, 450, 486 P.2d at 1096–97.
112 See, e.g., M. Cohen, "Property and Sovereignty," 13 *Cor-
    nell L. Q.* 8 (1927); M. Cohen, "The Basis of Contract," 46
    Harv. L. Rev. 553 (1933); F. Cohen, "Transcendental Nonsense
    and the Functional Approach," 35 *Colum. L. Rev.* 809 (1935);
    Hale, "Bargaining, Duress, and Economic Liberty," 43 *Colum. L.
    Rev.* 603 (1943).
113 Some of these paired justifications or maxims appear to be in
    flat contradiction, whereas others could be reconciled in the
    sense that one part of the pair could be seen as a qualification or
    limited exception to the other. Compare the famous sets of
    "thrusts and parries" involving canons of statutory construction
    in K. Llewellyn, *The Common Law Tradition* 521–25 (1960).
114 Thus, many writers on tort law of the last fifty years whose
    works have been referred to in notes herein have been cited in
    appellate opinions. Without doubt, they have influenced the
    perceptions and directions of courts. The writers frequently
    cited by courts in contexts relevant to this chapter's analysis of
    justifications include Guido Calabresi, William O. Douglas,
    Richard Epstein, George Fletcher, Leon Green, Fowler Harper,
    Fleming James, Page Keeton, Robert Keeton, Richard Posner,
    William Prosser, and Warren Seavey.
115 The early and obvious illustration would be the workers' com-
    pensation laws. Judicial understanding of their ideals and pur-
    poses bears a close relationship to later judicial ideals and
    purposes in developing tort law. In *Ives* v. *South Buffalo Ry. Co.*,

201 N.Y. 271, 94 N.E. 431 (1911) (holding N.Y. law unconstitutional), the court stated: "[The law] is based upon the proposition that the inherent risks of an employment should in justice be placed upon the shoulders of the employer, who can protect himself against loss by insurance and by such an addition to the price of his wares as to cast the burden ultimately upon the consumer; that indemnity to an injured employ[ee] should be as much a charge upon the business as the cost of replacing . . . machinery . . . ; that, under our present system, the loss falls immediately upon the employ[ee] who is almost invariably unable to bear it, and ultimately upon the community which is taxed for the support of the indigent. . . ." Id. at 294, 94 N.E. at 439.

In *New York Central Railroad Co. v. White*, 243 U.S. 188 (1917) (sustaining a New York law as constitutional), the Court stated: "The pecuniary loss resulting from the employee's death or disablement must fall somewhere. It results from something done in the course of an operation from which the employer expects to derive a profit. . . . [Employer and employee] voluntarily engage in [the employment] as co-adventurers, with personal injury to the employee as a probable and foreseen result. . . . And it is evident that the consequences of a disabling or fatal injury are precisely the same to the parties immediately affected, and to the community, whether the proximate cause be culpable or innocent. . . . One of the grounds of [the statute's] concern with the continued life and earning power of the individual is its interest in the prevention of pauperism, with its concomitants of vice and crime." Id. at 205–7.

Borgnis v. Falk Co., 147 Wis. 327, 133 N.W. 209 (1911) upheld the Wisconsin law over a constitutional challenge. The court referred to the problem of the "toll of suffering and death which . . . industrialism levies" as "distinctly a modern problem. . . . Accidents there were in those days [of manual labor] and distressing ones, but they were relatively few, and the employ[ee] who exercised any reasonable degree of care was comparatively secure from injury. There was no army of injured and dying. . . ." The law was "framed to meet new economic conditions and difficulties. . . ." Id. at 347–48, 350, 133 N.W. at 215, 216.

In 1980, Congress enacted hazardous-waste legislation, the Comprehensive Environmental Response, Compensation, and Liability Act of 1980, 94 Stat. 2767. The legislative background to that Act included S. Rep. No. 848, 96th Cong., 2d Sess. (1980), a Report of the Committee on Environment and Public Works recommending an alternative, more ambitious measure, S. 1480, which failed of enactment. In explaining the reasons for strict-liability provisions for owners, transporters, and disposers of hazardous wastes (applicable in part to the enacted legislation) and for compensation of victims, the Report stated: "Strict liability is applied to these and other cases for a variety of reasons. Chief among these are questions of fairness and equity. One additional purpose of S.1480's strict liability scheme is to assure that the costs of injuries resulting from defective or hazardous substances are borne by the persons who create such risks rather than by the injured parties who are powerless to protect themselves. . . . By holding the factually responsible person liable, S. 1480 encourages that person . . . to eliminate as many risks as possible. But some risks cannot be eliminated. The question then is whether the loss should fall on the victim or the person who created the risk. The issue is really one of fundamental fairness. . . . In [cases of two blameless parties] the costs should be borne by the one of the two innocent parties whose acts instigated or made the harm possible." The Report then referred to "two benefits" flowing from strict liability: "(1) the adverse impact of any particular misfortune is lessened by spreading its cost over a greater population and over a larger time period; and (2) social and economic resources are more efficiently allocated when the actual costs of goods and services (including the losses they entail) are reflected in their prices to the consumer." Id. at 33–34.

CHAPTER 4. SOCIAL VISION

1 In developing the concept of social vision described in this chapter, I have benefited from several writings that are informed by closely related jurisprudential or social theoretical concepts. I here describe relevant aspects of two such writings about law.

Roscoe Pound, in "The Theory of Judicial Decision (Part I)," 36 *Harv. L. Rev.* 641 (1923), describes three elements that make up law: (1) legal precepts; (2) ideas about how precepts should be interpreted and applied and a related legal technique for developing precepts; and (3) "a body of philosophical, political, and ethical ideas as to the end of law . . . held consciously or subconsciously" with reference to which precepts and traditional ideas and techniques are continually reshaped. Pound illustrates this third element by referring to criteria by which courts determined if English doctrines were applicable to American conditions. "In fact, they determined what was applicable . . . by reference to an idealized picture of pioneer, rural, agricultural America of the fore part of the nineteenth century, and this picture became part of the law." Or, when passing upon social legislation toward the end of that century, courts "turned to an idealized picture of the economic order" involving maximum abstract individualism and self-expression.

"[W]e deceive ourselves grossly when we devise theories of law or theories of judicial decision that exclude such things from 'the law.' When such ideal pictures have acquired a certain fixity in the judicial and professional tradition they are part of 'the law' quite as much as legal precepts. Indeed, they give the latter their living content and in all difficult cases are the ultimate basis of choosing, shaping, and applying legal materials. . . ." Pound asserts that "[i]deal pictures of the social order" direct growth and change in law "so as to maintain the general security." Although ideal pictures change, and hence influence change in precepts and techniques, they are understood by Pound largely as a rationalizing and stabilizing force in law. "[W]e must learn how to supply substantially the same ideal picture of the social order to all our judicial magistrates, and to make it the best, the most critical, and the most complete that is compatible with social progress." Id. at 645, 652–54, 657, 662.

The second writing is an unpublished draft by my colleague Richard Parker, "Political Vision in Constitutional Argument," Part I (draft of February 1979). Parker describes the life of constitutional law as constitutional argument. He explores the "practice of constitutional argument as a cultural artifact, a figurative mode of political legitimation, shaped by our vision of the present reality and possible perfection of our political life." Such practice constructs and communicates "an ideology of political order." Constitutional argument constitutes "one mode of political legitimation," explaining and justifying the phenomenon and use of power.

Parker sets forth the requirements that political argument must meet to constitute a mode of political legitimation, and then describes his "conception of political vision as the spring of constitutional argument." Conventional modes of constitutional

argument "figuratively communicate ideological assumptions—
general assumptions of political life—through their characteristic rhetoric and their characteristic metaphor. . . . They also
. . . spring from just such ideological assumptions." The assumptions conveyed by argument are drawn from those "that
are dominant, and so will ease persuasion, in the political
culture." Beneath a mode of argument, "structuring it, is a particular combination of prescriptive and descriptive pictures of
political life." Particular modes of constitutional argument, and
thus underlying ideological constructs, change throughout history as the "needs of legitimation" change. Political vision "de-
notes the *medium* or the *prism* through which we take on the tacit
ideological enterprise of satisfying the requirements of legitimation." It involves an *"imaginative construction* of political life tacitly going on under constitutional argument." Thus the
understanding of political vision is meant to illuminate the phenomenon of argument "as the expression of a profound political
ideology—of several competing visions of the reality and perfection of political life. . . ." (Quotations are taken from pp. 1–3,
77–87 of the February 1979 draft.)

A reading of chapter 4 will best reveal the relation between
my use of social vision and the concepts in the cited writings
(very different from each other) of "ideal pictures" and "political
vision." The similarities are evident. My concept, too, is meant
to illuminate the character of argument as well as the different
types of rhetoric that inform it. I, too, emphasize the degree to
which vision underlies and permeates argument, and illustrate
ways in which social vision has both descriptive and prescriptive
elements involving at once the description and creation of a social reality.

But "social vision" as used herein differs in important ways.
It is less characterized by ideal pictures or evocative metaphors
or basic ideologies about the polity at large, and more characterized by perceptions of varied and concrete phenomena of social life. It expresses how courts comprehend and evaluate what
they see, how they grasp the situation before them. It expresses
their insights and intuitions about that situation rather than
their imaginative constructions of social life or their responses to
the need for legitimation of power. My use of "vision" is, if you
will, less visionary. It has more to do with modes of perception
and less to do with emotive pictures of the world or with ideologies.

2 See note 7 (chapter 3), supra, for comments about my method in supporting observations about justifications. Here, too, I should note that my organizing concepts as well as many particular observations cannot be directly supported—in, say, the detailed manner of doctrinal observations—by quotation from the opinions. But my argument is that these concepts inhere in the opinions, and that the particular observations about social vision can be derived from my descriptions of and quotations from appellate opinions throughout this essay. Given the breadth of my themes, there is an inevitable need for inference and extrapolation. For example, I ground my claim about a systemic social vision in what courts have said about doctrine, insurance, loss spreading, behavior modification, and so on. At times I push my analysis further, to seek out more detailed implications of judicially expressed justifications and elements of social vision. Thus, my comments about the changing vision of the corporation grow out of quotations from earlier cases that liability could intimidate or ruin a defendant, quotations from modern cases alert to possibilities of market spreading, and so on. See p. 105, infra.

3 See Schwartz, "Tort Law and the Economy in Nineteenth-Century America: A Reinterpretation," 90 *Yale L. J.* 1717 (1981), for a description of California and New Hampshire cases expressing sympathy for the injured, rigorously applying the negligence standard against corporate defendants, and restricting the scope of contributory fault. See particularly pp. 1749, 1752, 1755–56, 1760–63.

4 See cases cited in note 70 (chapter 3), supra.

5 In *Dippel* v. *Sciano*, 37 Wis. 2d 443, 155 N.W.2d 55 (1967), the court observed: "We have long since passed from the unsure days of industrial revolution to a settled and affluent society where we must be concerned about the just claims of the injured and hapless user or consumer of industrial products. The doctrines of *laissez nous faire* and *caveat emptor* have given way to more humane considerations." Id. at 450, 155 N.W.2d at 58.

6 Legal scholarship has been attentive to this rise of liability insurance and its relevance to the justifications for strict liability. See the discussion of the implications of the development of liability insurance in Douglas, "Vicarious Liability and Administration of Risk," 38 *Yale L. J.* 584, 591 (1929); F. James, "Accident Law Reconsidered: The Impact of Liability Insurance," 57 *Yale L. J.* 549, 551–70 (1948); Gardner, "Insurance against Tort Liability—An

Approach to the Cosmology of the Law," 15 *Law & Contemp. Prob.* 455, 461–63 (1950); Jaffe, "Damages for Personal Injury: The Impact of Insurance," 18 *Law & Contemp. Prob.* 219 (1953). See generally C. Crobaugh and A. Redding, *Casualty Insurance* (1928) (tracing evolution of liability and other forms of insurance); McNeely, "The Genealogy of Liability Insurance Law," 7 *U. Pitt. L. Rev.* 169 (1941).

7 The court stated in *Barker* v. *Lull Engineering Co., Inc.*, 20 Cal. 3d 413, 434–35, 573 P.2d 443, 457 (1978), a case involving a design defect: "The technological revolution has created a society that contains dangers to the individual never before contemplated. The individual must face the threat to life and limb not only from the car on the street or highway but from a massive array of hazardous mechanisms and products. The radical change from a comparatively safe, largely agricultural, society to this industrial unsafe one has been reflected in the decisions that formerly tied liability to the fault of a tortfeasor but now are more concerned with the safety of the individual who suffers the loss." Courts perceive and signal other types of change in society that occasion accidents. *Trentacost* v. *Brussel*, 82 N.J. 214, 412 A.2d 436 (1980) involved a claim that a landlord had failed to provide proper security to prevent a crime against the plaintiff. The court noted that crime "is an inescapable fact of modern life. Its presence threatens the suburban enclave as well as the inner city." Modern apartments were "not habitable" without reasonable measures of security against crime. Id. at 227, 412 A.2d at 443. See also note 29 (chapter 4), infra, and note 8 (chapter 5), infra.

8 Here, as elsewhere in this essay, I do not mean to suggest a clear boundary between older and modern cases, but a trend. A perception of growing numbers of accidents related to industrialization was apparent in some nineteenth-century opinions, though the phenomenon was viewed differently and not thought to point toward heightened liability. For example, *Beatty* v. *Central Iowa Railway Co.*, 58 Iowa 242, 12 N.W. 332 (1882) refused to impose liability on a railroad for an accident at a crossing. The court observed: "It is not possible that a highway crossed by a railroad shall be as safe as before the railroad was constructed. There will and always must be some danger from collision, and from fright to animals, which did not exist before." Id. at 248, 12 N.W. at 335.

9 This understanding is most vivid in opinions dealing with legislative regulation or plans. An early case is *Borgnis* v. *Falk Co.*, 147 Wis. 327, 133 N.W. 209 (1911), upholding the state workers' compensation law and referring to the "army of injured and dying, with constantly swelling ranks" as "distinctly a modern problem." Id. at 348, 133 N.W. at 215. Decisions passing on the constitutionality of no-fault automobile plans are rich in statistical understanding of the automobile-accident problem. See, e.g., *Pinnick* v. *Cleary*, 360 Mass. 1, 271 N.E.2d 592 (1971) and *Shavers* v. *Kelley*, 402 Mich. 554, 267 N.W.2d 72 (1978). Compare the discussion in *American Textile Manufacturers Institute* v. *Donovan*, 452 U.S. 490, 495–505 (1981) (reviewing the cotton-dust standard set by OSHA), of the external costs of accidents. There are numerous cases in a common-law context that refer to the developing or the "well-known" and serious costs or incidence of injuries in one or another setting. See, e.g., *McConville* v. *State Farm Mutual Automobile Insurance Co.*, 15 Wis. 2d 374, 382–83, 113 N.W.2d 14, 19 (1962) (automobiles).

10 Contemporary approaches of courts to mass accidents, including the use of class actions, are summarized in P. Keeton, R. Keeton, L. Sargentich, and H. Steiner, *Tort and Accident Law* 805–808 (1983).

11 Numerous decisions, for example, dealing with car accidents have commented on their growing incidence. *Marcus* v. *Everett*, 195 Neb. 518, 239 N.W.2d 487 (1976) involved application of the family-purpose doctrine to such an accident. The court said: "The family purpose doctrine was developed as a response to the advent of motor vehicle transportation and the inevitable, numerous, and often serious mishaps resulting from the use of the car." It stressed the relevance to its decision of "the policy considerations concerning the alleviation of the burden of costs in the aftermath of often traumatic and expensive auto accidents." Id. at 530, 239 N.W.2d at 494. *Immer* v. *Risko*, 56 N.J. 482, 267 A.2d 481 (1970), involving a question of interspousal immunity, stated: "In a day when automobile accidents are unfortunately becoming so frequent and the injuries suffered by the passengers are often so severe," it was unjust to deny all claims for negligence between spouses because of fear of fraud against the insurer. Id. at 495, 267 A.2d at 488. *Spier* v. *Barker*, 35 N.Y.2d 444, 323 N.E.2d 164 (1974) involved the issue of reduction of damages because of plaintiff's failure to use a seat belt. The court

observed: "Highway safety has become a national concern. . . ."
Id. at 452, 323 N.E.2d at 168.

12 *Chavez* v. *Southern Pacific Transportation Co.*, 413 F. Supp. 1203
(E.D. Cal. 1976) dealt with the problem of abnormally dangerous activities and observed (quoting from an earlier case) that
the defenseless victim's losses were apt to be substantial, an
"overwhelming misfortune to the person injured." Id. at 1209.
An accident stemming from a water-main break in *Bridgeman-
Russell Co.* v. *City of Duluth,* 158 Minn. 509, 197 N.W. 971 (1924),
led the court to state: "If a break occurs in the reservoir itself, or
in the principal mains, the flood may utterly ruin an individual
financially. . . . It is too heavy a burden upon one." Id. at 511,
197 N.W. at 972. *Beshada* v. *Johns-Manville Products Corp.*, 90 N.J.
191, 447 A.2d 539 (1982) observed in a setting of product liability: "Although victims must in any case suffer the pain involved, they should be spared the burdensome financial
consequences of unfit products." Id. at 209, 447 A.2d at 549.
Compare an older decision, the Nitro-Glycerine Case [*Parrot* v.
Wells, Fargo and Co.] 82 U.S. (15 Wall.) 524 (1872), concluding
that the injury was the result of an "unavoidable accident" so
that the defendant was not liable: "The consequences of all such
accidents must be borne by the sufferer as his misfortune." Id. at
538.

13 The courts upholding the constitutionality of and interpreting
the early workers' compensation acts were sensitive to these di-
mensions of the new legislation. See the quotations from *New
York Central Railroad Co.* v. *White,* 243 U.S. 188, 205–7 (1917), note
115 (chapter 3), supra. *Borgnis* v. *Falk Company,* 147 Wis. 327, 133
N.W. 209 (1911) referred to "the toll of suffering and death
which . . . industrialism levies and must continue to levy upon
the civilized world." Id. at 347, 133 N.W. at 215. Whatever legislation might be enacted about safety or recovery within the common law, "the army of the injured will still increase, the price of
our manufacturing greatness will still have to be paid in human
blood and tears." Id. at 348, 133 N.W. at 215. Contemporary
courts evince ever-greater concern for the external as well as private costs of accidents. *McConville* v. *State Farm Mutual Automobile Insurance Co.*, 15 Wis. 2d 374, 113 N.W.2d 14 (1962) dealt
with the guest-host rule and assumption of risk in the context of
an auto accident. The court commented that the guest-host rule
may have been acceptable decades ago when accidents "were
less frequent and probably had less disastrous results. The se-

rious consequences following automobile accidents today are well known. . . . In view of the seriousness of many injuries, and the burdens falling upon the community as well as the individual and families affected," the court doubted that assumption of risk should bar recovery. Id. at 382–83, 113 N.W.2d at 19.

14 Courts have linked the availability of insurance to loss-spreading justifications for modern heightened liability for decades. See, e.g., the concurrence of Justice Traynor in *Escola* v. *Coca-Cola Bottling Co. of Fresno,* 24 Cal. 2d 453, 150 P.2d 436 (1944): "The cost of an injury and the loss of time or health may be an overwhelming misfortune to the person injured, and a needless one, for the risk of injury can be insured by the manufacturer and distributed among the public as a cost of doing business." Id. at 462, 150 P.2d at 441. Courts have come to stress availability of insurance as part of the justification for vicarious liability. For example, *Fruit* v. *Schreiner,* 502 P.2d 133 (Alaska 1972) observed that insurance "is readily available for the employer so that the risk may be distributed" among the insureds and costs could be spread through product pricing. Id. at 141. In characterizing a salesman as an agent rather than a servant, so that vicarious liability did not apply, a court has noted that the salesman-driver, "as owner, can distribute the risk of driving . . . by taking out insurance better than, or at least as well as, his principal." *Stockwell* v. *Morris,* 46 Wyo. 1, 22, 22 P.2d 189, 195 (1933). For a discussion of the relevance of liability insurance, today and during earlier periods, to the doctrine of nonliability for acts of independent contractors, see *Becker* v. *Interstate Properties,* 569 F.2d 1203, 1210 (3d Cir. 1977).

Insurance has also been important to the expansion of liability within the framework of the negligence system. See, e.g., *Pierce* v. *Yakima Valley Memorial Hospital Ass'n.,* 43 Wash. 2d 162, 172, 260 P.2d 765, 771 (1953) (immunity of charitable institution); *Sidle* v. *Majors,* 536 F.2d 1156, 1158–59 (7th Cir. 1976) (guest-host statute).

15 For example, *McConville* v. *State Farm Mutual Automobile Insurance Co.,* 15 Wis. 2d 374, 113 N.W.2d 14 (1962), holding that neither the guest-host rule nor the doctrine of assumption of risk barred recovery in a claim based on an automobile accident, stated: "Liability insurance is widely prevalent today. In few cases will the new rule shift the burden of loss from the injured guest to the negligent host personally. In the great majority of

cases it will shift part or all of the burden of loss from the injured individual to the motoring public." Id. at 383, 113 N.W.2d at 19.

16 See *Holodook* v. *Spencer,* 36 N.Y. 2d 35, 324 N.E.2d 338 (1974), for a detailed analysis of the implications of the likelihood or not of a defendant being insured for a liability rule, there for the question of a parent's liability to children for negligent supervision leading to their injury by a third party.

17 In *Borer* v. *American Airlines, Inc.,* 19 Cal. 3d 441, 563 P.2d 858 (1977), the court refused to recognize a cause of action in children for loss of consortium with their parents. "We cannot ignore the social burden of providing damages for loss of parental consortium merely because the money to pay such awards comes initially from the 'negligent' defendant or his insurer. Realistically the burden of payment of awards for loss of consortium must be borne by the public generally in increased insurance premiums or, otherwise, in the enhanced danger that accrues from the greater number of people who may choose to go without any insurance." Id. at 447, 563 P.2d at 862. See the dissenting opinion in *Mayer* v. *Housing Authority of the City of Jersey City,* 44 N.J. 567, 210 A.2d 617 (1965), which treats the liability imposed by the majority on a public housing authority as effectively "strict," resting on the notion that "the party best able to bear or distribute the loss should be liable." Availability of insurance "undergirds" such theory, but the theory may be "constructed on sand." Public liability insurance is difficult to obtain and costly, and if as a practical matter it is unavailable, "the risk is not distributed." Even if it is available, the extra costs from insurance may rest on tenants as well as taxpayers, but only if the latter bear the cost is there "a true distribution of risk." Id. at 579–80, 210 A.2d at 624–25.

18 The fundamental principles and conceptions (risk, loss, insurance categories, and so on) are explicated in basic texts such as H. Denenberg, R. Eilers, J. Melone, and R. Zelten, *Risk and Insurance* 3–78, 149–69, 211–30 (2d ed. 1974), and R. Mehr and E. Cammack, *Principles of Insurance* 16–43 (7th ed. 1980).

19 Compare *Ryan* v. *New York Central Railroad Co.,* 35 N.Y. 210 (1866), limiting the liability of a railroad for a negligently caused fire to the first structure damaged. "A man may insure his own house. . . . In a commercial country, each man, to some extent, runs the hazard of his neighbor's conduct, and each, by insurance against such hazards, is enabled to obtain a reasonable security against loss." Id. at 216–17. In *Mahowald* v. *Minnesota Gas*

Co., 344 N.W.2d 856 (Minn. 1984), the court refused to hold a gas distributor strictly liable for injury from a leak in a gas main located on public streets and over which the distributor did not have exclusive control. In discussing the insurance rationale for strict liability, id. at 861, the court said: "If adopted, the ratepayers pay the damage for those few who may sustain damage to person or property. On the other hand, in the typical explosion case involving a home, such as the one at bar, the insurance rationale is likewise present under the negligence standard. For example, the record here shows that the [plaintiffs] had homeowners insurance." The court noted the lesser liability of the distributor under a negligence standard but said, id. at 862: "However, in most cases, as in this case, it is not the innocent victim who bears the loss, but rather an insurance company which collected premiums to insure the loss for which it may seek recoupment if the utility was, in fact, negligent."

Offshore Rental Co., Inc., v. *Continental Oil Co.*, 22 Cal. 3d 157, 583 P.2d 721 (1978) involved a choice-of-law issue in the context of a tort action permitted under California law but denied under Louisiana law. In resolving that issue in favor of Louisiana law, the court found the question of availability of insurance to be relevant. It compared arguments that the plaintiff (a California corporation) ought to have taken out first-party insurance to protect itself, or that the defendant (doing business in Louisiana) ought to have aquired liability insurance. In the circumstances, it concluded that the "burden of obtaining insurance for the loss at issue here is most properly borne by the plaintiff corporation." Id. at 169, 583 P.2d at 729. Note that all three opinions treat property or business losses rather than personal injury, which would make relevant the victim's health insurance.

20 See, e.g, *Helfend* v. *Southern California Rapid Transit Dist.*, 2 Cal. 3d 1, 465 P.2d 61 (1970); *Reid* v. *District of Columbia*, 391 A.2d 776 (D.C. App. 1978).

21 One of the most powerful expressions of such ideas remains that of Justice Traynor in his concurrence in *Escola* v. *Coca-Cola Bottling Co. of Fresno*, 24 Cal. 2d 453, 150 P.2d 436 (1944): "Manufacturing processes . . . are ordinarily either inaccessible to or beyond the ken of the general public. The consumer no longer has means or skill enough to investigate for himself the soundness of a product. . . . [H]is erstwhile vigilance has been lulled" by the efforts of manufacturers to build confidence through advertising and trademarks. Id. at 467, 150 P.2d at 443. *Henningsen*

v. *Bloomfield Motors, Inc.*, 32 N.J. 358, 161 A.2d 69 (1960), a case invalidating the disclaimer of an implied warranty, observed that warranties had been developed "in the interest of and to protect the ordinary consumer who cannot be expected to have the knowledge or capacity or even the opportunity to make adequate inspection of mechanical instrumentalities . . . and to decide for himself whether they are reasonably fit for the designed purpose." Id. at 375, 161 A.2d at 78. The court said in *Codling* v. *Paglia*, 32 N.Y.2d 330, 340, 298 N.E.2d 622, 627 (1973): "Today as never before the product in the hands of the consumer is often a most sophisticated and even mysterious article." Consumers cannot investigate its structure, and "its functional validity and usefulness often depend on the application of electronic, chemical or hydraulic principles far beyond the ken of the average consumer." Advances in technology "have put it almost entirely out of the reach of the consumer to comprehend why or how the article operates. . . ."

22 Thus, a court will note that, with respect to medication, a consumer "is virtually helpless to protect himself" against injuries from defective drugs. *Sindell* v. *Abbott Laboratories*, 26 Cal. 3d 588, 611, 607 P.2d 924, 936 (1980). Or a court will note that, in modern multifamily dwellings, "the tenant is almost wholly dependent upon the landlord" to keep common areas safe. *McCutcheon* v. *United Homes Corp.*, 79 Wash. 2d 443, 446, 486 P.2d 1093, 1095 (1971).

23 See notes 105–9 (chapter 3), supra.

24 See note 35 (chapter 3), supra.

25 See the excerpts from *Beatty* v. *Central Iowa Railway Co.*, 58 Iowa 242, 12 N.W. 332 (1882), note 36 (chapter 3), supra.

26 See note 70 (chapter 3), supra.

27 Compare the discussion of the rhetoric of individualism and altruism in Kennedy, "Form and Substance in Private Law Adjudication," 89 *Harv. L. Rev.* 1685, 1713–24 (1976).

28 Several writings on contemporary civil litigation seeking structural reform (such as desegregation suits or suits to reform prisons) and involving class actions, complex injunctive decrees, and bureaucratic institutional defendants, have characterized phenomena that they describe in ways analogous to my description of systemic and dyadic visions of social life in tort opinions. See, e.g., Chayes, "The Role of the Judge in Public Law Litigation," 89 *Harv. L. Rev.* 1281, 1291, 1302 (1976): "The class suit is a reflection of our growing awareness that a host of important

public and private interactions . . . are conducted on a routine or bureaucratized basis and can no longer be visualized as bilateral transactions between private individuals." The subject of lawsuits in the "public law" idiom "is not a dispute between private individuals about private rights, but a grievance about the operation of public policy."

My colleague Lewis Sargentich, in "Complex Enforcement" (unpublished draft of March 1978), describes judicial activity "stimulated by the perception that society may be deeply at odds with the norms of its own legal order," so that "adjudication must not only denounce but also transform offending social practice." Sargentich stresses the "systematic conception of the wrong to be addressed," a wrong that "has a kind of system and structure to it that may be captured in the idea of wrongful practice." He describes complex enforcement as "a type of adjudication in which the wrong is a practice, the remedy is a plan, and the party structure aims at collective resolution." The practice "involves on-going behavior" so that adjudication leading to complex enforcement "by nature has a prospective concern about how the future ought to be organized."

Sargentich also describes the norm brought to bear on the practice as systemic rather than discrete, systemic norms expressing substantive legal principles that "may be brought to bear upon behavior having the character of a practice" whereas discrete norms "include all the law that addresses particular collisions that may occur in social life, discrete clashes and breakdowns. . . ." Relief, a complex injunctive decree, shares the systemic character of the criticized practice and the critical norm, for "the remedy in a practice suit takes the form of a system of prescriptions, or a plan, and in this respect it has the character of the thing it addresses." (Quotations are taken from pp. 3, 8, 12, 15, and 24 of the March 1978 draft.) Although Sargentich analyzes a distinct phenomenon of American law within a distinct conceptual vocabulary, there are analogies between his polar concepts (systematic and discrete, practice and conduct), and my use of the polarity of systemic and dyadic to capture the changing vision within substantive tort law.

29 Three diverse contexts for judicial comments suggest something of the range of systemic perceptions. *Payton* v. *Abbott Labs*, 83 F.R.D. 382 (D. Mass. 1979) involved a class action by actual and potential victims of an allegedly defective drug. The court said, with respect to marketing of drugs: "Traditional models of litiga-

tion, pitting one plaintiff against one defendant, were not designed to, and cannot, deal with the potential for injury to numerous and geographically dispersed persons that mass marketing presents." Courts must adapt traditional methods to these problems—as by use of the class action under Fed. R. Civ. Proc. 23(b)(3)—or face the choice of "leaving large numbers of people without a practical means of redress." F.R.C.P. 23(b)(3) offered the best means of adapting "an established and tested structure to a modern phenomenon." Id. at 390.

McCutcheon v. *United Homes Corp.*, 79 Wash. 2d 443, 486 P.2d 1093 (1971) involved an exculpatory clause in a lease. The court stated that leases could not be characterized as a matter of private concern rather than of public interest. This was no longer a society of occasional rental of rooms in private houses. The leasing business "has developed into a major commercial enterprise directly touching the lives of hundreds of thousands of people who depend upon it for shelter." The case didn't involve "an isolated contract specifically bargained for by *one landlord and one tenant* as a purely private affair. Considered realistically, we are asked to construe an exculpatory clause, the generalized use of which may have an impact upon thousands of potential tenants." Id. at 449–50, 486 P.2d at 1097.

The opinion in *Cities Service Co.* v. *State of Florida*, 312 So. 2d 799 (Fla. App. 1975) justified a *Rylands*-style strict liability for an abnormally dangerous activity. "In a frontier society there was little likelihood that a dangerous use of land could cause damage to one's neighbor. Today our life has become more complex. Many areas are so overcrowded, and even the non-negligent use of one's land can cause extensive damages to a neighbor's property." Id. at 801.

30 See the illustrations from nineteenth-century opinions in notes 35 and 36 (chapter 3), supra.

31 *Fruit* v. *Schreiner*, 502 P.2d 133 (Alaska 1972), a vicarious-liability case, expresses some of the ambiguity and paradox in the notion of interdependence. The court notes that older work relationships were more communal. Present-day division of labor and anonymity led to the sacrifice of the older "communal spirit and shared commitment." Nonetheless, the court stressed the "duty of every enterprise to the social community which gives it life and contributes to its prosperity." The corporation could not insulate itself from the social consequences of its action. Id. at 140–41. *Lyshak* v. *City of Detroit*, 351 Mich. 230, 88 N.W.2d 596

(1958), expanded the duty of a landowner toward a child trespasser. The court explained: "A simple agrarian society has been replaced by a crowded urban industrial society." Landowners were no longer absolute owners, and their rights "are not absolute but are relative." "The community has an interest in the life of a child. The preservation of that life is a proper factor to be weighed against a landowner's right to the exclusive possession of his land and the use he makes of it." Id. at 241–42, 244, 88 N.W.2d at 602–3.

32 In *Shingleton* v. *Bussey*, 223 So. 2d 713 (Fla. 1969), the court struck down a contractual "no joinder" clause in an automobile-liability insurance policy and allowed the victim to sue the tortfeasor and insurer jointly. In other states this result is reached through a "direct action" statute. Many issues remain to be resolved in such circumstances—for example, whether the victim or insurer should be allowed to inform the jury of the policy limits.

33 See Chayes, "The Role of the Judge in Public Law Litigation," 89 *Harv. L. Rev.* 1281 (1976); Fiss, "The Forms of Justice," 93 *Harv. L. Rev.* 1 (1979). For classic instances of injunctive relief for groups in the context of long-continuing class-action litigation involving institutions for the mentally ill and retarded, see two lower-court opinions: *Wyatt* v. *Stickney*, 344 F. Supp. 387 (M.D. Ala. 1972), and *Halderman* v. *Pennhurst State School & Hospital*, 446 F. Supp. 1295 (E.D. Pa. 1977). (For later appellate decisions in these two instances of structural-reform litigation, see *Wyatt* v. *Aderholt*, 503 F.2d 1305 (5th Cir. 1974), and *Pennhurst State School & Hospital* v. *Halderman*, 104 S. Ct. 900 (1984).

34 For a list of recent class actions involving tort claims, see P. Keeton, R. Keeton, L. Sargentich, and H. Steiner, *Tort and Accident Law* 807–8 (1983).

35 See note 7 (chapter 5), infra.

36 See *Bichler* v. *Eli Lilly and Co.*, 79 A.D.2d 317, 436 N.Y.S.2d 625 (1981), aff'd, 55 N.Y.2d 571, 436 N.E.2d 182 (1982).

37 See the discussion in P. Keeton, D. Dobbs, R. Keeton, and D. Owen, *Prosser and Keeton on The Law of Torts* 322–30 (5th ed. 1984).

38 *Sindell* v. *Abbott Laboratories*, 26 Cal. 3d 588, 607 P.2d 924 (1980) (reversing lower court's dismissal of complaint and remanding).

39 See notes 6 and 18 (chapter 4), supra.

40 See, e.g., *Woodill* v. *Parke Davis & Co.*, 79 Ill. 2d 26, 402 N.E.2d 194 (1980).

41 The court in *Hall v. E. I. DuPont De Nemours & Co.*, 345 F. Supp. 353 (E.D.N.Y. 1972), observed, with respect to loss-spreading justifications for strict liability, that despite all care, some accidents were inevitable. "Accidents and injuries, in this view, are seen as an inevitable and statistically foreseeable 'cost' of the product's consumption or use." What was "important" in enterprise liability was the general foreseeability of risk that an enterprise was likely to create rather than the idea in the negligence standard of risk of specific conduct in specific circumstances. Liability for harm from the typical risks of an activity were thus (quoting Ehrenzweig, "Negligence without Fault," 54 *Calif. L. Rev.* 1422, 1457 (1966)) "calculable and reasonably insurable." Id. at 368–69.

    Courts earlier made similar observations when drawing on analogies to workers' compensation, as occurred in a vicarious-liability case, *Kohlman v. Hyland*, 54 N.D. 710, 210 N.W. 643 (1926). The court there described the "underlying philosophy" of workers' compensation to be that industry bear the risk of injury. "There is always present the possibility of injury to employees, notwithstanding every conceivable precaution may be taken to guard against it. So it is when we look at the situation from the viewpoint of the public. There is an everpresent risk that third persons will suffer injury because somebody's servant is careless, disobedient, or unfaithful to his master. This . . . risk . . . is clearly one which industry, on the analogy of the Compensation Acts, may well be required to carry, within reasonable bounds." Id. at 716, 210 N.W. at 645.

42 See, e.g., *Usery v. Turner Elkhorn Mining Co.*, 428 U.S. 1 (1976) (presumptions for black-lung disease). See S. Rep. No. 848, 96th Cong., 2d Sess. (1980), accompanying a bill (S. 1480) that failed of enactment. Pp. 108–22 of the Report treat Section 4 of the bill (compensation of victims) and issues of causation.

43 For a proposal that courts, particularly in the context of class actions, determine causation under a proportionality rule that would hold manufacturers of toxic agents liable for the proportion of total injuries attributable to their products, see Rosenberg, "The Causal Connection in Mass Exposure Cases: A 'Public Law' Vision of the Tort System," 97 *Harv. L. Rev.* 851 (1984). See *In re "Agent Orange" Product Liability Litigation*, 597 F. Supp. 740 (E.D.N.Y. 1984), tentatively approving a settlement in a class action between plaintiff class and defendant chemical companies. In discussing the settlement, the court (at 833–43)

considered approvingly the role of a pro rata or proportionate liability rule, based on statistical evidence of causation, in class-action settlements. The court noted (at 748): "At the present time, however, it is doubtful whether the legal system is ready to employ this [pro rata] device except, perhaps, as part of an overall settlement plan voluntarily entered into by the parties."

44 E.g., *Stubbs* v. *City of Rochester,* 226 N.Y. 516, 524–26, 124 N.E. 137, 139–40 (1919); *Allen* v. *United States,* 588 F. Supp. 247, 404–43 (D. Utah 1984) (use of statistical evidence to show that fallout from testing of atomic devices was a substantial factor in causing plaintiffs' cancers).

45 *Sindell* v. *Abbott Laboratories,* 26 Cal. 3d 588, 607 P.2d 924 (1980), involving the drug DES. The court attached several conditions to such a several liability, including a requirement that the plaintiff join in the action a sufficient number of defendants so that they collectively represent a "substantial share" of the relevant market for the product. The market-share approach contrasts with a more traditional conception, that of a joint tort liability among joint tortfeasors. To prevail on that basis, plaintiff must prove that the defendant before the court engaged in concerted action with other manufacturers of the product. See *Bichler* v. *Eli Lilly and Co.,* 79 A.D.2d 317, 436 N.Y.S.2d 625 (1981), aff'd, 55 N.Y.2d 571, 436 N.E.2d 182 (1982).

46 The court in *Sindell* v. *Abbott Laboratories,* 26 Cal. 3d 588, 612–13, 607 P.2d 924, 937–38 (1980) stated: "Under this approach, each manufacturer's liability would approximate its responsibility for the injuries caused by its own products. . . . [U]nder the rule we adopt, each manufacturer's liability for an injury would be approximately equivalent to the damages caused by the DES it manufactured."

47 For early and prescient speculation about the effect of public law—at that time, the effect of the workmen's compensation acts—on the attitudes and doctrine of the courts developing tort law, see Smith, "Sequel to Workmen's Compensation Acts," 27 *Harv. L. Rev.* 235, 344 (1913).

48 See p. 129, infra, for description of the private-public distinction.

49 Some examples are cited in notes 7, 9, and 10 (chapter 5), infra.

50 See note 12 (chapter 2), supra.

51 E.g., Indiana Medical Malpractice Act, Ind. Code Am. §16, Art. 9.5 (Burns 1975) (as amended).

52 See note 4 (chapter 1), supra.

53 See Landis, "Statutes and the Sources of Law," in *Harvard Legal Essays* 213 (1934).

54 E.g., *Kohlman v. Hyland,* 54 N.D. 710, 716, 210 N.W. 643, 645 (1920).

55 E.g., *Henningsen v. Bloomfield Motors, Inc.,* 32 N.J. 358, 371–73, 161 A.2d 69, 76–77 (1960).

56 E.g., *Spur Industries, Inc. v. Del E. Webb Development Co.,* 108 Ariz. 178, 184, 494 P.2d 700, 706 (1972).

57 See note 115 (chapter 3), supra.

CHAPTER 5. REFLECTIONS

1 The writings of the legal realists long ago exposed the fallacy and inadequacy of such strong conceptions. See note 112 (chapter 3), supra.

2 These visions of separate spheres within the liberal political tradition reach back to theorists like Locke. They figure prominently in the writings of twentieth-century theorists. See, e.g., F. Hayek, *The Road to Serfdom* (1944). Hayek (in chapters 5 and 6) distinguishes the liberal-individualist tradition from the collectivist-communist tradition by stressing autonomous spheres of thought and action in which individual ends are supreme. "Within the known rules of the game the individual is free to pursue his personal ends and desires, certain that the powers of government will not be used deliberately to frustrate his efforts." Id. at 73. Historical and contemporary conceptions of the private-public distinction and evaluations thereof are set forth in "Papers from the University of Pennsylvania Law Review Symposium on the Public/Private Distinction," 130 *U. Pa. L. Rev.* 1289–1608 (1982). For a brief review of the different meanings that distinction has borne, see Horwitz, "The History of the Public/Private Distinction," id. at 1423. See also note 99 (chapter 3), supra. See Rakoff, "Contracts of Adhesion: An Essay in Reconstruction," 96 *Harv. L. Rev.* 1173, 1197–1220 (1983) for use of concepts of private and public law as organizing categories for analysis of adhesion contracts.

3 The legal literature within the critical legal studies movement frequently portrays structures in law, sometimes in an effort to identify a dominant ideological structure—see, e.g., Klare, "Critical Theory and Labor Relations Law," in D. Kairys (ed.), *The Politics of Law* 65 (1982)—and sometimes to portray compet-

ing structures—see, e.g., Kennedy, "Form and Substance in Private Law Adjudication," 89 *Harv. L. Rev.* 1685 (1976). The theme of contradiction figures importantly in this literature. See, e.g., Kennedy, "The Structure of Blackstone's Commentaries," 28 *Buffalo L. Rev.* 205 (1979), and Olsen, "The Family and the Market: A Study of Ideology and Legal Reform," 96 *Harv. L. Rev.* 1497 (1983). See generally Gordon, "Critical Legal Histories," 36 *Stan. L. Rev.* 57, 114–25 (1984) for an account of recent historical and other writings treating such themes as indeterminacy, structure, and contradiction. See also Trubek, "Where the Action Is: Critical Legal Studies and Empiricism," 36 *Stan. L. Rev.* 575, 575–79 (1984). The author there characterizes the critical legal studies movement as developing a critique of legal order based on four principles: indeterminacy, antiformalism, contradiction, and marginality. That essay seeks to trace the "full implications" of the four principles.

4 Two contemporary illustrations of such scholarship draw respectively on the utilitarian and right-fairness traditions to explain and justify legal doctrine: R. Posner, *Economic Analysis of Law* (2d ed. 1977), and C. Fried, *Contract as Promise: A Theory of Contractual Obligation* (1981).

The relationship between this essay and postrealist jurisprudence of recent decades is more complex. I refer to such prominent and influential authors within the broad tradition of legal idealism—stressing the role of purposes, policies, and principles in resolving legal controversies and making judicial law— as R. Dworkin, *Taking Rights Seriously* (1977); Fuller, "The Forms and Limits of Adjudication," 92 *Harv. L. Rev.* 353 (1978); and H. Hart and A. Sacks, *The Legal Process: Basic Problems in the Making and Application of Law* (tentative ed. 1958). Such works attempt, as does this essay, to impress some structure on legal argument. But the conceptions of structure in law and of the role of moral ideals are quite different in such writings from what they are in my essay. Ultimately, the differences appear more significant than the similarities.

Consider, for example, some themes in this essay and in chapter 4, "Hard Cases," of Dworkin's book. Like Dworkin, I stress the inescapable, vital, and historically prominent role of ideals in legal argument. Like Dworkin, I note and illustrate that moral ideals serve both to justify and rationalize extant law and to criticize and develop law. But our purposes differ. My effort has been to describe the character or structure of legal argument and common-law change by attention to what courts have said, to describe how law has changed through relationships among doctrine and justification and social vision, rather than to develop (as does Dworkin) a normative theory of the character or structure of adjudication. Thus, my essay suggests no equivalent to Dworkin's descriptive and heuristic notion of a "right answer." Through its stress on structures of justification and vision, this essay suggests limits on judicial choice and invention. Nonetheless, unlike Dworkin, I advance no theory of a proper resolution of the tension between judicial freedom and judicial constraint (expressed by Dworkin in several ways, including the argument that a principle employed by a court should fit most doctrine even if it criticizes some).

Rather, I have emphasized the historical contingency of theories of justification and the ongoing conflicts and choice among them. Moreover, my conception of legal justifications is more closely linked to visions of social life informing the justifications—visions themselves in conflict and changing. That is, I describe justifications as less disembodied or abstract or autonomously instituted in law than is suggested by Dworkin. Finally, unlike Dworkin, this essay, in its description of the role of moral argument in judicial decision, attaches no differential significance to "policies" (utilitarian-based) and "principles" (right-fairness based).

5 Few authors stressing indeterminacy in law have carried their thesis to such an extreme. For a representative legal-realist portrait of indeterminacy (uncertainty, competing available premises), see Llewellyn, "Some Realism about Realism— Responding to Dean Pound," 44 *Harv. L. Rev.* 1222, 1233–47, 1251–56 (1931). Perceptions of indeterminacy in legal argument, and of the degree to which legal doctrine and justifications can be employed to support a given argument or course of action as well as their opposites, have figured importantly within the critical legal studies movement. See, e.g., Frug, "The Ideology of Bureaucracy in American Law," 97 *Harv. L. Rev.* 1277, 1292–93, 1341–43, 1364–65 (1984); Klare, "The Law-School Curriculum in the 1980's: What's Left?", 32 *J. Legal Educ.* 336, 339–41 (1982); Tushnet, "Legal Scholarship: Its Causes and Cure," 90 *Yale L. J.* 1205, 1206–15 (1981).

6 For proposals for the reform of accident law that have radical redistributive implications, see Abel, "A Critique of American Tort Law," 8 *Brit. J. L. & Soc.* 199 (1981). The author urges a "so-

cialist approach to injury and illness" that would involve state-provided comprehensive medical care, a guaranteed minimum income, and a compensation system the "paramount criterion" for which should be equality of treatment among victims. That system would eliminate compensation for damages to property or individual earning power above a certain level. Protection for such traditionally covered elements of damages would have to be achieved through loss insurance.

7 The explanations for and appropriate responses to the problems in insurance rates and availability are sharply disputed. Product manufacturers, doctors, and insurance companies tend to locate the explanation in the expansion of tort liability and damages and to locate at least part of the cure in legislative measures that would reduce both liability and damages. Consumer groups, labor unions, bar-association groups, and varied critics stress structural factors in the insurance industry, the lack of adequate antitrust and rate regulation of that industry, and its short-sighted rating and investment practices in the early 1980s.

The debate is frequently concentrated on medical malpractice. The academic writing on that field linking malpractice issues to the problems of liability insurance includes S. Law and S. Polan, *Pain and Profit: The Politics of Malpractice* (1978) and P. Danzon, *Medical Malpractice: Theory, Evidence, and Public Policy* (1985). Important aspects of this debate are captured in reports of professional associations, such as American Medical Association (Special Task Force), *Professional Liability in the '80's*, Report 1 (October 1984) and Report 2 (November 1984); and American Bar Association Special Committee on Medical Professional Liability, *Report to the House of Delegates* (1986). Recent journalistic accounts of the charges and countercharges about tort liability and the insurance industry include *Time*, 24 March 1986, 16; and *New York Times*, 8 March 1986, 35.

There is no doubt that pressures on legislatures for tort reform have been strengthened by concern over liability insurance. Those pressures have led to acts or bills in numerous states that affect all of tort accident law, as by placing caps on damages or limiting joint and several liability. Other acts or bills affect particular fields of tort law, such as medical malpractice or suits against municipalities. A summary of recent legislation and pending bills appears in *New York Times*, 31 March 1986, 1.

For illustrations of recent legislation restricting the possibility of recovery in product-liability actions through rules bearing on time limitations, the defense of "state-of-the-art," and contributory or comparative fault, see Product Liability Act of Kentucky, Ky. Rev. Stat. §411.300 et seq., (1978), and Utah Product Liability Act, Utah Code Ann. §§78-15-1 et seq. (1977). See also S. Rep. No. 476, 98th Cong., 2d Sess. (1984) of the Sen. Comm. on Commerce, Science and Transportation, reporting favorably on a Product Liability Act, S. 44, 98th Cong., 2d Sess. (1984). The bill was not enacted. In early 1986, officials of the Reagan administration had drafted a bill that would preempt inconsistent state law on product liability and restrict that liability. *New York Times,* 21 April 1986, 8–9.

8 In a case involving claims of several thousand women across the United States injured by an allegedly defective intrauterine device, the court said: "The latter half of the twentieth century has witnessed a virtual explosion in the frequency and number of lawsuits filed to redress injuries caused by a single product manufactured for use on a national level. Indeed, certain products have achieved such national notoriety due to their tremendous impact on the consuming public, that the mere mention of their names—Agent Orange, Asbestos, DES, MER/29, Dalkon Shield—conjure[s] images of massive litigation. . . ." In re: Northern District of California "Dalkon Shield" IUD Products Liability Litigation, 526 F. Supp. 887, 892 (N.D. Cal. 1981), vacated and remanded sub nom. Abed v. A.H. Robins Co., 693 F.2d 847 (9th Cir. 1982). See note, "The Manville Bankruptcy: Treating Mass Tort Claims in Chapter 11 Proceedings," 96 *Harv. L. Rev.* 1121 (1983); P. Brodeur, *Outrageous Misconduct: The Asbestos Industry on Trial* (1985); Rabin, "Dealing with Disasters: Some Thoughts on the Adequacy of the Legal System," 30 *Stan. L. Rev.* 281 (1978).

9 E.g., Nev. Rev. Stat. §41A.100 (1975) (amended 1979), limiting to five described circumstances the use in medical malpractice cases of a "rebuttable presumption that the personal injury or death was caused by negligence."

10 E.g., Wis. Stat. Ann. §895.045 (West 1971).

11 See note 51 (chapter 4), supra.

12 For descriptions of such legislative schemes by courts passing on their constitutionality, see *Wright* v. *Central DuPage Hospital Ass'n,* 63 Ill. 2d 313, 347 N.E.2d 736 (1976), and *Johnson* v. *St. Vincent Hospital, Inc.,* 404 N.E.2d 585 (S. Ct. Ind. 1980). See also "Model Periodic Payment of Judgments Act," 14 *Unif. Laws Ann.* (1984 Cum. Ann. Pocket) §2 et seq.

13 The scholarly literature has long made such suggestions. See, e.g., Jaffe, "Damages for Personal Injury: The Impact of Insurance," 18 *Law & Contemp. Probs.* 219, 221–32 (1953) (questioning damages for pain and suffering as liability expands).

14 See, e.g., *Feldman* v. *Allegheny Airlines, Inc.*, 524 F.2d 384 (2d Cir. 1975) (discount rate and inflation); *Grimshaw* v. *Ford Motor Co.*, 119 Cal. App. 3d 757, 174 Cal. Rptr. 348 (Ct. App. 1981) (punitive damages). For proposals for remedial innovation in class actions involving damage scheduling (awarding compensation to claimants not on basis of personal characteristics but on basis of characteristics of class of which individual victim is a member) and insurance-fund judgments (ordering defendant to insure disease-risk claimants against risk of disease), see Rosenberg, "The Causal Connection in Mass Exposure Cases: A 'Public Law' Vision of the Tort System," 97 *Harv. L. Rev.* 851 (1984). For a recent illustration of a complex settlement in a class action involving compensation arrangements departing in concept and detail from the common law, see *In re "Agent Orange" Product Liability Litigation*, 597 F. Supp. 740 (E.D.N.Y. 1984).

15 Compare the concept of transformative law in Sargentich, "Complex Enforcement" (unpublished draft of March 1978), note 28 (chapter 4), supra, a concept related to the notions of systematic wrongs and systemic norms that were referred to in the earlier note. Compare also the concepts of expanded and deviationist doctrine in Unger, "The Critical Legal Studies Movement," 96 *Harv. L. Rev.* 561, 576–83 (1983).

16 Numerous opinions treating tort liabilities express this perception of the greater possibilities of legislative schemes. In *Maloney* v. *Rath*, 69 Cal. 2d 442, 445 P.2d 513 (1968), the court noted that it was aware of the "growing dissatisfaction" with the negligence law governing compensation "for the increasingly serious harms caused by automobiles." But working out strict liability for auto accidents was too complex a task for the judiciary. "Who is to be strictly liable to whom in such cases?" Judicially imposed strict liability "would only contribute confusion to the automobile accident problem." Only the legislature could avoid such difficulties through a "comprehensive plan" for compensation displacing or adding to negligence law. Id. at 445–46, 445 P.2d at 514–15. See *Hammontree* v. *Jenner*, 20 Cal. App. 3d 528, 97 Cal. Rptr. 739 (Dist. Ct. App. 1971). The court in *Wights* v. *Staff Jennings, Inc.*, 241 Or. 301, 310, 405 P.2d 624, 628–29 (1965) cautioned that a loss-spreading rationale had no limits and could

extend to all business-related accidents. Were such an extensive
move toward strict liability made, there would be an argument
to impose limitations on damages and other elements of the recovery, as in workers' compensation. But a legislature alone had
the power to impose such limits.

17 See note 4 (chapter 1), and note 115 (chapter 3), supra.

18 See the Comprehensive Environmental Response, Compensation, and Liability Act of 1980 (CERCLA), 94 Stat. 2767. Section
211 of CERCLA imposes "environmental taxes" on raw materials
(including crude oil and petroleum products) that are used in
many processes generating hazardous wastes. See S. Rep.
No. 848, 96th Cong., 2d Sess. (1980) for a description of bolder
proposed legislation, including compensation from a superfund
for victims of hazardous wastes, that was not enacted. For example, chemical-feedstock producers would contribute to a superfund from which funds for remedial measures and for
compensation for some losses are drawn, even though the immediate accident may have stemmed from disposal by other
producers of wastes containing the particular chemicals.

19 See the proposed scheme in Pierce, "Encouraging Safety: The
Limits of Tort Law and Government Regulation," 33 Vand. L.
Rev. 1281 (1980). Compare the New Zealand Accident Compensation Act as described in T. Ison, Accident Compensation: A Commentary on the New Zealand Scheme (1980). See P. Atiyah,
Accidents, Compensation and the Law 617–31 (3d ed. 1980); Sugar-
man, "Doing Away with Tort Law," 73 Cal. L. Rev. 558, 642–64
(1985).

20 See the new §85, "Principles of Compensation in American
Legal Systems," of P. Keeton, D. Dobbs, R. Keeton, and
D. Owen, Prosser and Keeton on The Law of Torts (5th ed. 1984), for
an analogous way of relating the common law (but there including only the common law of strict liability) to the plans. Strict
common-law liability and accident plans are both there associated with the principle of "strict accountability" in contrast with
two other principles—the "fault principle" yielding the negligence system, and the "welfare principle" (compensation to victim not from actor causally related to injury, but by society
through the medium of one or another governmental scheme).

21 See p. 123, supra.

22 See Abel, "A Socialist Approach to Risk," 41 Md. L. Rev. 695
(1982). The author notes three ways of responding to risk of
physical harm: compensate for harm, punish those who cause

harm, and control risk before it results in harm. He argues that the first two responses must be subordinate to the third (and handled in separate systems distinct from efforts to control risk). Abel then develops proposals looking toward greater autonomy (control by each individual of the risk to which he is subjected) and equality for people in their encounters with risk (as through reduction in the division of labor, and job rotation). Abel notes several criticisms of regulation as a way of controlling risk, including: "Welfare capitalism and social democracy can soften the rigors of a pure laissez-faire approach to risk. Regulation can set a floor that forbids certain extreme risks. But this leaves untouched the vast inequalities that remain above that floor and indeed legitimates them by suggesting that what is not regulated represents an acceptable level of inequality." Id. at 717.

23 See the introductory discussion of such systems at pp. 11–12, supra.

24 A recurrent theme in the scholarship on tort law has been a preference for strict liability over welfare systems as a way of compensating victims precisely because of the causal connection to business defendants within tort law. See, e.g., note 20 (chapter 5), supra; Seavey, "Speculations as to 'Respondeat Superior'," in *Harvard Legal Essays* 433 (1934). In recognizing the strength of arguments for liability insurance and beyond-fault liability, Seavey responds to a criticism that such liability constitutes a "levelling process" by stating that "in view of the modern temper which requires all to be taken care of, it would seem preferable to have industry rather than the state perform the function of protection." Private firms are better managed than public bureaucracies, and it is better for the injured to be compensated from the cause rather than from the community. Id. at 463 note 41.

25 For an account of and explanation for that evolution, see Vogel, "The 'New' Social Regulation in Historical and Comparative Perspective," in T. McCraw, ed., *Regulation in Perspective: Historical Essays* 155 (1981).

26 See p. 73, supra.

27 For earlier discussions of these and related problems, see Jaffe, "The Effective Limits of the Administrative Process: A Reevaluation," 67 *Harv. L. Rev.* 1105 (1954); J. Landis, "1960 Report on Regulatory Agencies to the President-Elect," Sen. Comm. on the Judiciary, 86th Cong., 2d Sess. (1960). See also McCraw,

"Regulation in America: A Review Article," 49 *Bus. Hist. Rev.*
162, 162–83 (1975); G. Stigler, *The Citizen and the State: Essays on
Regulation* (1975); S. Breyer and R. Stewart, *Administrative Law
and Regulatory Policy* 131–32 (1979); R. Litan and W. Nordhaus,
Reforming Federal Regulation (1983); T. McCraw, *Prophets of Regulation* (1984).

28 See *American Textile Manufacturers Institute* v. *Donovan*, 452 U.S.
490 (1981), for conceptions of a feasibility standard and comparison with a cost-benefit standard.

Index

DESIGNED BY MIKE BURTON
COMPOSED BY BAILEY TYPOGRAPHY, NASHVILLE, TENNESSEE
MANUFACTURED BY BOOKCRAFTERS, CHELSEA, MICHIGAN
TEXT AND DISPLAY LINES ARE SET IN PALATINO AND OPTIMA

Library of Congress Cataloging-in-Publication Data
Steiner, Henry J.
Moral argument and social vision in the courts.
Includes index.
1. Torts—United States   2. Accident law—United
States.   3. Judicial process—United States.
4. Sociological jurisprudence.   I. Title.
KF1250.S76   1987   346.7303′22   86-28121
ISBN 0-299-11010-9   347.306322